D0778734

atlas

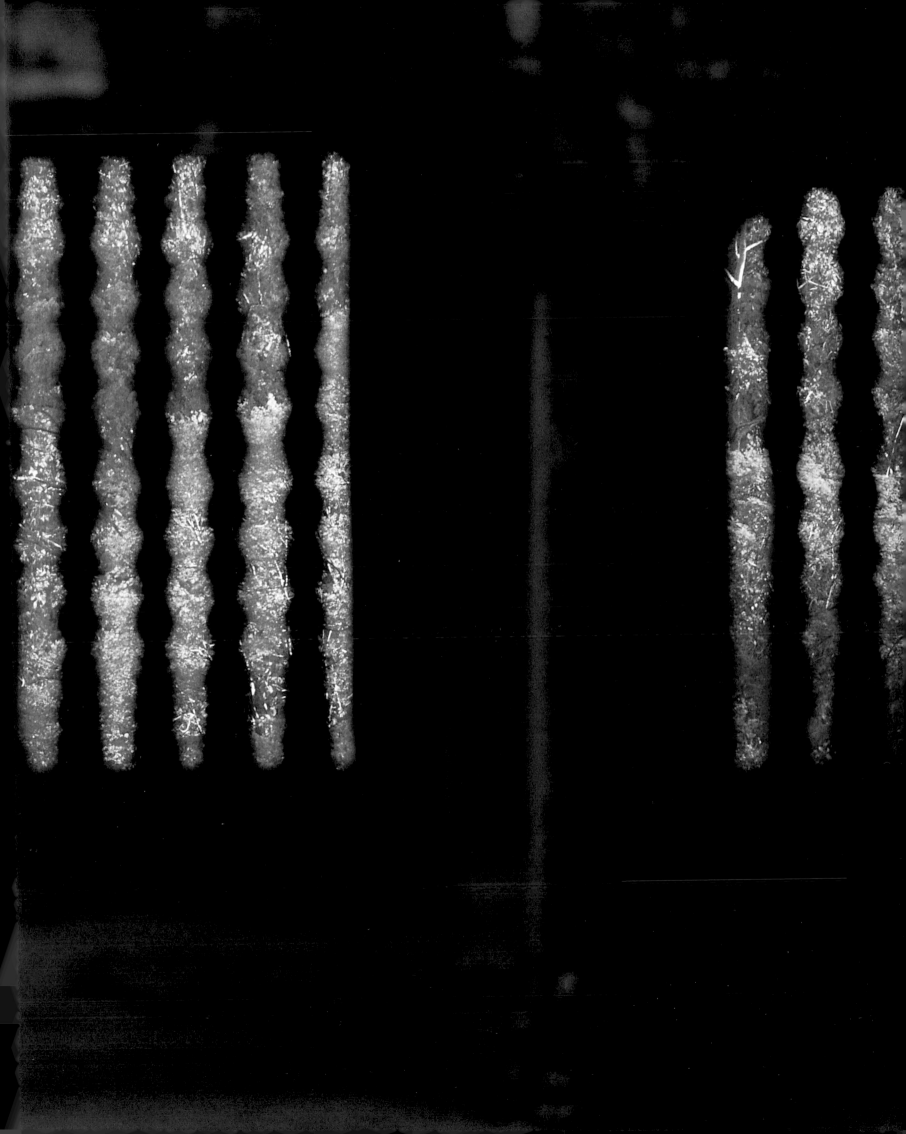

HERBERT YPMA

HIP
HOTELS

atlas

Thames & Hudson

EUROPE

Gannerhof
La Colombe d'Or
Château de Bagnols
Le Domaine de la Baronnie
La Huchet
Le Mas de Peint
Villa Marie
Babington House
Hotel Tresanton
Hotel Bratsera
Katikies
Atelier sul Mare
Castello di Falconara
Hotel Raya
La Posta Vecchia
Parco dei Principi
Villa Cimbrone
Relais La Suvera
Villa Feltrinelli
Le Sirenuse
Pousada de Nossa Senhora da Assunção
Casa de Carmona
Hacienda Benazuza
La Sacristía
The Ice Hotel

AFRICA

Adrère Amellal
Shompole
Caravanserai
La Gazelle d'Or
Auberge Tangaro
Kasbah Ben Moro
Riad Kaiss
Lebombo Lodge
Sweni Lodge

ASIA

Begawan Giri Estate
The Balé
La Résidence d'Angkor
Amansara
China Club
Fuchun
Devi Garh
Nilaya Hermitage
Samode Haveli
Surya Samudra Beach Garden
The Tawaraya
Three Sisters Inn
Amanjiwo
The Apsara
Cheong Fatt Tze
Dwarika's
Doornberg
Taru Villas
Amanpuri
Costa Lanta
Evason Hideaway

AUSTRALIA

Bay of Fires Lodge
The Prairie Hotel

NORTH AMERICA

Carlisle Bay
The Landing
Korakia
Dunton Hot Springs
The Home Ranch
Round Hill
Hotelito Desconocido
Cotton House
The Wawbeek
Hix Island House
Cibolo Creek Ranch
Sundance
Canoe Bay

SOUTH AMERICA

Yacutinga Lodge
Los Notros
Pousada Picinguaba
Vila Naiá
Pousada Etnia
Explora Atacama
Hotel Monasterio
Machu Picchu Lodge
La Posada del Faro

introduction

The desire to travel is universal. We all have a need, now and then, to get away from it all. Inevitably, this leads to the question 'Where should I go?' and, just as importantly, 'Where should I stay?' In a world of ever-expanding options – particularly in the context of accessibility and affordability – the choice is bewildering. Thus even the most well travelled among us can benefit from a book that offers travel and accommodation ideas on a global scale, and that spares us the nightmare of any nasty surprises.

In every corner of the globe there are Highly Individual Places to stay. Some are big, some small, some expensive, some not: the thing they have in common is that these are the hotels that help make travel memorable – the places that provide stories for many a dinner party to come. Not only can they generate travel experiences to be treasured, but they are also destinations in their own right.

This book, divided into six continents – Europe, Africa, Asia, Australia, North America and South America – is an atlas of global opportunities; a worldwide guide to the kind of hotels we all want to find, if only we knew where to look. Unusual, unique, interesting, out of the way, and almost always charming, the places that fill this book make travel what it should be, namely exciting and rewarding.

The diversity on offer is spellbinding. From a restored seventeenth-century mud kasbah built on the old African slave route in the Sahara, to a collection of open-plan contemporary timber bungalows set amongst the boulders of a hidden beach in Vietnam, to a Frank Lloyd Wright cabin on a North American pond in the woods of Wisconsin, this book lets you experience the kinds of places once found only on the pages of James Bond novels.

The temples of Luang Prabang, the shores of Sri Lanka, the wilds of Tasmania, the ruins of Angkor Wat, the turquoise treasures of the Bahamas, the colourful 'pueblo' traditions of Mexico, the magnificence of India's Raj, the peasant charm of Provence, the Zen of old Japan, the mystery of ancient Egypt, the breathtaking beauty of Italy's Renaissance…. All of these need not merely be admired; they can now be experienced. Name a travel fantasy and the book will not only place you smack bang in the middle of it, but you'll also be able to spend the night. You, the traveller, become integrated into your surroundings. It's a new kind of tourism that involves 'being', as opposed to merely seeing. This book provides a unique global perspective on precisely the sorts of places that make you want to pack your bags and escape!

EUROPE

Geographically, it is possible to 'do' Europe in a week, but why would you want to? Rome, Paris, London and Madrid can be seen in seven days, but the experience will not leave you with much other than jet-lag and exhaustion. If you stand in line to see the Eiffel Tower, Big Ben or the Colosseum, you'll find they're no different from the postcard, only bigger.

To experience the real Italy, the genuine France, the authentic Spain and so on, my advice is to forget the cities: just choose a destination in the countryside, and stay there. You'll be able to experience the beauty, charm, history and gastronomy of Europe without stress or strain. No guide, no agenda, and no '(playing) trains, planes and automobiles'.

Italy, France, Greece, Austria, Spain and Portugal may all share the same currency, but that's about it … and it is precisely the differences between these countries that makes them so compelling. The food, the culture, the people and the architecture are like a code that shape our imagination. Most of us have a picture in our mind of what we expect, or more accurately what we want, from a location. These idyllic images are exactly what you will find in the pages of this atlas.

The Italy of romantic palazzos and Renaissance art; the France of aristocratic châteaux, rural villages and gourmet indulgence; the England of Georgian country houses, rolling green hills, afternoon tea and corner pubs; the Spain of Moorish haciendas, scorching sun and flamenco: all of these can be yours with the right address. Why not reside in the kind of place that's normally found only on a sightseeing schedule? Who cares if they're clichés? They're what your imagination wants.

In any case we're not talking about staying in a museum. These are hotels that use history, tradition and culture as inspiration, but never to the point of compromising a guest's comfort or pleasure.

All the hotels in these pages, whether a medieval hunting lodge on a Sicilian beach, a cliffside dwelling on a volcanic Greek island, a historic villa on a picturesque Italian lake, a cutting-edge conversion of a Portuguese convent, or a Scandinavian fantasy constructed entirely in ice, have one thing in common – you're not likely to forget staying in them. And without reading a single guidebook or taking a single guided tour, you will have learned more about a place than any package tour will teach you, no matter how many sights you take in.

gannerhof

The Villgratental in Austria's Osttirol is the one that got away. Somehow this mountain valley has totally escaped the all-embracing grip of Austrian ski tourism. Innervillgraten, the village located in the Villgraten valley, consists almost entirely of three- and four-hundred-year-old farmhouses. The only exceptions are the church and the town hall. Farming and timber, not tourism, are the industries of this valley.

Until 1962, the grandfather of the present proprietor of Gannerhof was a farmer. For his son, however, three cows and a paddock were not enough; he sidestepped family tradition, and that's how his son, Herr Mühlmann, came to run Gannerhof. He too was a farmer at first until he decided he could do better by turning his inheritance from farmhouse to guesthouse. Local bankers didn't think it was a good idea at all: who would come? And what for? All the valley could offer was farmhouses and the odd timber yard…. They were right of course, but as locals they didn't appreciate that unspoilt Alpine valleys are not as common as they used to be. Bankers be damned, Mühlmann pursued his dream. The old family *Bauernhaus* yielded eleven basic but handsome guestrooms, a new *Stube*, two old *Stuben* (one originally from the 1700s), a new kitchen and a sauna where the chickens used to live. The Gasthof

Gannerhof opened for business in 1992. It didn't take long for a local wit to point out that there was one *hof* too many in Innervillgraten – a dig at the rather awkward name. Point taken, the Mühlmanns dropped the Gasthof part and decided to use the single appellation without a der, die or das to spoil its simplicity.

It was clear that the Mühlmanns were going to do things their own way. Although Alois and Monika always intended to base Gannerhof's cuisine on local fresh farm produce, they had not actually planned on doing the cooking. But one night, the chef didn't show and Frau Mühlmann stepped in. For more than eighteen years she ran the kitchen, and she made quite a name with her unique and *ländlich* cuisine. At Gannerhof they bake their own bread, churn their own butter and grow the herbs to make their own *Kräutertee* (herbal tea), even though Frau Mühlmann has now handed over the reins to a new chef. Ducks, chickens, geese, goats: everything on the menu, if not straight from the backyard, is reared in the valley. The animals are part of the ambience, and some guests have grown very attached to them. One couple were particularly anguished to discover – half-way through dinner – that they were eating their friend Ushi the duck.

Although Alois only lasted two years in farming, its culture is clearly in his blood. There is definitely a farmer's mentality in his and his wife's straightforwardness and decency. For example, much as I wanted to photograph other bedrooms, they would not allow it out of respect for their guests' privacy even though they were all off skiing. Frau Mühlmann was a bit surprised by my enthusiasm. 'They are just bedrooms,' she said, 'they have a bed and a place to hang your clothes, nothing more!' Given that some of the rooms feature Grandpa Alois's antiques, and others combine a simple pine interior with the avant-garde artistry of a local blacksmith, such modesty was a surprise.

Despite all the awards and commendations the kitchen at Gannerhof has garnered over the years, no one outside of Austria seems to have ever heard of it. It's extraordinary. Perhaps the Austrians from nearby Lienz are keen to keep Gannerhof to themselves. Interestingly, despite its isolation, and despite the fact that Innervillgraten has no ski shops, no boutiques, no ski service or rental, the local skiing area – less than ten minutes away – is one of the biggest in Osttirol. The south-facing pistes of the Hochpustertal are only a ten-minute drive from Gannerhof. And for advanced skiers looking for a challenge, the 3,000-metre (9,000-foot) peaks of the Hohe Tauern are less than half an hour away. Gannerhof represents an extremely rare opportunity to combine the ambience and cuisine of an authentic Austrian *Bauernhaus* with some excellent skiing in the eastern Alps.

Frau Mühlmann has a great story: one day, a lady called and wanted to know what there was for children to do. 'Nothing,' replied Monika. 'What do you mean, nothing?' asked the caller. 'Nothing. Our children were raised in and around this house, there are fields to run in and animals and mountains, but beyond that nothing.' 'Good,' said the caller, 'that is exactly what I am looking for.'

---

address Gannerhof, A-9932 Innervillgraten 93, Austria
t (43) 4843 5240 **f** (43) 4843 5506 **e** gannerhof@aon.at
room rates from € 62

la colombe d'or

Picasso, Matisse, Calder and Delaunay all came here for the food, or so it is sometimes said. The famous Colombe d'Or *entrées* and the signature basket of salad were the attraction. Even when Matisse was ailing towards the end of his life, he would come in his chauffeur-driven Bentley to be served by Mme Roux in the back of the car. But my suspicion is that what they loved most was the artistic intelligence that is so strongly in evidence here.

The original proprietor, Paul Roux, had a true artist's attitude. In his later years he was encouraged by Picasso to start painting, and some of his work now hangs in the hotel. But you don't have to look too hard to find more general evidence of his sensibilities. For example the chairs on the famous terrace that serves as the summer dining room might look just like typical wooden Provençal farm chairs, but in fact they are *fer forgé*, wrought iron made to look like patinated wood. This is just the kind of twist so typical of an artist's way of thinking. The same is true of the bronze shells that illuminate the paintings in the dining room, the Eames-like bar tables and the rugged Noguchi-style stools.

It's true that the walls are covered with art that the world's top museums would kill for. But Paul Roux's grandson François, who now oversees the day-to-day running of La Colombe d'Or, is not like other Picasso owners. He doesn't stop at each painting to pump you full of detail, nor is he particularly precious about these family jewels. The clear impression is that they are there to be enjoyed and appreciated, not revered. There's something quite wonderful about a giant Calder mobile perched on the edge of a simple but handsome swimming pool. This is how art should be – relaxed and accessible, lived with rather than viewed from a respectful distance with your hands clasped demurely behind your back.

There's an ease to the decor that belies the creativity that went into it. Just as Picasso could turn an old TV stand into a sculpture of a horse, the Roux family transformed a *maison de village* into an art-filled wonderland. It does help that the mountaintop village of St-Paul-de-Vence is one of the prettiest in the Côte d'Azur hinterland. But these days that can be more of a disadvantage than an advantage, particularly in summer, when the streets are full of sightseers no longer deterred by the long winding road up. Still, once inside this old mansion, the atmosphere is at once seductively avant-garde and reassuringly Provençal.

The Roux family take the reputation of their restaurant very seriously. An army of classically clad waiters – black

The hilltop village of St-Paul-de-Vence in the Côte d'Azur hinterland is one of the prettiest in the south of France

The massive proportions of the old architecture of La Colombe d'Or are complemented by modern art

A gigantic mural by Fernand Léger dominates the secluded leafy courtyard that serves as the summer dining room

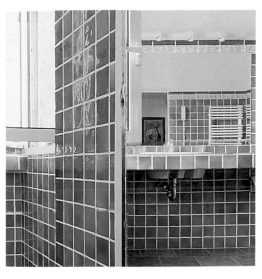

While most of the hotel is eclectic and rustic,
the bathrooms are pure function,
simply tiled in local faience

A large mosaic by Braque framed by
towering cypresses is the backdrop
to the poolside recliners

Rustic and romantic: the bedrooms
combine stone fireplaces, four-poster beds
and old Persian rugs

trousers, white shirts, black tie – prepare the tables and bring out dishes that were first served here more than half a century ago. Yet they started almost unimaginably modestly. Paul Roux, veteran of the First World War and son of a Provençal peasant, took on a small inn in St-Paul-de-Vence on his return from the front. The menu offered *hors d'œuvres*, trout and chicken, and the sign read '*ici on loge à cheval, à pied ou en peinture*' (lodgings here for horses, pedestrians and artists). But by 1929 La Colombe d'Or had become the winter salon of international celebrities. To tell all the stories that took place on its legendary terrace would fill more than a few books. Even the abridged version of the legend of Colombe d'Or – the ubiquitous visitor's book – runs to seven volumes. Charlie Chaplin, Groucho Marx, Hubert de Givenchy, Winston Churchill, Jean Cocteau, Marlene Dietrich, Maria Callas, F. Scott Fitzgerald, David Niven, Rita Hayworth, Orson Welles, Cary Grant, Clark Gable, Alfred Hitchcock, Brigitte Bardot, Michael Caine, Robert de Niro, Madonna – the list goes on and on and on.

All the stars and all the art almost make one forget that architecturally this is quite a place – an eclectic arrangement of vaulted spaces, corridors, terraces and more terraces, all constructed in great slabs of rugged stone that give it a monastic quality. This stone was hauled here in three-hundred-odd lorry loads from a dilapidated château in Provence which Roux purchased and demolished for the purpose. It is said that when Roux died, Picasso was devastated, and his was one of the few funerals the artist ever attended. But for me the best example of the artistic attitude of La Colombe d'Or is the story of when King Leopold of Belgium came to stay. He had the nerve to announce to Paul Roux that he didn't like the paintings by Picasso, to which the owner replied: '*Monsieur, vous êtes un sauvage.*'

address La Colombe d'Or, Place du Général de Gaulle, 06570 St-Paul-de-Vence, France

t (33) 4 93 32 80 02   **f** (33) 4 93 32 77 78   **e** contact@la-colombe-dor.com

room rates from € 220

château de bagnols

Château de Bagnols is not just a castle converted into a hotel – it's a slice of French history. From the tumultuous Middle Ages through the Renaissance to the glory years of the Bourbon kings and then the upheaval of the Revolution, there's not a period of the past eight hundred years that has not left its mark on this château nestled in the picturesque countryside of the Beaujolais Valley.

Through death, marriage and inheritance the estate changed hands many times. But it was always the residence of one wealthy Lyonnais family or another. Perhaps that's the key to its charm. It's grand, but still on a domestic scale. Like an old face that shows the evidence of an eventful life, Bagnols is filled with traces of the wars and famine, prosperity and tragedy it has witnessed over the years.

The first castle was built in the thirteenth century with a loan from the bishop of Lyons: the Church in those days was willing to swap financial support for protection. Lifestyle was a low priority in the original architecture; far more important was defence against marauding bands of ultra-violent mercenaries and bandits. The castle thus was not much more than a stone box surrounded by a dry moat and drawbridge. There were no windows – only slits just big enough to shoot an arrow through. Husbands waged war; wives stayed in dark halls to oversee the cooking and raise those children who survived the pestilence and violence that plagued the times.

As this part of France became more secure and prosperous, some domestic refinements were added. Tapestries were woven to provide adornment (and protection from draughts) and fresco paintings were commissioned. The Medici, who established businesses in Lyons, brought with them the influences of the Italian Renaissance. The odd window was installed, but still the lion's share of architectural refinements were defensive. Special holes were made to allow the newly invented guns to be accommodated, while machicolation and stone buttressing created an overhang perfect for pouring hot oil on intrepid intruders.

The families under whose auspices the fort evolved over the centuries are too numerous and complex to list, but in general the function of the fort slowly changed from protective to domestic. By the eighteenth century, it had become an aristocratic estate dedicated to the enjoyment of life. Large windows were knocked through the five-foot thick walls, and ceilings were raised and adorned with timber beams. Fireplaces were installed to warm the

The west wall of the château, topped with machicolation, leads to the grove where breakfast is served in summer

The massive towering walls of the courtyard reveal the building's military origins

Frescoes throughout the château are in the distinctive colours and style of Burgundy

A detail of the old well reveals the medieval heritage of the thirteenth-century Château de Bagnols

A canopy of chestnut trees is the summer breakfast room, with a view over the entire valley

The medieval fireplace, renovated in the 1800s, is the original hearth of the great hall, now used as a dining room

An old hay cart reminds the visitor that until recently this was a working estate

Bathrooms differ in size and design, but all have sumptuous Napoleonic baths and lavish amounts of space

With a commanding view of the Beaujolais Valley, the grounds of the château are fringed by fragrant lavender

This being Burgundy, food plays a big role;
the new head chef at Château de Bagnols
trained under Michel Troisgros

In summer a canopy runs the length of the ramp
leading to the dining room; the space
is used for lunch and drinks

Deciding which frescoes to keep and which
to peel away was one of the most stressful
aspects of the renovation

A magnificent *lit à la polonaise* is the centrepiece
of a suite distinguished by its combination
of panelling and frescoes

The ornate stonework of the main portico
was added during the Renaissance

The round swimming pool is a recent addition.
As the landscape matures it will be
the centre of a cherry grove

Centuries-old frescoes appear throughout
the guest rooms and suites
of the hotel

One of the most vivid of Château de Bagnols'
surviving frescoes shows a typical
eighteenth-century boar hunt

Much of the decor dates to a makeover
in the late 1700s, when lifestyle at last
began to take priority over defence

spacious apartments, and luxurious fabrics and furniture were introduced. Despite the conversion to genteel life, however, the protective features of the building – crenellations, arrow slits, even the drawbridge – were preserved, for they were still symbols of status and power. Not surprisingly, they fell victim in 1789 to the Revolution: the crenellations on the towers were destroyed in an act equivalent to punitive castration. The towers still stand, but their roofs slope off in a manner more like a grain silo than a military watchtower.

All this heritage was like a giant puzzle that Lord and Lady Hamlyn took on when they purchased the forlorn château in 1987. It was in a state of complete neglect and disrepair, but it was exactly what the couple were looking for. Lady Hamlyn embraced its challenges with such purpose and sensitivity that the finished result, which took more than four years to complete, earned her the title *Chevalier des Arts et des Lettres*.

In the process, numerous difficult decisions had to be taken. Some rooms had been decorated and redecorated many times over centuries, and the choice had to be made of which era to go back to – in particular, how many layers of fresco to remove in the likelihood of finding something better underneath. It was not a job for the fainthearted. This was a restoration on an industrial scale achieved with archaeological precision. Expensive and excruciatingly slow, the job was further complicated by the plan to make the place a luxury hotel. All the functional bits – smoke detectors, emergency exits, fire extinguishers, heating, plumbing and catering facilities – had to be allowed for without affecting the historic character. But the end result is not only inspiring, it's unique. Château de Bagnols is the only hotel in France that is classified as a *Monument Historique Classé*. It's a completely indulgent alternative to a history book – not that I don't like history books, but this is definitely better!

address Château de Bagnols, 69620 Bagnols, France
t (33) 4 74 71 40 00 **f** (33) 4 74 71 40 49 **e** info@bagnols.com
room rates from € 425

le domaine de la baronnie

St-Martin is the kind of town that makes you want to buy a 2CV, learn to play *boules*, and never again drink anything but wine. Beautifully built and beautifully situated, it is the old capital of the Île de Ré, a twenty-mile island off the coast of La Rochelle. With fortifications and an ornate entry designed by Vauban, engineer to Louis XIV, St-Martin is a perfectly preserved fishing port. Unlike other famous ports (such as St-Tropez), tourism has not yet turned every beautiful building here into a Body Shop or a Gap. The old centre remains largely residential. It has a Place de la République, a harbour crammed with fishing boats, lots of elegant eighteenth-century mansions, and original cobblestone streets.

The island traditionally made its living from oysters, salt and wine. Today its charms attract plenty of Parisians, but in the past it was the Dutch and the English who were most interested in its wealth and strategic location. The English were particularly unwelcome. Time and again they tried to capture Ré, but without success. The Duke of Buckingham was most persistent. He laid siege to St-Martin, and came close to triumph: the town's bread supplies ran out on the very day that Louis XIII's reinforcements arrived. The aggressive intentions of the English were never forgotten.

Even today the women who work the salt marshes in the north of the island wear a hat of folded cloth called a *quiche notte*, which derives from the English 'kiss me not'.

The attitude towards foreign visitors is largely academic since for the most part the Île de Ré serves as a weekend retreat for Parisians. But that does not mean it is dominated by hotels and high-rise apartment buildings – quite the opposite. Church steeples and lighthouses are the only structures higher than two storeys. This no-nonsense, unpretentious island enjoys the official status of a protected historic treasure, and restrictions on development are blessedly severe.

If St-Martin is the most beautiful village on Ré, its most beautiful house is without doubt the Domaine de la Baronnie. Proprietors Pierre and Florence Pallardy are not *Retais*, as the locals are known, so they harbour no resentment of the English. Here Italians mingle easily with the ubiquitous Parisians and, yes, even the odd *rosbif*.

This stone house, located around the corner from the thriving port, was built in 1700 on the site of the château of the medieval barons of Ré. Behind its impressive gate is a tree-lined drive that leads to a court in front and a substantial garden behind. When the Pallardys took it on it was a noble

ruin. Since the Second World War it had been owned by a wealthy bachelor who would spend August each year on Ré with his Portuguese maid. The rest of the time it stood empty. He came less and less as he grew older, and had little reason to keep the house on, but it was never put on the open market. The Pallardy family would not have bought it if it hadn't been for a chain of events that began with an unlikely encounter in the nearby town of Flotte.

Pierre Pallardy is well known in France as the healing osteopath with the magic hands, and his model wife is equally famous. They were drowning their sorrows one afternoon in Flotte after a disastrous property deal when, despite his dark mood, Pallardy couldn't resist asking why the bistrot owner limped. He promptly offered to treat the problem. Some manipulation of the man's ligament produced a miracle. The healed proprietor had overheard their talk and was eager to repay his debt. Hence they

were privy two years later to a whisper that the old man with the Portuguese maid might be prepared to sell, though only to a buyer he trusted to keep the place intact and restore it to the highest standards. Negotiations took a year, but the Pallardys eventually won out.

The Domaine de la Baronnie thus became the house of *bien être*. Here you can benefit not only from the salty air and nearby beaches but from the healing hands of Pierre Pallardy, who has set up a clinic in one of the outbuildings. Guest rooms are suitably baronial: vast suites with high ceilings, decorated with eclectic combinations of fleamarket and auction antiques found by Florence. And for those who cannot keep away from the sea, there's even a widow's-peak duplex suite that features a bedroom in a lookout upstairs, where once upon a time the lady of the house would have been found keeping an eye on the Atlantic, waiting for her seafaring husband to return.

---

address Le Domaine de la Baronnie, 21 rue Baron de Chantal, 17410 St-Martin-de-Ré, France

t (33) 5 46 09 21 29 **f** (33) 5 46 09 95 29 **e** info@domainedelabaronnie.com

room rates from € 160

la huchet

Part of La Huchet's attraction is that it is so difficult to find. Getting there can feel like embarking on an old-fashioned treasure hunt. Armed with a rudimentary hand-drawn map, you're faced with at least twenty different ways to get lost. 'Now is that the second path following the bridge immediately after the nudist camp, or the first?' is the sort of thing you are likely to find yourself asking.

The route – if you follow it correctly – takes you through ever smaller towns, as the autoroute from Dax to Bordeaux fades into distant memory. La Huchet really is in the middle of nowhere – but what a nowhere to be in the middle of! Following an extremely narrow and bumpy dirt road through the pine forest – the largest forest in western Europe – you turn a corner to find that the trees have suddenly stopped and you are faced with miles and miles of undulating dunes. You can't see the ocean, you can only hear the faint crashing of the waves beyond the tallest dunes.

Painted red and cream, and constructed in typical Atlantic coast style, La Huchet seems marooned like a shipwreck in the dunes. How did anyone ever come to put a hotel here, you may wonder. The answer is simple: it was only recently converted into a hotel. For two centuries before that it was a hunting cottage (though 'cottage' only

in the sense that a Georgian estate is a shack in the English countryside). For the noblemen who came to shoot here, there was clearly a limit to the extent they were prepared to rough it. With twenty-foot ceilings, enormous chandeliers, and fireplaces in every room, it's not exactly your average shooting lodge. And because it was so soundly built, with secure stone foundations, it has survived despite the sandy terrain – which is just as well because the spectacular dunes of Les Landes have long since been a nature reserve and all new building strictly forbidden.

Before La Huchet opened, the beaches and dunes of Les Landes were largely the preserve of daytrippers and campers. This coastal area on the southernmost Atlantic shores of France lies between Biarritz and the Bassin d'Arcachon. It is defined by endless beaches, towering sand dunes and the white surf of the Atlantic. An hour's drive from Biarritz and a couple from Bordeaux, it's not an area that most French are particularly familiar with, and it's certainly not as popular as Cap Ferrat or the Île de Ré further north. A more exclusive destination than La Huchet is hard to imagine.

La Huchet's exclusivity is not just a matter of isolation, however; the hotel also has a unique eligibility programme.

Even if you could find it, you couldn't just call, book and drop in. For the only way to stay at La Huchet is to have stayed first at one of Michel Guérard's operations in Eugénie-les-Bains. Guérard set up La Huchet believing that his guests might appreciate a spell on the beach before returning to the real world following the intensive spa treatments at Eugénie-les-Bains. It's an attractive proposition – first you purify and spoil yourself in the green surroundings of Eugénie, with its beautiful gardens, natural hot springs and Guérard's acclaimed cuisine; then, when you're all exfoliated, massaged, mud-bathed and burnished to a glow, you take your Jolly Roger map and lose yourself for a few days among the sand dunes of the Atlantic.

Since La Huchet accommodates a maximum of ten people, it is never a crowded experience. Christine Guérard's design makes the place feel more like a private beach compound than a hotel. In fact you are only reminded that this is a hotel by the welcome bits – the immaculate service, the delicious cuisine and the freshly ironed linen, which, in this case, really is linen. And with Guérard as proprietor, you would be right to imagine that the food goes far beyond the standard of your average beach shack.

The aristocratic proportions of all the guest rooms are suitably grand, while the furnishing style creates the feel of an old, moneyed beach house by its clever mix of sober seaside simplicity, colonial souvenirs from Indochina and lots of rustic ephemera. But most impressive of all are the two beach lofts set in separate, smaller pavilions adjacent to the main lodge. Misleadingly simple from the outside (they look like sun-bleached storage huts), they have twenty-six-foot-high ceilings, open fireplaces, a separate mezzanine for children accessed by a wrought-iron spiral staircase, and the enormous bathrooms that have become a signature of Guérard's approach to hospitality.

---

address La Huchet (Les Maisons Marines d'Huchet), 40560 Vielle Saint-Girons, France

t (33) 5 58 05 05 05 **f** (33) 5 58 51 10 10 **e** guerard@relaischateaux.fr

room rates from € 260

le mas de peint

If there's a French equivalent of 'Marlboro Country', then this is it. Le Mas de Peint is a converted ranch in the Camargue, a sun-bleached marshland south of Arles home to black bulls, white horses and colourful gypsies. The music here is flamenco (the 'Gypsy Kings' are from the Camargue), the favourite spectator sport is a local version of bullfighting in which agile *razeteurs* try to pluck a coloured ribbon from the bull's horns and exit the ring before being skewered, and men and women proudly wear the brightly coloured block-printed fabrics made famous by companies such as Souleiado. The Camargue is quite unlike any other part of France. There are no châteaux – only simple whitewashed ranches; and there is no legacy of aristocracy – ranch owners and their 'cowboys' work side by side. In style it has more in common with New Mexico, or the *estancias* of Argentina, than with the manicured refinement of northern France.

Jacques Bon, proprietor of Le Mas de Peint, was born and raised in the Camargue, and he takes his cowboy heritage very seriously. He still takes part in the round-up of horses and cattle, often spending the better part of the day on a horse (a white one, of course), and wears only the uniform of the Camargue cowboy – paisley-printed shirts, moleskins and riding boots. Together with his wife Lucille, an architect, he decided a decade ago to convert part of his family ranch into a small luxury hotel. But he is not out of the ranching business altogether. He still keeps forty white horses and three hundred black bulls.

From the very beginning both Jacques and Lucille Bon had very clear ideas about what kind of place it should be. Above all they believed it should retain the rugged character that is so much the signature of the Camargue. They did not want their guests to be cosseted and pampered in a five-star, 'yes sir, no sir' kind of way. That is not the way of the Camargue. The atmosphere they had in mind was that of friends coming over to help round up the horses. They would naturally eat in the kitchen, spend the day on horseback and collapse in a neat but not too 'tarted up' room. No glitz, no glamour, just the rosy glow of genuine hospitality, good food and being outdoors all day. The experience of Le Mas de Peint comes remarkably close to this vision. Everybody eats together in the kitchen, rooms are spacious but sparsely furnished, and guests are encouraged to ride along to help round up the herds.

Every evening around ten there is a ritual that the Bons adhere to faithfully. Jacques and his wife emerge from their

The famous white horses of the Camargue
are born grey; they turn white
as they get older

Le Mas de Peint's pared-down decor shows
an architect's preference for neutral tones
and natural fabrics

The wild rice displayed on a table in the
reception area is a special hybrid
variety grown on the property

Le Mas de Peint is a typical *mas* or
stone farmhouse converted into
a small luxurious hotel

Embroidered white linen and old brass beds:
this is farmhouse style with a
minimalist twist

The Camargue is France's cowboy
country. The hotel interior reflects
the region's ranch culture

private quarters and do the rounds in the kitchen, greeting and chatting with their guests. On the first night that I witnessed this ritual Jacques Bon appeared like a French rodeo star. He was wearing moleskins with a red pinstripe down the side and a red silk paisley-patterned shirt. He speaks not a word of English, but that didn't deter him from slapping backs, cracking jokes and working the room like a politician. The next day it was the same – only this time he wore black moleskins and a black silk paisley shirt. With his handlebar moustache and his colourful 'cowboy threads', Jacques Bon is quite a character. Magazine reviews have dubbed him the Jack Palance of the Camargue. He and Lucille are the perfect hosts for a genuine Camargue experience. He adds the colourful local flavour and she contributes the urbane design touch that makes Le Mas de Peint such a pleasurable retreat. For, despite Jacques Bon's insistence that he doesn't want to pamper guests, Le Mas de Peint is significantly more luxurious than your average Camargue ranch. The guest rooms are large, bed linen is immaculate (and embroidered with the brand of the ranch) and the en suite bathrooms are of a size and design standard you would expect in a sophisticated city hotel. A large swimming pool with a stone-tiled terrace is hidden in one of the paddocks and one of the large barns has been converted for use as a party space.

I had always rather cynically assumed that the famous white horses, black bulls, gypsies and whitewashed ranches of the Camargue were about as real as windmills and wooden shoes in Holland – in other words just something staged for the tourists. But, unlike other parts of Europe, the Camargue has not been sanitized by tourism and a uniform suburban culture. Here people cling fiercely to their way of life. Where else could you meet a character like Jacques Bon?

---

address Le Mas de Peint, Le Sambuc, 13200 Arles, France
t (33) 4 90 97 20 62 **f** (33) 4 90 97 22 20 **e** hotel@masdepeint.net
room rates from € 205

villa marie

St-Tropez is a circus. With its Russian hookers, Swedish bankers, Italian playboys, American billionaires, Dutch industrialists, Australian sailors, German fleshpots and French celebrities, there is no place in the Mediterranean, French or otherwise, that can match St-Tropez for scandal, sex and all-out price-is-no-object exhibitionism. St-Tropez, as they, say is *trop*. And that's what has made it a magnet for the summer jetset for over forty years.

Traffic in the high season is almost as bad as London or Paris, prices are even higher, crowds are getting bigger, as are the mega-yachts pretentiously parked along the old fishing port's quay, screaming out 'Look at me, I'm filthy stinking rich'. St-Tropez is anything but discreet. Every year the world's travel writers predict that the bubble is about to burst. St-Tropez, they say, has finally crossed the line of acceptable gaucheness. Yet every year it becomes more difficult to get a table at Club 55 for lunch and you have to get up earlier and earlier to guarantee a coveted beach parasol. True, the scene is over the top. But that's what makes it so much fun. Shocked, yes, scandalized, perhaps, but you will never, ever be bored here. Besides, what all St-Tropez regulars will tell you is that the scene is there when you want it and when you don't you simply stay poolside at your villa. The problem is of course that not everyone has a villa. Until now, the choice for the St-Tropez visitor *sans villa* was some high-profile accommodation in the town itself, such as Byblos or Maison Blanche, or the rustic Moulins on the Route des Plages. For those interested in peace and quiet as well as flash and decadence, the choice was very limited indeed.

There was not just a gap in the market but a huge gaping void, and hoteliers Jean-Louis and Jocelyne Sibuet had been aware of it for quite some time. Having made their name with the now famous Fermes de Marie, Le Lodge Park, Hotel Mont Blanc and Au Coin du Feu in Megève, they knew a thing or two about what the more demanding customers are looking for and what they expect. Thus they were keen to apply their unique formula of quality and character to a summer version of their winter resorts. After many years of looking, they found the ideal property high in the hills, immediately behind St-Tropez's famous beaches. By St-Tropez standards it was an immense stretch of land: six hectares, blessed with the two most desirable attributes – a view and seclusion. Jean-Louis knew this was it, and he and his wife did not hesitate to make an offer. The only problem was, the proprietor kept changing his mind.

Sometimes it would be for sale, but by the time they got around to negotiating, it was not. For five years the Sibuets played real estate cat and mouse with the owner, who was also the proprietor of all the vineyards as far as the eye could see. But finally the reluctant vendor signed on the dotted line and the Sibuets ended up with not only a prime piece of St-Tropez real estate but, more importantly, one that already had a hotel on it. Without this, they would have stood little chance of securing the necessary planning permission for their project.

The Sibuets immediately set about putting their signature on the property. To keep the project on track, Jean-Louis and his team of builders and craftsmen moved to St-Tropez for two full years. The plan was simple: reorient the rooms to take better advantage of the view, and create interiors evoking the Italian heritage of the area, an aesthetic hybrid of Provençal and Tuscan. The result is a low-key villa – one that creates the impression that it might once have been a more humble farmhouse. It is surrounded by lush gardens that cascade in spectacular fashion down the steep hillside. Fountains, potted fruit trees, imposing wrought-iron gates, cypress pines and olives create a decidedly Mediterranean ambience. Inside the approach continues with plenty of colour – red, orange, green, dark brown – and a particularly eclectic combination of art, objects and furniture that gives the place the feel of an old Italian playboy's villa: drawings by Matisse, Picasso and Cocteau, 1950s patinated garden furniture and the odd gilded Louis XVI piece. The rooms are spacious and unconventional, like mini Tuscan lofts. Creatively speaking, the hotel is a big success. But perhaps the most telling compliment came from the previous owner who, on a tour of the property just prior to opening, commented rather bitterly: 'If I'd known the rooms had such a view I'd never have sold.'

---

address Villa Marie, Route des Plages, Chemin Val Rian, 83350 Ramatuelle, St-Tropez, France
t (33) 4 94 97 40 22 **f** (33) 4 94 97 37 55 **e** contact@villamarie.fr
room rates from € 190

babington house

'Of all the great things that the English have invented and made part of the credit of the national character, the most perfect, the most characteristic, the only one they have mastered completely in all its details so that it becomes a compendious illustration of their social genius and their manners, is the well-appointed, well-administered, well-filled country house.' So thought Henry James, and it's difficult not to agree. There's a romantic fantasy that pervades the English country house – an irresistible combination of nature, history and style. Sloshing through windswept fields in rubber boots; coming home to a roaring fire and a game of billiards … the invigorating pleasures of outdoor sports are perfectly complemented by the cosy comforts indoors.

Babington is an English country estate, and a Georgian one at that – the style that has not only become the most enduring signature of English architecture but is far and away the most covetable. Babington is a particularly beautiful example; in fact it may be the perfect English country house – not least because someone else launders the sheets and tidies up the mess. At Babington it is as it used to be: live like a lord and let someone else take care of the chores. But thankfully the food is not as it used to be. Instead of 'roast something or other and one vegetable'

Babington brings the urban food culture of London to the country. It must be the only country estate with a wood-fired oven (producing delicious home-made pizzas) and an industrial-strength cappuccino machine.

Babington is equally adventurous in its approach to the interior. Tradition has been abandoned, and with great flair. The design signature shows a very healthy disrespect for frumpy chintz and family antiques. Modern and Georgian complement one another well, as no one who has been to Babington would dispute. Cynics might respond that this is a country house for people who don't really like the countryside, but if you have ever endured the 'romance' of a few nights in the country without modern comforts such as central heating, plenty of hot water and decent coffee, you would confirm that it is not romantic … just uncomfortable. The reality is that these stylish Georgian boxes demand an awful lot of maintenance and obscene amounts of money to heat properly. So the idea of running a country house as a club is rather ingenious. The old dining room is now a funky bar, and there are two restaurants and a fifty-seater cinema. The bedrooms are sumptuously equipped with bathrooms that feature showers big enough for two and claw-foot baths that stand before marble fireplaces.

Yet all of this pales beside what has been accomplished with a bunch of old barns. The Cowshed, Babington's fitness centre, has a juice bar, a dance studio, a cardio training room and two swimming pools – both heated, both open all year round, one outside and one inside. A cold winter's day takes on new meaning when you start it with a swim through rising steam in an outdoor pool nestling among cow fields.

But none of these city-slicker luxuries takes anything away from the authenticity of the house and the surroundings. Set in fifteen acres of grounds, Babington is a genuine country estate that has always been a community unto itself. It still has its own picturesque chapel set at the end of an elegant tree-lined drive. Babington was first documented in the 1370s, and the seven-bay facade that gives the building its Georgian signature was not added until 1702. The house is in fact anything but pure Georgian. Ornate moulded ceilings are Queen Anne in period and

style and the staircase is distinguished by a superb fifteenth-century stained-glass window. The dominant view from the interior is defined by a series of man-made lakes that cascade into one another; cherry blossom marks the arrival of spring; and immaculate lawns, dotted with old oaks, spread in every direction with not a hint of a road, building or telegraph pole to spoil the Arcadian scene. Capability Brown, the famous landscape gardener, could not have conceived a more convincing example of the idyllic English country estate.

Gardens, architecture, historical pedigree … Babington has it all, including the most essential ingredient of any successful country house, an interesting guest list. As the country counterpart of Soho House, London's most fashionable club, Babington mixes the elite from the worlds of film, television, radio and art with paying non-members, creating a laid-back atmosphere charged with a very English potential for scandal.

---

address Babington House, near Frome, Somerset BA11 3RW, Great Britain
t (44) 1373 812266 **f** (44) 1373 812112 **e** enquiries@babingtonhouse.co.uk
room rates from UK £235

hotel tresanton

'Fish, tin and copper' goes the famous Cornish drinking toast – because until relatively recently, this southwestern tip of England was a hardy area that earned its living by fishing pilchards and mining tin and copper.

Life was hard, survival all-consuming. Its location gave Cornwall military importance (it was from here that the English defeated the mighty Spanish Armada) but in peacetime Cornwall was the forgotten corner of England. Before the Industrial Revolution and the rail network, the journey to the Cornish peninsula from London would average forty-eight hours. Thus, apart from a few strategic forts such as the castle at St Mawes and the odd private estate built from mining wealth, it was always an isolated, humble part of England with its own language and its own traditions.

In a bitter twist, life got even grimmer in the late nineteenth century, when the great schools of pilchards that the fishermen relied on stopped migrating past the Cornish coast. At the same time the expansion of empire led to the discovery of far greater and more accessible sources of tin and copper. Thus the two main industries of Cornwall collapsed almost simultaneously. An already tough life became almost unsustainable.

It was because times were so bad for so long that Cornwall stayed the same while the rest of Britain changed at breakneck speed. Its quaint fishing villages, idyllic harbours, white sandy beaches and rolling countryside are all intact. And therein lies the main reason why Cornwall is today considered the Riviera of the British Isles: no industry, no people – it's that simple. That, and the weather. By courtesy of the Gulf Stream, Cornwall has the most moderate climate in the British Isles. With a frost once in ten years, it's the only place tropical plants will survive at such northern latitudes. The whole of Cornwall, and the southern tip in particular, has a microclimate in which the temperature is usually several degrees higher than the rest of Britain. But the tag Riviera doesn't just refer to the unspoilt beauty and the balmy climate. It's also an indicator of price. So popular is Cornwall today that property prices are almost as high as in London and little thatched cottages in seaside villages almost never come on the market.

Olga Polizzi knows this area well. Her husband's family has had a holiday home on the bay of St Mawes for years. The Tresanton, only a few doors down, was opened in the late forties by her husband's godfather, Jack Siley. In its heyday it was one of the smartest hotels in Cornwall.

St Mawes castle was built by Henry VIII
to safeguard England's south coast

Hotel Tresanton has redefined the English
seaside vacation: fewer frilly bits,
more style

St Mawes is the perfect picturesque
fishing village – a Cornish cliché
come true

Each room is different – what they have
in common is a simple pared-down
sophistication

The dining room combines classic
fifties Race chairs with
tongue-and-groove panelling

The games room adjacent to the bar
has sweeping views of the bay
of St Mawes

The chef, like the table setting, is urban:
Jock Zonfrillo has worked with Marco Pierre White
and Gordon Ramsay

The main salon combines a massive open
fireplace with floppy sofas and the
odd scattering of antiques

Bathrooms look like they belong
on a yacht, all pristine
and panelled

The rooms at the front are typical
of a Cornish country cottage

Despite a laid-back ambience, the food and
service are impeccable: no buffet breakfast
at Tresanton

The nautical theme is reinforced in
the espresso bar by a compass motif
in the mosaic tiled floor

Mosaic medallions decorate
the dining-room floor

Olga Polizzi's design approach is bright
and modern but comfortable

The idyllic bay of St Mawes is a popular
place for yachting in the summer

The adjacent gardens were created by a
New Zealander, who imported many
of the exotic plants from down under

A microclimate created by the Gulf Stream
allows some unlikely species to flourish
in the subtropical gardens

An urban design signature contrasts
successfully with the cosy cottage
architecture of Cornwall

But with the advent of affordable international travel in the seventies it went into a slow, gradual decline. 'Each time,' recalls Polizzi, 'my husband and I stayed at the Anchorage we'd walk past Tresanton and he'd say "you ought to buy it and rescue it" … I toyed with the idea for years.'

Her temptation is understandable. As the daughter of Lord Forte, she has hotels in the blood. For most of her working life she has worked alongside her brother, Sir Rocco Forte, taking charge of building and design for such family jewels as the Eden in Rome, the George V in Paris and the Waldorf in London. Then in 1995 the Granada group staged a hostile takeover coup and seized control of the family business. This was her opportunity to realize a hotel of her own. The Tresanton, by then a tired affair teetering on the edge of collapse, had the potential; Polizzi had the time, the expertise and (after Granada's buyout) the money.

The result redefines the English seaside holiday. It brings style to Cornwall, as well as a restaurant on a par with London's best. Chef Jock Zonfrillo, a Scottish Italian, learned to cook with Marco Pierre White and Gordon Ramsay. The hotel is distinguished by what one London magazine described as 'a robust absence of prissiness'. There are no paper doilies, no mini-bars and not a floral print in sight. Instead the interior is all gleaming wooden floors, painted tongue-and-groove panelling and the odd antique – like a boat, simple and buttoned-down.

Despite its quickly gained reputation as the most stylish little English hotel outside London, Tresanton remains a family affair. Polizzi often pops in to lend a hand when the hotel is short-staffed, and her two daughters, Alex and Charlie, have been known to serve the odd meal. Even her husband, writer and biographer William Shawcross, occasionally gets to lug guests' baggage to their rooms.

---

address Hotel Tresanton, Lower Castle Road, St Mawes, Cornwall TR2 5DR, Great Britain
t (44) 1326 270055   **f** (44) 1326 270053   **e** info@tresanton.com
room rates from UK £195

hotel bratsera

Litmos, Naxos, Patmos, Paros, Mykonos, Zakinthos, Lesbos … the sheer number of Greek islands presents a bewildering choice. With so many options, which do you choose, and why?

One of the smallest stands out. Hydra is unlike all other Greek islands – and not just because it doesn't end in '-os'. It hasn't been marred by mass tourism, and it's one of very few islands that doesn't allow vehicles of any kind – cars, motorcycles, scooters, mopeds, even bicycles. Horses, mules, donkeys and feet are the only available means of transport. This means that Hydra has avoided that most irritating plague of the Mediterranean – teenagers and tourists on whining, two-stroke-engined two-wheelers circling the town like Sioux Indians on the warpath until the early hours of the morning.

The only motors you will hear on Hydra are the burbling engines of the hydrofoil or the high-speed catamaran ferry that pulls in briefly to drop off and pick up passengers to the mainland. Hydra is a perfectly charming cluster of traditional houses hugging an old horseshoe-shaped harbour with the odd windmill and some remote monasteries in the barren hills beyond. It has no high-rise buildings, no hideous concrete bunkers and no huge hotel.

But wait – it gets better. Hotel Bratsera, like Hydra itself, is one of a kind. Architecturally, I admit I was sceptical. What, I thought, could possibly be done with a whitewashed house except something simple and predictable? Blue doors, thatched wooden chairs, that sort of thing. I was certainly not prepared for a building that won a Europa Nostra diploma in 1996 for outstanding restoration.

Until the mid-eighties, Bratsera was a factory – a sponge factory. Established by Nickolaos Verneniotis in 1860, this was where his family's eighteen-odd boats and their divers would return with sea sponges plucked from the Mediterranean. In the factory the sponges were cleaned, bleached and trimmed into neat shapes, and then placed in a massive press to compact them ready for shipping. Customers were as far-flung as the Swedish post office, which used sponge for wetting stamps, and French porcelain manufacturers, who used it for protective packaging. But a once-thriving business was transformed in the years after the Second World War by the availability of cheap plastic sponges. At the same time, the countries bordering the Med started to police their national waters more vigorously. Greek sponge divers found themselves no longer welcome in the waters of Lebanon, Syria, Turkey and Cyprus.

The current proprietor of the Bratsera hotel, Christine Nevros, grew up surrounded by sponges. The factory was her family's business, and up until 1986 she was in charge of exports. But as the years went by, it was ever more difficult to stay afloat, and it was she who made the decision to convert from sponges to hospitality. The factory, a stone's throw from the picturesque harbour, was the perfect venue for a highly individual hotel. It was spacious enough to house a bar, restaurant, courtyard swimming pool, gallery, and hall with capacity for over one hundred; and it provided the raw ingredients and the inspiration for a highly inventive design approach.

Architect Dimitris Papaharalambous successfully integrated the signature features of the sponge factory into a highly effective design scheme. The doors of the twenty-three guest rooms, for example, were constructed from recycled packing crates, with their stencilled destinations still legible.

The sponge press and other old factory equipment adorns the public areas as carefully placed sculpture. Vintage black and white photos from the heyday of the sponge factory decorate the guest rooms. But the industrial theme goes beyond cleverly conceived decoration. It is present in the very construction materials: in the window frames of robust angle steel, in the staircase composed of two massive steel girders, in the rough and rugged stone walls, and in floors of unfinished broad pine planking. Together with the polished-granite ground floor, it all combines to create a style and ambience that is not only thoroughly individual but entirely unexpected for a hotel in such an idyllic little village.

The most telling Hydra statistic is the fact that more than forty Athens-based architects have houses here: Greece's cultural and aesthetic elite have chosen Hydra as their weekend getaway and summer retreat. It's no accident that the island remains so unspoiled.

---

address Hotel Bratsera, Hydra 180 40, Greece

t (30) 22980 53971 **f** (30) 22980 53626 **e** bratsera@yahoo.com

room rates from € 125 (including breakfast)

katikies

When we think of the Greek islands, we think of blue water, blue sky and simple whitewashed villages twinkling in the sun. The combination of white and azure blue is so Greek that even the nation's flag follows this predominant duotone. But nowhere I have come across takes it to the extreme of Katikies, this cliffside hotel in the picturesque town of Oia (spelled Ía in Greek). The place is literally blindingly white. Without sunglasses, you wouldn't last long here. The steps, the terraces, the roofs, the furniture, the outdoor curtains and cushions, the staff uniforms, the china – everything is white. Contrasted against the deep blue of Santorini's sea and sky, it makes a bold, vivid package.

There's a mythical angle to add to the intrigue. It has long been rumoured that Santorini is what remains of the fabled lost city of Atlantis. The ruins, according to legend, lie at the bottom of Santorini's deep, dark blue crater. A few decades ago, none other than Jacques Cousteau arrived with his exploration vessel, *Calypso*, to have a look, but the Greek authorities, intent on retaining the enduring appeal of the unsolved mystery, refused him permission to dive, and so the tantalising possibility remains exactly that.

In any case, Santorini does not really need the possibility of submerged archaeological wonders to enhance its attraction. Even without myths, it is unlike anywhere else in the Mediterranean, suspended as it is from towering, near vertical cliffs that tumble without respite into the bluest water on the planet.

It's true that Katikies, unlike perhaps other hotels on islands of this ancient archipelago, is not situated on an idyllic little sandy beach, complete with colourful fishing boats, but it nonetheless feels like it is. With its low-key minimal dress code, its sunglasses-only brightness, and its colour-scheme typical of a beach house, Katikies is 100% a beach destination even if you never get any sand between your toes.

Still, let's assume you are not the type to hang around the pool, and sand below that bare foot is the aim, after all. Most conveniently located is Baxedes beach, just to the north. It is walking distance and has the added advantage that the 200-odd steps that lead down to it (and back up again) discount any need for further sweating in the gym. The beach also happens to be next door to a small fishing harbour which is home to the Paradhisos Taverna, not a bad place to grab a late lunch. Linger over a dish of freshly caught fish or octopus on the terrace overlooking the port and the local fishing fleet. With more adventure in mind,

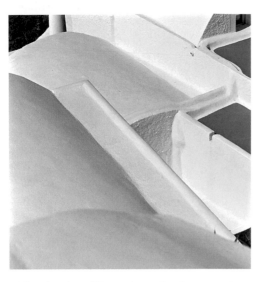

The gleaming whiteness is continually renewed –
the surfaces at Katikies are repainted at least
once a month

From one of two horizon pools, you can
contemplate the possibility that the fabled
lost city of Atlantis lies below you

Lunch, and life, are alfresco –
with virtually no chance of rain in the summer,
every moment is spent outdoors

The hotel's arrangement of space is completely vertical – tiny, winding steps take you up and down the cliff face

The ubiquitous whitewash of Katikies makes it startlingly, blindingly bright – just don't forget your sunglasses

The traditional domed roofs of these cliffside structures have their origins in simple peasant dwellings

you can rent a boat and head over to the two volcanic islets of Palea Kameni and Nea Kameni, where you can swim in sulphurous mudbaths heated by hot springs.

On Santorini, you can even colour-code your beach itinerary. The island has black beaches, white beaches and even a couple of red beaches. The red is the one that got my attention. Kokkini Ammos (literally red sand) is definitely not walking distance from Katikies, but still certainly worth the effort. Located only a few hundred yards from the ruins of the ancient city of Akrotiri, its red sands framed by red cliffs make a spectacular sight. This southwestern tip of the island offers a more pure, restrained and mythic aspect. The frantic fracas of Fira (Santorini's main town – avoid if you can) is replaced by solitary churches carved into impossibly steep cliff faces. On the way home you can stop at the Glaros Taverna for lunch and take in the site of Akrotiri before heading back to Oia.

Santorini's legendary beauty is not exactly a best-kept secret, and at the height of the season the cruise ships do tend to hover off its volcanic cliffs. Thankfully, however, the water, right up to the shore, is too deep for them to anchor, so they don't stay long. And even in the busiest months (July and August) it's possible to find complete isolation on nearby Tharissia, whose landscape is untouched by tourism. A short boatride from Katikies, Tharissia has nothing: no shops, no hotels, no bars, no nightclubs, no cruise-ship escapees, just a crystal-blue Aegean, lots of rocks and the odd goat.

Volcanoes, ancient civilizations, age-old trade routes, modern mythology, Santorini has it all – including the fervent belief, which persisted well into the twentieth century, that the island was home to a much feared population of vampires. It's a nice touch. And a perfect excuse never to go to bed.

---

address Katikies, Oia (Ía), Santorini (Thíra), 84702, Greece

t (30) 22860 71401   **f** (30) 22860 71129   **e** info@katikies.com

room rates from € 225 (including breakfast and beach transfers)

atelier sul mare

Sicily has been a hub of civilization since the earliest days of Mediterranean history. Egyptian, Phoenician, Roman and Greek empires have used the conveniently located island as a foothold in conducting trade around the region. Once virtually a colony of ancient Greece, Sicily has been a stomping ground for European culture for three thousand years. Two hundred years ago Nelson parked the collective might of the British fleet in the bay of Palermo and was reluctant to leave, and just over a century ago Garibaldi led his Red Shirts to an astounding coup, ending the Bourbon iron grip over southern Italy and paving the way for the first unification of the Italian peninsula since Roman times.

It's perhaps fitting that an island with so much history should play host to such a modern phenomenon as Atelier sul Mare. Founded by entrepreneur Antonio Presti, son of a local cement magnate, Atelier sul Mare is this Sicilian businessman's second major project patronizing modern art on a monumental scale. The first was Fiumara d'Arte – 'Art Stream' – a sculpture park that features the commissioned work of nine international contemporary artists. The spectacular works are each the size of two- and three-storey buildings and wind along the course of the River Tusa in the Nebrodi Mountains Park of northeast Sicily.

Presti's campaign to bring art to this forgotten corner of Sicily was followed by Atelier sul Mare, a hotel that introduces the idea of living with art. Unlike the famous Colombe d'Or in the south of France, which is decorated with a collection of works by some of the world's greatest modern artists, at Atelier sul Mare artists were invited to each turn an entire guest room into an art installation. With the only two restrictions being that there had to be somewhere to hang clothes and a mattress to sleep on, the artists (many of whom also participated in the Fiumara d'Arte) were restricted only by their imaginations. One contributor, Chilean film director Raoul Ruiz, conjured a minimalist planetarium: a thirty-foot circular black tower with a revolving round bed at the base and a sliding roof that opens to the sky. Video artist Fabrizio Plessi created a room called 'The Sea Denied' that is panelled on all sides with old doors to completely block all evidence of the hotel's seaside location ... except for a row of half a dozen video screens playing a tape of waves repeatedly crashing on a shore.

But without a doubt the craziest room is the one created by Presti himself as a tribute to his hero, the Italian poet and film director Pier Paolo Pasolini. This entire room

One room, conceived as a tribute to Italian poet and film director Pasolini, recreates the interior of a Yemeni hut

Located on Sicily's rocky northeast coast, Atelier sul Mare is literally on the water's edge

'Nest' by Paolo Icaro is a concrete-walled, oval-shaped sanctuary in which even the bedcover mimics feathers

'Energy' by Maurizio Mochetti is a red and white glowing fantasy that entirely shuts out the blue of the Mediterranean

Fourteen of the forty rooms were designed by internationally acknowledged contemporary artists

The bar, originally an old garage, is decorated inside and out with local graffiti art

is covered wall to wall in red mud, in reference to Pasolini's favourite country, Yemen. This has been inscribed with a graphic white border of Pasolini's words written in Arabic. Even the telephone is hidden under a mud-covered flap in the floor. But that's nothing compared to the bathroom. Called the Car Wash (because Pasolini died beneath the wheels of a car), it's a spaghetti tangle of copper pipes that spring from the walls like snakes from the head of the Medusa and spray water in every conceivable direction. Children, predictably, absolutely love it.

And that, for Antonio Presti, is the point – to make art fun. He's convinced that art has been ruined by heavy-handed intellectuals and investment buyers. It dismays him that people are so rarely exposed to works of art and when they are it's in the stifling environment of a museum. So despite the fact that some of the artists involved have international reputations, this is not an elite project. Quite

the opposite. It actually helps if you don't know much about modern art, for then you are free to experience the hotel with a totally open mind.

And that is certainly what happens every morning, in an unlikely ritual in which guests throw their keys into a large stone bowl on the reception desk and are then invited to grab a set and take themselves on a tour of the other rooms. It sounds like a formula for disastrous invasions of privacy – what about those forgotten underpants left hanging in the bathroom? But because the management is relaxed about it, so is everyone else.

Not one aspect of Atelier sul Mare accords with convention. The bar is a graffiti-painted garage, while the lobby contains a monumental kiln in which guests can fire their own crockery designs (there is, as a result, not a matching cup and saucer on site). It all expresses the delightfully twisted imagination of proprietor Antonio Presti.

---

address Atelier sul Mare, Via Cesare Battisti 4, Castel di Tusa, Messina, Sicily, Italy
t (39) 0921 334 295 f (39) 0921 334 283 e ateliersulmare@interfree.it
room rates from € 85 (half board)

castello di falconara

Take Isak Dinesen's *Out of Africa*, throw in Prince
Lampedusa's *The Leopard*, mix it all together and you
have some idea of what to expect from this twelfth-century
Norman castle on Sicily's southern coast.

Like Dinesen, aka Baroness Karen Blixen, Baron Roberto
Chiaramonte Bordonaro used to have a farm in Africa (farm,
of course, being an aristocratic diminutive for a plantation –
a coffee plantation). And like Blixen, whose famous book was
written after she reluctantly abandoned her plantation and
returned to her native Denmark, this Sicilian baron's family
also miss their Kenyan property terribly. Antonella, the baron's
wife, describes it as having been paradise on earth. Judging
from the number of African mementoes and souvenirs that
dominate Castello di Falconara, it's clear that their lifestyle
in Africa was very much à la Hemingway. There are faded
photos throughout this old hunting lodge featuring the baron,
his father and grandfather dressed in head-to-toe khaki with
a big gun in hand, kneeling beside various successful big
game kills. Rhino, crocodile, water buffalo, ostrich, antelope,
gazelle … you name it, Baron Bordonaro and his forebears
have shot it. The proof hangs on the walls of Falconara.

Even if, decoratively speaking, this may not be
everyone's thing, it is nonetheless impressive. Moreover,

given the history of the property, it is also quite appropriate.
The square tower, a seafront fortification built to protect
against barbarian invaders, dates back to Norman times.
It was presented in 1392 by King Martino of Aragon to
Ugone di Santapau for services rendered in protecting the
monarch's holdings from his enemies. Like most medieval
castles, it was not primarily a residence but a fort, occupied
by professional soldiers and domestic animals. The
mercenaries slept in a loft suspended under the ceiling,
while the animals were kept in the great hall. Then in 1540
the castle became the property of Ambrogio di Santapau
Branciforte, Prince of Butera, who finally set about turning
it into a residence befitting a nobleman. Its function shifted
from military defence to the pursuit of pleasure, and the
original tower became a place for raising falcons for the
hunt, hence its present name.

In the 1800s Castello di Falconara passed by dowry
to a German officer, Count Wilding, and then on his death to
his brother. During the risings of 1848, the latter decided to
sell up and go home. Thus the property – and the title that
came with it – were acquired by Antonio Chiaramonte
Bordonaro. It is at this point that the story of Falconara
starts to resemble the life described in Giuseppe Tomasi

di Lampedusa's romantically melancholy novella. Set in the late 1800s, *The Leopard* chronicles the life of the Bourbon aristocracy in the old Sicily just before Garibaldi's bold effort at unification, when Palermo and Napoli were still ruled as part of the 'Kingdom of the Two Sicilies'. Not only is the current baron's great grandfather the spitting image of Burt Lancaster in Visconti's film based on the book, but his lifestyle even today is not too different from that evoked in the novel. Bordonaro's life revolves principally around his exquisite Belle Epoque palace in Palermo, but in summer the family move, staff and all, to their country estate, Castello di Falconara.

The only difference is that today the aristocracy of Sicily are no longer as wealthy as they once were, and as a result, they have to generate an income. Not unlike the royal families of India, Bordonaro has decided to make his properties viable via hospitality. His Palermo residence,

Carlotta, is used as a venue for catered events, and Falconara is available as paid accommodation. But he bristles rather haughtily at any mention of the word hotel. He prefers 'family seaside estate' – for him the word 'hotel' is too far removed from 'house', which is what he considers it to be. In any case, it's only available to rent in its entirety, and only then when he wants it to be. Otherwise, it remains the family's summer seat. One does get the impression, however, that if it were to be booked the whole time, he really wouldn't mind.

The Baron's proud sense of proprietorship is perfect for the experience – it keeps it authentic. There are plenty of examples in Sicily of important properties ruined by conversion to 'grand hotels'. At Falconara there are no bell boys, receptionists, chambermaids or waiters; nor is there a fax or phone in every room – just age-old aristocratic ambience.

---

address Castello di Falconara, Butera (Caltanissetta), Sicily, Italy
t (39) 091 329 082   **f** (39) 091 589 206   **e** info@castellodifalconara.it
rates from € 5,750 (per week)

hotel raya

Without Raya, I'm not sure that Panarea would hold the same attraction. One of the smallest Aeolian islands, Panarea is nowhere near as beautiful as Salina or as dramatic as Stromboli. What it does have going for it, however, is one of the most refined hotels in the Mediterranean.

Raya is all white, perfectly pristine and totally the place to be. Whitewashed all over, it is the architectural equivalent of a perfectly ironed white linen shirt – immaculate to look at, cool to be in. Detailed with the odd strategically placed urn or giant shell, Raya is my – and no doubt other people's – fantasy of what a Mediterranean island hotel should be. The place is so perfectly styled it only requires five items of clothing: black linen pants, a white shirt, white linen pants, a black t-shirt, and a swimsuit. Every year the white gets repainted and any scratched white floor tiles in the rooms are replaced. The hotel understands the most basic lesson of minimalism, which is that it must be maintained to an immaculate standard.

When Myriam Beltrami and Paolo Tilche, an adventure-seeking, globe-trotting couple, first arrived here in the 1960s, Panarea was well on its way to being abandoned. Most of the population had emigrated and just a handful of families continued the age-old struggle to make a living from the sea. Myriam and Paolo, however, didn't see a hapless, waterless, minuscule piece of seabound volcanic rock; they saw a place of exquisite untouched beauty – rugged and unforgiving but also blessed with the clearest emerald-green water in the Mediterranean. Here they could realize the lifestyle of their fantasies: swimming, diving, fishing, a return to nature without the price-tag of most Mediterranean retreats. They built their house on the island's prime location, a small rocky outcrop looking straight at the active volcano of Stromboli. Understandably, within the shortest space of time, friends were lining up to share their newfound paradise. In those days there was at most a boat every two weeks that stopped at Panarea, and then only when the weather permitted – the island is notoriously exposed. None of this deterred people from visiting. Paolo drew on building skills learned during a stint on the Greek island of Hydra to create accommodation for his guests. Slowly, inevitably, the project grew into a hotel, as they added on another house each time they could afford it. At the same time, many friends, captivated by the uncomplicated life on Panarea, asked Myriam and Paolo to find a piece of land and build a house for them. Thus Panarea began its gradual transformation

from nearly abandoned island of dirt-poor fishermen to stylish Italian retreat. All in all, Myriam and Paolo built about thirty houses, and it's largely to them that the island can attribute its consistent and culturally authentic architecture, not to mention its total lack of cars, motorbikes, trucks or buses. In many ways, this island is strikingly similar to Hydra: both prohibit vehicles, both have a small harbour as the town centre, and both lack big hotels, apartment blocks or offices that might spoil the indigenous architectural charm.

There was at first some local hostility to Panarea's gradual reinvention (Myriam and Paolo's joint was more than once burned to the ground), but Panarea has now become the envy of the Tyrrhenian Sea. Its low-key, well-planned and aesthetically responsible tourism has only done good for the island. And things are unlikely to change. For a start there are far more private houses than hotels, and those hotels that do exist are small in scale. At Raya, the simplicity is absolute: there are no televisions to distract from the wild-island experience. Its properties, all built in the traditional Aeolian form, conform to a strict and beautifully appropriate colour scheme: the only contrast to the overall whitewash are a powder blue, soft ochre yellow and terracotta-tinted pink. As a result, walking around the island is a complete pleasure. Even with no knowledge of Aeolian tradition, you will sense that everything is true to it – it simply looks right.

If ever a group of well-travelled aesthetes were to get together to design a Mediterranean island from scratch, they would probably come up with something very like Panarea. It has Malta's sunshine, Pantelleria's untouched rugged beauty, Sardinia's emerald-green water, Sicily's food, Capri's style, and the whitewashed consistency of Mykonos. And at night – most amazing of all – you can dine on Raya's all-white terrace and watch the spectacle of glowing lava spurting out of the volcano of Stromboli, just across the water.

---

address Hotel Raya, Via San Pietro, 98050 Panarea, Aeolian Islands, Italy
t (39) 090 983 013 **f** (39) 090 983 103 **e** info@hotelraya.it
room rates from € 118

la posta vecchia

Be Agnelli for a day. When the urge grabs you to be surrounded by beauty from all ages and in all shapes and sizes, from Roman busts to baroque mirrors to exquisite Renaissance furniture, then La Posta Vecchia is the place. Nowhere in Europe will you find such treasures in such a location. In fact the person who originally owned this villa, the one who piled it so full of irreplaceable things, was even richer than Agnelli. In his day, J. Paul Getty ranked as the world's richest man, and La Posta Vecchia was a reflection of his passion for antiques. Although he always intended it to be his last real home, Getty abandoned La Posta Vecchia after his grandson was kidnapped by the Red Brigades. Disgusted, he turned his back on Italy and never returned. The house with all its contents was sold as one. That is how such an extraordinary property with such extraordinary contents came to be available to the paying guest.

For centuries, this impressive double-fronted villa in Palo Laziale on the coast northwest of Rome was part of the hereditary estate of the Odescalchi family. It was built in 1640 as a residential hotel for tradesmen; the name derives from the fact that it became one of the official stops for the coaches transporting the royal mail. Getty was acquainted with the descendants of the Odescalchi family, and on

occasion he leased their nearby castle for the summer. But it was the Renaissance structure next door that really caught his eye, despite its dilapidated state. In 1918 La Posta Vecchia had been largely destroyed by fire, but Getty never relented in trying to convince Prince Ladislao Odescalchi to sell it to him. Getty's legendary will and persistence eventually prevailed and in 1960 the family agreed to sell La Posta Vecchia together with a sizeable portion of land.

J. Paul Getty had a serious appetite for classical antiquities, but with La Posta Vecchia even he may have got more than he bargained for. It all started with the pool. In spite of the private black-sand beach that came with the property, Getty nonetheless wanted a swimming pool, and workmen started digging in the garden to prepare for one. Halfway through, the work had to stop when they uncovered the ruins of a Roman seaside villa, and a significant one at that, attributed to the Emperor Tiberius no less. Archaeologists were brought in and a booty of amphorae and objects was uncovered slowly – very slowly. A new location was selected in the garden for the swimming pool, and digging started afresh ... only to discover yet another villa from ancient Rome. The archaeologists returned and work slowed back down to handbrush pace.

Tiramisu finished with a swirl of peppermint
is a speciality of the kitchen

La Posta Vecchia is a Renaissance villa
bang on the Mediterranean coast

Every space, every corner is testament
to the most exquisite attention to
detail money could buy

The indoor swimming pool in one of the
villa's wings has an entire history
of its own

When J. Paul Getty sold the villa in 1975,
his cook stayed on. One of her best
dishes is pasta with scampi

Many of the bathrooms come complete
with magnificent marble fireplaces

A connecting corridor space serves
as a small private living area

The dining room occupies the opposite wing to
the one containing the swimming pool

A solid marble bathtub with
bronze swan-shaped taps

The front of the villa is right on the
sea wall; to the rear it looks over acres
of formal classical gardens

Getty employed an art historian for the
better part of a decade to find
the pieces to furnish the villa

A detail of the red velour antique bedhead
in one of the guest rooms

Scagliola – polished marble inlaid with coloured
lime mortar – on a table top in one
of the reception spaces

Getty filled the house with priceless pieces
that were then sold with the
property when he left

The bathroom in what was Getty's own
suite is a masterpiece of solid
pink marble overkill

The present owners have experimented for
years to find exactly the right shade of
terracotta for the external walls

Opulent, spacious, grand – the guest suites
at La Posta Vecchia recall the days when
this was a private villa

Getty was a firm fan of antiquity.
The classical figures that decorate
the corridors are of museum quality

Not one to give up easily, Getty decided to build a pool complex under the house. To do this the entire palazzo had to be suspended on steel beams to secure its structure before the excavation underneath commenced. No points for guessing what they found. Only this time, the Roman villa was bigger and better, with original mosaic floors intact and enough artefacts to fill a museum – which is exactly what Getty did. He turned the excavated space beneath the house into a museum to display his own hoard of Roman antiquity. As for that damned pool – Getty had no choice but to build it in the one place where he could be guaranteed not to find an ancient villa – inside the house.

The pool is not the only Getty eccentricity guests can enjoy at this extraordinary hotel. If you are lucky enough to score the Getty Suite, you will sleep in a gilded Renaissance bed that once belonged to a Medici. Some bathrooms have fireplaces larger than you would find in a Tuscan farmhouse,

baths are carved from solid blocks of marble, and the taps are gilded swans – what else did you expect? The pay phone in the corridor that Getty used to make his guests use is no longer there, but the irreplaceable antiques and works of art are: portrait busts of the emperors Agrippa and Vespasian with faces in white marble and togas in coloured stone; Flemish tapestries hanging in the library; a Piranesi drawing in the study. Even the dining tables are in a rare antique yellow marble.

La Posta Vecchia is all about arriving with all those books you have always wanted to read, and not leaving its paradise compound before you absolutely have to. Breakfast, lunch and dinner are served on a terrace by the Mediterranean, and no activity should take you more than a hundred yards from the villa and its seventeen acres of gardens. Be Agnelli for a weekend; but be warned – any longer and returning to real life could be painful.

---

address La Posta Vecchia, 00055 Palo Laziale, Ladispoli, Italy

t (39) 06 994 9501 **f** (39) 06 994 9507 **e** info@lapostavecchia.com

room rates from € 570

parco dei principi

The Amalfi coast is one of Italy's most enduringly beautiful landscapes, a continuous strip of volcanic mountains that plunge into an emerald-green Mediterranean. The established haunt of writers, directors, film stars and royals, this is where Liz Taylor and Richard Burton escaped to for their torrid affair while filming *Cleopatra* in Rome, where American author and society wit Gore Vidal lives for several months a year, and where Franco Zeffirelli has entertained American film stars and British royalty alike.

The Amalfi coast combines the seductive climate and passion of the southern Mediterranean with a culture defined by almost three millennia of civilization. From the ancient Greeks to the Bourbon kings, this stretch south of Naples has been coveted by a non-stop succession of powerful rulers. Hence you will find Roman ruins (Pompeii and Herculaneum), Renaissance palazzi, Belle Epoque villas, medieval churches and, of course, the timeless little fishing villages that appear on all the postcards. What you don't expect to find, perhaps because it seems so modern amid all this antiquity, is a masterpiece by Italy's most famous twentieth-century architect, Gio Ponti.

Ponti is to Italy what Frank Lloyd Wright is to America – a creative giant whose work shaped and redefined the aesthetic direction of a nation. Ponti designed Milan's landmark skyscraper, the famous Pirelli Building; he founded *Domus*, the world's most prestigious design and architecture magazine; and he designed ceramics and furniture for Italy's top factories. Although one automatically associates his work with a slick city environment like Milan, one of his most enduring projects and certainly one of his funkiest stands on the Amalfi coast. Hanging a few hundred metres above the sparkling Mediterranean on the edge of Sorrento's typically spectacular cliffs, Parco dei Principi is a testament to the timeless originality of Ponti's work. It is still as fresh and surprising and utterly stylish today as when it was completed more than thirty years ago.

For Parco dei Principi, Ponti designed every single element: the building, the furniture, the blinds, the wall decoration, the plates and even the tiles. As a result this hotel is a complete original … a total one-off. There is simply nothing else like it in the world. Outside it's like a giant piece of white card with geometric cutouts; inside it resembles a huge, modernist beach cabana, all blue and white.

Gio Ponti had a thing about using a single colour – he believed it was the only way to approach interior design.

For Parco dei Principi he chose a palette of blues. Glossy blue concrete eggs are embedded in white walls, Venetian blinds in different shades of blue form bold planes of horizontal stripes, lobby furniture is upholstered in navy blue wool, and even the telephones were specially commissioned in a particular shade of blue. But it was for the floors that Ponti really put his 'one colour' theory to the creative test. Working with a local tile manufacturer, he designed numerous variations of geometric patterns in three different shades of blue with white. So mesmerizing are the floors that I was all prepared to photograph each and every pattern … until the management tactfully reminded me that Ponti had designed a hundred different tile patterns for Parco dei Principi. This, after all, is the Amalfi coast and there are better things to do than look at the floor all day.

From May to October this a hedonistic pleasure playground with few equals. It has the weather (hot and sunny), the people (slim, sexy and suntanned), and the food (a mix of dishes from Tuscany and the more spicy tomato-based cuisine of Calabria), not to mention the pizzas for which the Neapolitans are famous. Life is all about renting a scooter and zipping around the idyllic coastal roads, finding a little restaurant in a fishing village, and then diving into the sea after lunch.

An elderly Belgian couple I met at the hotel had been coming to Parco dei Principi for a month every year for the past twenty years. When they first made the excursion from Belgium their daughter was just a baby; now she had dragged her boyfriend along, and they were sure they would eventually be bringing the grandchildren to continue the tradition. I doubt that they even knew who Gio Ponti was – what they loved about the hotel was the fact that it was still, after twenty years, the most stylish and original they had ever seen.

---

address Hotel Parco dei Principi, Via Rota 1, 80067 Sorrento, Italy

t (39) 081 878 4644 **f** (39) 081 878 3786 **e** info@hotelparcoprincipi.com

room rates from € 185

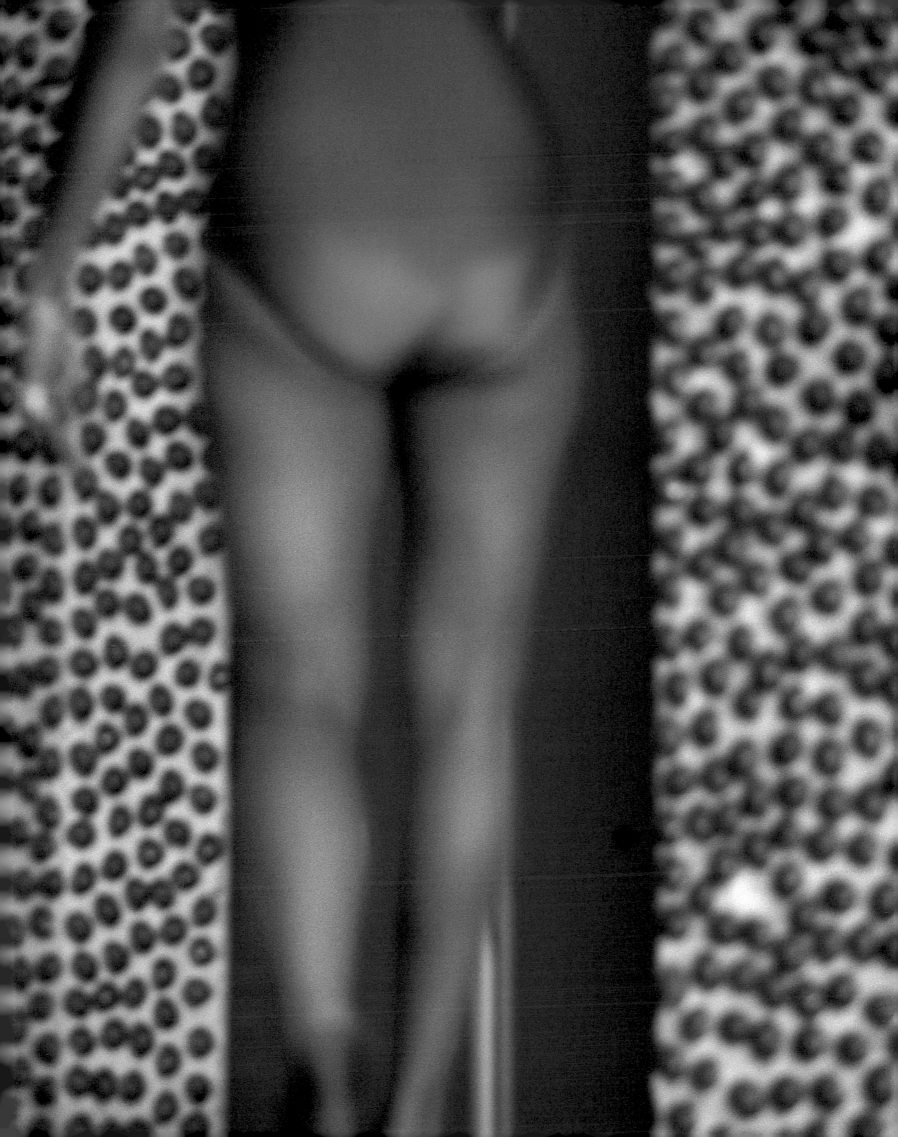

villa cimbrone

The prettiest villages on the Amalfi Coast are Positano and Ravello – on that, even the locals will agree. Amalfi, they will tell you, is too big; Sorrento too close to Naples; and Salerno too far away. Yet even though Positano and Ravello are always referred to together, they are as different as chalk and cheese. They are also further apart than most maps and descriptions make them seem. The winding, twisting, but all the while breathtaking Amalfi Coast road must surely be one of the most picturesquely impressive routes in the world. It can also be rather hair-raising: John Steinbeck observed that it was 'carefully designed to be a little narrower than two cars side by side'. Nothing has changed.

The road to Ravello, which starts at Amalfi, soon begins to climb in earnest, as the landscape turns from rocky coast with fishing villages suspended among the cliffs to one of granite peaks with chiselled verdant green terraces. The temperature drops a few degrees and the clouds descend from peak to peak in a dazzling chiaroscuro. Situated at the top of this tight winding road with a photo opportunity at every turn is the almost untouched village of Ravello, an enchanting place of small squares, narrow streets, steep alleys and hybrid architectural influences, including Romanesque, Byzantine and Arabic. Dominated by a

stone-clad piazza said to be among the prettiest in Italy, Ravello is not only close to aesthetic perfection, it's also quiet, since most of it is car- and moped-free.

From the piazza a lava-stone passageway leads further up to Villa Cimbrone. It's a ten-minute walk through alleys and lanes, passing convents and churches. The added beauty of this little trek, apart from the sense of expectation it creates, is its democracy. Everyone, regardless of who you are or how much money you have, has to approach Villa Cimbrone on foot (though there is a baggage service to transport your valise, so travellers with serious luggage shouldn't be put off).

The end destination is more than worth the scenic schlep. Seemingly perched on top of the world, Cimbrone is an ivy-clad palazzo flanked by one of the most spectacularly situated gardens anywhere in the world. Its climbing arbours, elevated rose gardens, rows of mature plane trees, cypress pines, vine-shaded walkways and lichen-covered statues all owe their existence to an English aristocrat. Once part of a monastery, the Villa Cimbrone was bought in 1904 by Lord Grimthorpe. This eccentric Yorkshireman dedicated most of his adult life to the creation of his garden in what had been the monastery's pasture and orchard. From a

series of beautifully considered vantage points, heroic lead statuary, magnificent urns, and lichen-covered marble busts set the scene for a breathtaking series of juxtapositions. The main path culminates in its star attraction: the Terrace of the Infinite, a cantilevered terrace decorated with Renaissance marble busts that is suspended over a sheer face that drops 1,600 feet down to the sea below. Looking out from here, the mind boggles as to how those Neopolitan princes and Franciscan monks ever managed to get up in the first place. The answer is simple: the hard way, via a staircase chiselled out of the stone cliffs that climbs all the way from the sea.

The interior of Cimbrone has been carefully restored, but it is difficult to compete with the visual grandeur of the garden. The salon features an impressive Renaissance fireplace and a collection of antique books, while the bedrooms have frescoed walls and high ceilings, and

bathrooms are detailed in intricate Neopolitan tiles. By and large, however, the decor is in deference to the garden and the view. After 6pm, when the gardens close to the public, they become a private sanctuary exclusive to hotel guests.

Merchant princes from Naples first built palaces in Ravello to escape the heat and enjoy the fruits of the town's wealth (derived from its abundant lemon trees and grapevines); later, the place gave Wagner the inspiration for Klingsor's magical garden in *Parsifal*; E.M. Forster, attracted by the mysterious atmosphere, came to write; Greta Garbo came to have an affair (she found sanctuary at Villa Cimbrone after eloping with Leopold Stokowski); and John Huston came to film *Beat the Devil*. Today the mayor of Ravello is proud to count Gore Vidal as a citizen. Vidal has his own villa, but aspiring authors can emulate their idols by taking a room at the Cimbrone. If this property can't provide inspiration, keep the day job.

---

address Villa Cimbrone, 26 Via Santa Chiara, 84010 Ravello, Salerno, Italy
t (39) 089 857 459 **f** (39) 089 857 777 **e** info@villacimbrone.it
room rates from € 250

relais la suvera

When Pope Julius II acquired this former medieval fort as a gift from the city of Siena in 1507, he set out to transform it into a proper palace. Fortunately for him he was able to call upon the services of the same artisans who were busy creating St Peter's for him. As a result, the best architects and artists of the day transformed Suvera castle into a Renaissance villa worthy of the leader of the Catholic Church. Architect Baldassare Peruzzi was responsible for the unique double-level portico, the great staircase and the ceiling frescoes that adorn the building to this day. Perched high on a hill overlooking the rich farmland outside Siena, La Suvera gave the pope cause to be extremely grateful to the Sienese republic (which, of course, was the intention).

This same view and situation charmed the Marchese Giuseppe Ricci and his wife Principessa Eleonora Massimo in the 1960s when they were looking for 'a small house that could be easily taken care of'. When they saw La Suvera, they knew they had found it … even though the papal villa hardly qualifies as small. It is blessed with an almost perfect location, not too far from (but equally, not too close to) Tuscany's major cities and cultural landmarks. Florence is less than an hour away, and Siena and San Gimignano less than thirty minutes.

La Suvera remained the Rome-based Riccis' country estate until 1989, when they decided to turn it into a hotel in order to raise revenue for restorations. Tellingly, they retained a private apartment in the villa, and still visit regularly for weekends and holidays. Far from resenting the intrusion of paying guests, they seem to enjoy their role as hosts. Their only daughter Elena, a graduate of hotel school in Lausanne and art school in Paris, has returned to continue what is now a family tradition of high-quality hospitality and exquisite decor. According to *National Geographic*, 'curators of New York's Metropolitan Museum of Art would jump through hoops' for the contents of the villa's twelve suites. It's true: the rooms, especially those in the main palazzo, are stuffed to the rafters with priceless pieces. Yet the effect is neither precious nor overpowering. The Marchese, an enthusiast of interior design, is disarmingly modest about the antiques, describing them as 'a few pieces from family palazzi'. In fact, the project was not achieved without some sacrifice. The Riccis had to sell one of their Rome properties in order to make present-day La Suvera a reality. Beyond the attention-seizing antiques, some serious investment was necessary. The arcaded eighteenth-century olive mill was converted to a restaurant (which has recently received

La Suvera's Papal Suite has a belvedere with delicate Renaissance frescoes and a view over the entire valley below

The Maiolica Suite is dominated by the impressive field bed of Tommaso of Savoy, Duke of Genoa

La Suvera is crammed with paintings, sculpture and other treasures, too much in fact to take in all at once

Arranged around a private piazza are the estate chapel, the old olive mill and the imposing villa itself

The opulent Papal Suite is on the top floor – too far, joke the Ricci family, for the rotund Julius II ever to climb up

Standing on the western slopes of the Sienese hills, La Suvera has had a strategic presence since around 1100

The rooms and suites abound with ancestral paintings belonging to the Marchese Giuseppe Ricci and his family

Each bathroom in each suite is entirely different, though all are decorated with precious antiques

The Renaissance gardens descend from the top of the hill down into a web of hidden corners and secret spaces

Named for the painter Emilio Farina, this suite
is white and romantic, with lots of blue glass
and walnut antiques

The suite dedicated to the Marchesa Rosalia
Eustace contains a stunning collection
of Biedermeier pieces

The huge bird cage that straddles a Renaissance
fountain contains no birds. The owners believe
birds should be free

A large antique Chinese marriage tapestry
decorates the bedroom
of the Fox Suite

Dedicated to San Carlo Borromeo,
the villa's church has remained
unaltered since 1571

The double-level loggia is a signature
of the great Sienese architect
Baldassare Peruzzi

The Farina Suite and its marble bathroom
are set beneath the original exposed
ceiling beams of the top floor

The swimming pool, complete with baroque
stone fountain, was fashioned from one
of the villa's fish ponds

La Suvera, the Marchese Ricci's former
summer residence, is an extraordinary
mix of grandeur and comfort

the much-coveted local accolade of the three golden keys of Gambero Rosso). The pool was created from one of the ponds of the well-preserved cascading formal garden. The old stables and farmhouse were converted to provide La Suvera's thirty-five rooms and suites. There is a sixteenth-century church dedicated to San Carlo Borromeo, as well as a lemon house, vineyards and a monumental aviary kept symbolically free of birds to remind us that birds are meant to be free.

The suites in the papal villa are arranged by historic theme. The Papal Suite is rich, dark and opulent, filled with red, purple and yellow velvets and an imposing carved four-poster Renaissance bed. The family joke is that the rotund Julius II was too fat ever to make his way up here. Honeymooners prefer the Maria Gabriella of Savoy Suite, dedicated to the first wife of Prince Camillo Vittorio Massimo. Its centrepiece is a large canopied bed with a gilded crown under a Bohemian crystal chandelier and a massive baroque gilded mirror. There's a Marie Antoinette Suite, and a Napoleon Suite with around a hundred statues and statuettes of Napoleon. My favourite is the Maiolica Suite, a long stately room with double doors opening onto a terrace with a view of the valley below. It is dedicated to the Principessa's great grandfather, the first Duke of Genoa, and features a magnificent framed wedding kimono given to the duke by the last empress of China. Its crowning piece, however, is the field bed that belonged to the duke himself, constructed from lacquered iron columns and decorated with gilded eagles and pine cones.

The architecture, the location and the history of this villa bring to mind Kenneth Branagh's film of Shakespeare's *Much Ado About Nothing*. Contrary to reports that Tuscany is becoming Chiantiville, places like La Suvera are a reassuring sign that all is well.

---

address Relais la Suvera, Pievescola, 53030 Siena, Italy

t (39) 0577 960 300   **f** (39) 0577 960 220   **e** reservations@lasuvera.it

room rates from € 360

villa feltrinelli

For one and a half infamous years, Villa Feltrinelli became Villa del Duce. At the tail end of Mussolini's rule, shortly after he was kidnapped by the Italian resistance, the dictator's Nazi allies decided to keep him here under heavy guard to avoid having to rescue him again. But Mussolini didn't own the house, nor did he make any changes to its furnishings or structure. In truth, the real story of this villa is the story of the Feltrinelli family.

The Feltrinellis originally amassed their substantial fortune from lumber. In the 1890s they purchased one of the finest pieces of waterfront real estate on Lake Garda, just outside the picturesque village of San Gagnano, where they proceeded to build an ornate neogothic fantasy castle in step with the scope of their fortune. An extraordinary array of custom-designed neogothic furniture was made from a collection of different exotic woods, and even though the family had grown rich on trade in European timber, they imported rare species from the American Northwest for their intricately laid parquetry floor. They also built a boathouse, a guest house, and an impressive *limonaia* to grow lemon trees all year round.

The Feltrinelli achievement did not end there. From timber they expanded – logically enough – into paper, and from there the next generation took the family into the publishing industry. Many of Italy's twentieth-century literary classics made their debut under the Feltrinelli imprint. But entry into the world of progressive prose had its risks for a capitalist dynasty. With so much contact with the radical thinkers of their day, it was perhaps inevitable that a Feltrinelli would some day get more involved in politics than in business. The last Feltrinelli to occupy the lakefront villa was a dyed-in-the-wool anarchist. With a lack of commercial leadership, the family fortunes declined, and, sadly, eventually the villa ended up on the market. Its prospects were uncertain. Its size and facilities had once made it the perfect summer venue for the well-to-do Italian family, but these were modern times and the place was much too big and too expensive for most potential suitors.

This was the point at which Bob Burns, of Regent Hotel fame, stepped into the picture. Having just sold his hotels to the Four Seasons group – including the magnificent property that is now the Four Seasons Milan – he had no further plan than to retire and spend his money. He fell for Villa Feltrinelli instantly: this was to be his retirement home.

First, however, it needed a bit of work – an understatement if ever there was one. The structure required

major reinforcement – the kind of work whose results you can't see but that costs the most money. Then there was the bureaucratic challenge of the interior. Every bit of it, including all the furniture, was protected. Apparently the last Feltrinelli tried to auction the contents separately, only to have an army of government deputies arrive on the very day of the sale to declare it illegal (a final lesson in the perils of mixing business and politics).

When the extremely elastic budget passed a particular milestone (around the $30 million mark), Mr Burns decided it might be more financially responsible to continue the project as a hotel. The result is a testament to determination and deep pockets. In the world of hotels, Villa Feltrinelli is a unique phenomenon. It has the Aman knack for seductive luxury (Aman founder Adrian Zeccha used to work with Bob Burns at Regent Hotels); the Rafael reputation for best location (Georg Rafael was also an ex-Regent Hotel man);

and the individuality of a place not originally conceived as a hotel. It's perfect in almost every detail.

The San-Francisco-based design team of Babey Moulton Jue and Booth managed to make something colourful, fun and funky from a rather sombre interior without sacrificing any of its grandeur (or running up against the heritage authorities). They retained the original interior configuration and as a result the guest rooms are exactly as one would expect of a villa – huge. Suffice to say no corners were cut on anything. So why then is it only almost perfect? Because, at the time I was there, Bob Burns was still awaiting delivery of his custom-built mahogany speedboat. Inspired by the old commuter speedboats that carried New York's Long-Island-based tycoons to work in the 1920s, the plan is to whisk guests to Verona, where they can attend the opera and then enjoy a champagne supper on the moonlit journey back. Even Aman can't compete with that.

---

address Grand Hotel a Villa Feltrinelli, 25084 Gargnano, Lake Garda, Italy
t (39) 0365 798 000   **f** (39) 0365 798 001   **e** grandhotel@villafeltrinelli.com
room rates from € 425

le sirenuse

In Greek mythology the sirens on Li Galli – the rocky outcrop just off the coast of Positano – sang so sweetly that Ulysses cupped the ears of his crew and had himself tied to the mast to avoid being lured to his doom.

Hotel Le Sirenuse is aptly named. Like a siren, it keeps tempting guests back. A couple I met from Los Angeles are typical: on their very first visit to Italy, they started at Positano and worked their way north to Rome and eventually to Tuscany. But after the first two days of what should have been a week on a farm in the hills outside Siena they were pining for Positano, and back they came.

They are certainly not the first to have been bewitched by this enchanting bit of the Amalfi Coast. Chiselled into a cliff face that plunges steeply into the calm Mediterranean, Positano is a village somehow suspended on the horizontal from a near-vertical surface. It's a triumph of human ingenuity. Positano is the kind of place that, no matter how often you have been, takes your breath away each time you round the last corner of the snaking Amalfi Coast road. It leaps into view as a cascading fan of yellow, pink, orange and ochre houses linked by a web of steps and alleyways plastered to the jagged limestone cliffs.

Positano seems so picture-postcard perfect that it's hard to grasp that until relatively recently it was really nothing more than a fishing village and a summer retreat for the odd noble Neopolitan family. Historically, the nearby town of Amalfi was much more important. In its day, Amalfi was not just one of Italy's great trading city-states (on a par with Genoa and Venice), it was the very first to get rich from the trade in spices, silks and perfumes from the Orient. The maritime republic of Amalfi was initially founded by people fleeing the fall of Rome and the murderous Huns who were rampaging their way through Italy. What they were seeking – and found – on this coast was both fortress and sanctuary, a place where they could not be discovered or attacked.

Today the business of this thirty-mile stretch of lemon-scented coast is very different. Tourism is the new trade, and in this respect, Positano is the capital. Although opinions differ as to which is the town's best hotel, all agree that it's a choice between Le Sirenuse and the San Pietro. The difference between the two is simple: San Pietro is perched on a point looking directly at Positano, whereas Le Sirenuse is in the absolute heart of Positano. The Hotel San Pietro is new and glamorous, while Le Sirenuse is an old family palazzo furnished with antiques. Which one is better?

Rooms facing the sea are much in demand.
The buildings of Positano cling to
an almost vertical cliff face

Like a favourite cashmere sweater,
Le Sirenuse's interiors cleverly combine
informality with discreet quality

The portrait of Cardinal Sersale attests to the
grand lineage of the Sersale family who
own and run Le Sirenuse

In winter, dinner is served in the ivy-clad
dining room that offers one of
the finest views in Positano

Originally the summer house of the Sersale family,
Le Sirenuse has been painted the same
oxblood red since the 1600s

Extraordinary antiques scattered about
the hotel help create an atmosphere
of aristocratic nonchalance

Given that the main attraction of Positano is the town itself I would prefer to be in the centre of the whole show, so Sirenuse gets the nod from me. Le Sirenuse is Positano's hotel of legend. Built in the eighteenth century for the Marchese Sersale, it retains the atmosphere and the style of a patrician residence, and almost every room faces the sea. The aristocratic charm of the place is perfectly in sync with the easy, relaxed pace of life on the Amalfi Coast. The travel press seems to agree. Le Sirenuse was voted by US *Travel & Leisure* magazine as Europe's best hotel.

It was the last marquis, Aldo Sersale, then also mayor of Positano, who first made the decision to convert the estate to a hotel. Rather fortuitously, this happened at the time that American writers were starting to discover Positano. In an episode reminiscent of *The Talented Mr Ripley*, John Steinbeck was brought here by fellow writer Alberto Moravia to discover the beautiful coast of Amalfi and escape the heat in Rome. Steinbeck described Positano as 'the sort of place one could imagine only in dreams and didn't seem real until one was actually there, yet whose profound reality only struck once one left it behind.' In a 1953 article for *Harper's Bazaar* he gave an early account of Positano, its mayor Aldo Sersale, and the Albergo Le Sirenuse, a hotel he described as first rate, every room with a balcony overlooking the sea.

Sadly, Positano is no longer the exclusive haunt of adventurers, artists and writers. But the corridors of Le Sirenuse are still lined with old maps, its public spaces are still decorated with family antiques, its restaurant is still one of the finest in town, and a Sersale – Antonio Sersale, nephew of Aldo – is still in charge. What's more, Steinbeck was right when he said tourism will never spoil Positano – no bus will ever fit on the small winding road leading into the village.

address Le Sirenuse, 30 Via Cristoforo Colombo, 84017 Positano, Italy
t (39) 089 875 066   **f** (39) 089 811 798   **e** info@sirenuse.it
room rates from € 250

pousada de nossa senhora da assunção

The convents of Portugal are as characteristic a feature of its countryside as the châteaux of France. Yet not all are as they used to be. Many suffered badly in the course of the nineteenth century, when the Church lost first its influence and then its land. Quite a few prime properties passed into private hands to be converted into country houses. These were the lucky ones. Many simply fell to ruin and neglect. Had it not been for a creative scheme developed in recent years by the government they might have disappeared altogether.

The Pousadas of Portugal is a national hotel project charged with restoring historical architecture, preserving regional values and enriching tourism with a sense of cultural integrity. Anyone who doubts that governments are able to do such things in a convincing and stylish manner should see the Pousada de Nossa Senhora da Assunção. Situated in a valley below the old city of Arraiolos in the sunbaked plains of Alentejo, seventy-five miles outside Lisbon, this imposing former convent had its beginnings as a private estate. In the absence of hereditary descendants, it was bequeathed to the order of St John the Evangelist, otherwise known as the Blue Canons because of the colour of their habits. The monastery here was founded in 1527 in

celebration of the day of the Assumption of our Blessed Lady. Built in a mixture of the Portuguese Manueline and Renaissance styles, it remained a monastery until the general abolition of religious orders in 1834, when it was returned to private hands. The Arraiolan family of Mexia Lobo Côrte-Real converted the monastery for use as a holiday home, which is how it stayed until 1983, when their descendants sold it to the state. By then it still had historical significance, but little else; the place was a wreck.

It is much to the credit of the Portuguese government that they chose architect José Paulo dos Santos to rescue it. Dos Santos defined his approach to this sensitive task in the phrase 'step forward and be silent'. The resulting Pousada is a place to be noticed while remaining true to the serene spirit of the cloister. Its elegant, meditative minimalism represents the kind of design statement that wouldn't be out of place in the hippest hotels of New York, Paris or London, and yet here, in the heart of the Portuguese countryside, it seems even more appropriate. The materials chosen for the renovation – granite, limestone and plaster – are those of the original structure. Even the furniture in the guest rooms evokes the centuries-old monastic tradition of functional simplicity. Enormous

terracotta pots punctuating the interior spaces and the outdoor courtyards recall the agricultural wealth of the Alentejan plains, and many of the stucco ceilings, carved relief panels and restored arcades are painted in the blue of the Canons. Even the surrounding land is once again given over to pasture for grazing horses and to olive groves for the production and bottling of oil.

Dos Santos's thoroughly modern, pared-down approach reinforces both the spiritual and the spatial qualities of the former monastery. Yet don't assume that because Pousada de Nossa Senhora retains its atmosphere of serenity it is a solemn place to stay. Only the peace is monastic. There is nothing austere in the experience of being a guest here. Among the labyrinthine vaulted spaces are two separate restaurants and a bar. The food is excellent – surprisingly so for a state-run affair. A typical menu might include soft cheese with penny royal sauce

followed by grilled dam fish with herbs. There is also a series of courtyards used for outdoor dining in the summer months, and the swimming pool, a vast stone-edged basin, is set on a purpose-built terrace that overlooks the surrounding farmland. Rooms are spacious and beautifully appointed with wooden floors, marble-panelled bathrooms and modern furniture with linen slip covers. There is nothing in the view to detract from the harmonious atmosphere. You cannot catch so much as a glimpse of highways, electricity pylons or other twentieth-century eyesores – only acres and acres of olive trees and verdant oaks marching up and down the rolling hills.

Pousada de Nossa Senhora da Assunção should be a role model for restoration projects. It is proof not only that the modern and the antique make a potent combination, but that even governments can make funky hosts when steered in the right direction.

---

address Pousada de Nossa Senhora da Assunção, 7044-909 Arraiolos, Portugal
t (351) 266 419340   **f** (351) 266 419280   **e** guest@pousadas.pt
room rates from € 125 (including breakfast)

casa de carmona

Carmona is one of the most important historic towns in Spain. Its civilization can be traced back five thousand years and over the ages it has been ruled by the Phoenicians, the Carthaginians and the Romans, among others. One of its surviving city gates ranks among the finest ancient Roman portals to be found anywhere in the former empire. But Carmona's greatest period was the eight hundred years of Moorish rule in the south of Spain. Moorish El Andalus included the cities of Seville, Cordoba and Granada, and the distinctive Arabic culture of this part of southern Spain was the most enlightened of all the regions conquered by the followers of Mohammed. While most of Europe was still floundering in the Dark Ages, Moorish Spain was spectacularly successful in science, architecture and the arts. Mathematics, music and highly skilled handcraft thrived under the enlightened and tolerant rule of southern Spain's Caids. The Moors were also great potters and ceramists, and their colourful glazed tiles played a significant role in defining Moorish culture and architecture. Since the depiction of living things was forbidden by the Koran, geometry became their art. Intricate compositions in small mosaic tiles decorated the walls and floors of already ornate buildings.

This golden age of Arabic culture wasn't to last. After centuries of warfare against the 'infidel' Moors, the Castilian north, under Queen Isabella and King Ferdinand, finally drove them out of Spain in 1492. Yet a glimpse of the splendour of El Andalus can still be found in a renovated Moorish palace in the heart of Carmona, now little more than a sleepy whitewashed village. When Doña Marta Medina, an aristocrat, art historian and architect from one of Seville's oldest families, first bought the dilapidated sixteenth-century palace in the late eighties she had no plans to make it a hotel. She wanted only to create a magnificent apartment for herself and to leave the rest in 'splendid ruin'. But the World Expo '92 in Seville changed all that. Inspired by the international attention the fair would draw to the area she decided instead to take on the mammoth task of renovating the entire building to create a small luxury hotel.

To hear Doña Marta tell it, building a new palace from scratch would have been easier. Walls of monumental stone blocks do not really lend themselves to the installation of modern essentials such as smoke detectors, automatic sprinklers and ducted air-conditioning, not to mention thirty bathrooms. Despite countless setbacks and

145

A detail of the studded front gate of
Casa de Carmona in Andalusia

The pool, in keeping with Moorish tradition,
is tucked into a courtyard of its own

Unmistakably Spanish, the massive
front gates set the theme

The front courtyard would originally have been
used for turning coaches around

The sheer scale of the staircase reveals the
architectural pedigree of what was once
a Moorish nobleman's palace

The vaulted spaces of the poolside
conservatory

Long, tall and narrow, the formal rooms (this is
the Music Room) are arranged around the
main courtyard

Ochre and terracotta: the colours
of the ancient Romans and the
Moors alike

Casa de Carmona is located in the
centre of Carmona, one of the oldest
towns in southern Spain

The grand apartment is one of the rooms
available to guests. It's also used
as a conference room

The impressive staircase leads from the
main courtyard to the first-floor
balcony level

The exterior of the poolside conservatory
where breakfast is served
in the summer

Enormous decorative terracotta pots are a
reminder of the wealth the area once
derived from olive plantations

A classical statue at reception recalls
Carmona's status as one of Spain's
key Roman cities

The library, a dark and soothing space where
pre-dinner drinks are served

Interior architect Doña Marta Medina
imported all the bath fittings
and taps from England

Another corner of the library, this
one overlooking the pool
courtyard beyond

Leading from the entrance gate is
the first of a series of courtyards

bureaucratic tangles, however, the entire project was completed in eighteen months, just in time for the Seville Expo of 1992.

Casa de Carmona is nothing less than a small palace. That's the best, indeed the only way to describe it. The paintings, the furniture, even the smallest decorative details are all of a quality and beauty that belong to a wealthy ancestral home. With every room, including all thirty-odd guest rooms, crowded with art and antiques, it's easy to imagine the Andalusian nobility residing here. The courtyards and gardens, the hidden spaces, the tall narrow rooms, the typical mosaic tile decoration, and the bold terracotta red of the walls all conspire to make this a place of considerable aesthetic impact. Set against the powerful Moorish architecture it becomes an irresistible experience – a chance to live amid the authentic style and opulence of one of the world's great cultures. And that was exactly the intention.

Doña Marta Medina is passionate about El Andalus and she laments the lack of scholarly attention devoted to the beautiful buildings, large and small, that the Moors left behind. Here she has made a practical effort to redress the balance, in the process creating a magical, intoxicating place to stay – so magical that it's tempting never to leave the confines of the house. With a pool, a courtyard garden, a library and of course a restaurant serving Andalusian specialities such as gazpacho, you need never be bored or go hungry … though you might very well miss the benefits of Carmona's extraordinary location. Seville, a heady mix of old and new, is only twenty miles away; Cordoba, with its famous Mezquita mosque, is only an hour's journey, as is the national park of Doñana with its unspoilt beaches and spectacular wildlife sanctuary. Thus Casa de Carmona is a handy place from which to explore Andalusia. But it's also a great place to hang around and do nothing – in great style.

address Casa de Carmona, Plaza de Lasso 1, 41410 Seville, Spain
t (34) 954 191 000 **f** (34) 954 190 189 **e** reserve@casa_decarmona.com
room rates from € 120 (including breakfast)

hacienda benazuza

Since the tenth century, the hacienda of Benazuza has been one of the most important estates in southern Spain. Founded in the time of the Moors, who planted 15,000 olive and fig trees on 5,000 acres of land overlooking the fertile plain of Seville, the continued prosperity of Benazuza was ensured by Ferdinand II. Ferdinand – canonized as Fernando el Santo – successfully reconquered Cordoba and Seville from the Moors and then was astute enough to seek their expert advice on matters of farming.

Even the term hacienda has its origins in Moorish times, when the architecture of the farm was dictated by what was being cultivated. Properties with olive groves were distinguished by a tower (allowing the proprietor to climb above the trees to observe the estate) whereas *cortijos*, farms for cereal crops, were lower and flatter. The haciendas of Seville have thus survived as a fascinating and very particular form of rural architecture. Some supported substantial populations and were extraordinary examples of industry and productivity.

When Ferdinand's son Alfonso X inherited the property he returned to Aragon, leaving Benazuza to the crusading order of the Knights of Santiago. It remained a monastery until the sixteenth century, when Charles I of Spain, hungry for funds to finance his campaigns against Italy and Turkey, reappropriated it and sold it to the Duke of Béjar in 1539, who, in turn, leased it to Francisco Duarte, purveyor of the imperial armies and navies. The Duarte family stayed for three centuries, and it was during their tenure that Felipe IV granted the title of Count of Benazuza to the head of the estate. The name Benazuza was that of the long line of Saracen princes who dwelled here for seven centuries prior to the Christian conquest.

So large had the workforce of Benazuza become by this time that civil and criminal law were administered from its salon by permission of the king. Only in the nineteenth century, with the Industrial Revolution and the spread of mechanization, did the prosperity that had sustained these communities for many centuries as virtually independent civic powers begin to be eroded. Many haciendas were abandoned, and only those able to reinvent themselves survived. Benazuza was lucky: it was sold to the Pablo Romero family, famous for breeding Spain's best fighting bulls.

Today, Benazuza has entered a new phase of its long, eventful history. It is now a five-star hotel just twenty minutes' drive from Seville. Its history gives an idea of the grandeur of

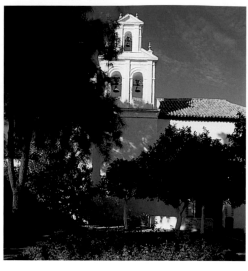

Hacienda Benazuza was a prosperous olive estate – a fact brought home by the size of the property's chapel

Like the architecture of the Andalusian *finca* or farmhouse, furniture is plain, sturdy and distinctly masculine

Whitewashed walls and the odd patch of red or ochre are deeply characteristic of the south of Spain

The old warehouse where the oil was pressed is now the hotel's reception area and guests' lounge

The Moorish style is still evident in Andalusian buildings – even, ironically, in Christian churches of the region

Oak beams, red upholstery and the rugged texture of roughly plastered walls typify the style of El Andalus

the architecture and design, but to their credit the new owners resisted the temptation to smother the former farmhouse with luxury. The church has been carefully restored (it is used today for weddings and other occasions), the stables are almost untouched, and the courtyard and pathways were repaved in a rugged manner that suits the heritage of the property. Rather than disguise its long life as an olive plantation, the tools of the hacienda's former industry have been used as decoration. The mills, pots and vats used for pressing and storing olive oil are arranged like sculpture throughout the public spaces. The massive stone pressing wheel, the copper cylinders for taking oil to market, the weighing mechanism (for olive oil was historically sold by weight) and the enormous terracotta pots buried up to their rims in the ground to catch the oil from the pressing wheel are artfully arranged around chairs and in little conversation corners. Thankfully there isn't an explanatory plaque in sight.

Haciendas were never meant to be glamorously furnished. That was what city palaces were for. Out here in the *campo*, utility and simplicity were of the essence. Terracotta paved floors, whitewashed walls with the odd splash of ochre and sturdy furniture in dark-stained solid wood are the decorative hallmarks of a typical Andalusian hacienda. The luxury is in the space and the serenity, and in the pleasure garden, another Arabic legacy.

A telling sign of the success of Hacienda Benazuza's makeover is that many of the guests are Spanish. The food probably has a lot to do with it. Like the architecture, it is simple but refined. As well as Andalusian specialities there is always a seasonal menu. The Benazuza kitchen has gained quite a reputation, and many residents of Seville will journey out into the country to experience it. You might find the restaurant empty at ten, but that's only because the Spanish are not likely to eat before midnight.

address Hacienda Benazuza, 41800 Sanlúcar la Mayor, Seville, Spain
t (34) 955 703 344 **f** (34) 955 703 410 **e** hbenazuza@elbullihotel.com
room rates from € 252

la sacristía

If you happen to be an architect who surfs, or a kitesurfer who designs, this is the place for you. La Sacristía is exactly how one would imagine a place in the deep south of Andalucia: exotic, mysterious, steeped in history and tinged with a strong Moorish influence. What one perhaps doesn't anticipate is a level of sophistication on a par with the best-designed hotels in world cities like New York, London and Paris. There are no bright surfer colours anywhere in this small, ten-room hotel – unless you count the odd gilded icon on a wall, or a low Japanese-style bed painted a handsome dark red. The interior is also not the whitewashed cliché that is so omnipresent in this neck of the woods. Instead, all the walls are a restrained and quite unexpected shade of fawn grey, the colour of their unpainted render. Rooms, corridors, café, shop and restaurant are unified by this single colour scheme, which imposes a tremendous calm on the historic building, a former inn in the old walled quarter of Tarifa dating back to the seventeenth century.

Colour may be uniform and spare, but the interiors are anything but plain or simple. Their beauty and diversity come mainly from clever use of space. Each room is entirely different, and each room is distinguished by a special antique: a Venetian mirror, an extraordinary bed, a beautiful lantern, a red Chinese lacquered cupboard, an English chair upholstered in a slinky damask, a heavy pair of Castilian wedding beds, etc. These very select pieces make such an impact because the interiors are otherwise so restrained.

The other thing all the rooms share is a tremendous sense of spaciousness, which perhaps reflects the fact that one of the proprietors, architect Miguel Arregui, used to design interiors for Oberoi resorts in India. 'Space to breathe and a place for peace' is how Arregui and fellow designer-proprietor Bosco Herrero sum up their creation. In a hyped-up surf town like Tarifa, they have a point. There are more surf shops here than on Bondi Beach. The prevailing aesthetic is strictly surfer: bright colours and ethnic twists, sandals, cargo pants, screen-printed t-shirts, bleached blond hair, and lots of beads and shark's-tooth pendants. Much as you may love the sport – surfing, kitesurfing, windsurfing – that doesn't necessarily mean you want to spend the night in a surf-themed bedroom. Even golfers don't do that. The arrival of La Sacristía provides a calm, pared-down, architecturally sophisticated accommodation option in Tarifa.

The surfing scene gives Tarifa its energy and vibrancy, and the weather (or rather the wind) gives it its reputation as

one of the top destinations for windsurfing, but it is Tarifa's history that makes it unique. Thirty minutes across the water lies Tangier, Morocco's most notorious city, whose lights are visible by night. The strategically situated, massively reinforced city of Tarifa remained a skirmish point between Moors and Christians long after the rest of Spain had capitulated to the Castilians from the north. But the town's rich history goes still further back. The cove of Bolonia, tipped by Tarifa locals as the most stunning beach in the area, was once the backdrop to the thriving Roman town of Baelo Claudia (named for Emperor Claudius, AD 41–54, who granted it the prestigious rank of municipality). Baelo Claudia owed its wealth to the production of garum, the fermented fish sauce that Romans ate with everything. Made from fish intestines mixed with salt, oil and lemon, Baelo Claudia's garum was exported all over the empire, and the success of the town's factory on the beach afforded its 3,000 residents a privileged lifestyle. The thirteen-hectare city, surrounded by a massive protective wall, boasted a forum, four temples, a theatre, baths, gardens, market, pharmacy, tavern and basilica. However, its prosperity was brought to an abrupt end in the second century by an earthquake, whose effects are still visible today in the buckled paving stones that line the streets. Abandoned in the sixth century, it remained untouched (except as a handy source of building materials) until the late 1960s, when work began in earnest to uncover its well-preserved ruins. Being in one of the more remote stretches of Spain was a blessing: before the tourism crush could spread to this unspoilt quarter, the government declared most of the area a national park.

So here's the twist for the style-savvy surfer. Stay in a 300-year-old Moorish villa inside the old town walls at night, and surf during the day just yards from the splendid ruins of an ancient Roman town. Who says surfers are a-cultural?

---

address La Sacristía, San Donato 8, 11380 Tarifa, Cádiz, Spain
t (34) 956 681 759 **f** (34) 956 685 182 **e** tarifa@lasacristia.net
room rates from € 115 (including breakfast)

the ice hotel

'The world's largest igloo' is how the brochure describes it, and technically this is correct. A fairy tale structure in the wintry landscape north of Sweden's Arctic Circle, the Ice Hotel is a fascinating example of a building in snow and ice. But this is no Eskimo hut – it's a palace, a castle cut from frozen crystal.

Consider the statistics: the Ice Hotel covers 40,000 square feet and accommodates over a hundred guests. It has an ice bar, an indoor curling lane, an ice cinema (specializing in films about northern adventure), a viewing platform (to catch the aurora borealis if you're lucky), a sculpture garden and an ice gallery, not to mention an ice chapel that is very popular for baptisms and weddings. All this takes about 30,000 tons of snow and 5,000 tons of ice to realize every winter … because, come May, the whole place simply melts away.

The ice used in constructing the Ice Hotel has little in common with your everyday ice cube. The pillars, bed frames, church pews, cinema seats, windows and even the fibre-optic-lit chandeliers are all cut from the ice of the adjacent River Torne. The ice of a flowing river is under constant pressure as it forms, giving it a structural strength that makes it suitable for use as a building material.

But even if its design is far more elaborate, the Ice Hotel still functions as an igloo. The science of an igloo is based on the fact that the best protection from a snow storm is, ironically, a shelter made out of snow. As Arne Bergh, creator of the Ice Hotel, will tell you, snow is a great insulator (against light and cold), and yet it also breathes. So the inside temperature of the hotel remains a constant minus 4–7° Celsius whether outside temperatures reach record lows of minus 40° or a positively balmy plus 5°.

Even so, why would anyone of sound mind and body travel to a place where the indoor temperature is 5° below zero? That's easy – because on this entire planet there is nothing, absolutely nothing like it. The beauty of the place is spellbinding. The colour of the ice changes according to the weather and the time of day – it can be green, blue, grey or turquoise, and the entire structure melts back into the river each spring. Even a cynic must admire the pure poetry of such a cycle.

Being spellbound by its beauty is one thing, but what's it like to stay here? That's the question most people ask. Surprisingly, this monument in snow and ice is more congenial than its average temperatures might indicate. The Swedes are completely unperturbed by below-zero

thermometer readings – for them it's simply a matter of 'appropriate' or 'inappropriate' clothing. It's true that standing in the Absolut Ice Bar nursing a hollowed-out block of ice filled with vodka is perfectly comfortable so long as you're wearing a cosy snowsuit. (The snow suits, boots and gloves are supplied by the hotel's ever-helpful 'igloo guides'.)

Beds are wooden platforms suspended on massive blocks of ice with a thin foam mattress covered in a thick layer of overlapping reindeer skins. Arctic sleeping bags make it possible to sleep in a room the temperature of a meat-packing plant. Dozens of candles are tucked into little ice nooks and crannies throughout the room. It might look rather romantic but any ideas of *amour* are cut dead by the fact that the sleeping bags are like quilted coffins, strictly for one person only. Besides, the effort of extinguishing all the candles and manoeuvring yourself (fully clothed) into the bag is exhausting. But you can forget worrying about having to get up in the middle of the night: once you're out … you're out cold!

The next thing you register is the cup of hot berry juice brought to your bedside in the morning by a smiling igloo guide. So now to the second most asked question: what is there to do? Lots! This is Swedish Lapland, a never-ending white wilderness that is home to the indigenous Sami people. It is a perfect playground for snowmobile safaris, cross-country skiing, downhill skiing, ice fishing and dog sledding. Winter lasts from November to April, and activities and facilities are all superbly organized (in typical Scandinavian fashion). The Ice Hotel maintains an entire fleet of shiny snowmobiles, not to mention an arsenal of clothing and accessories. Lapland is a popular destination, and there are regular flights from Stockholm. Swedes, it seems, need a fix of ice and snow in the way we need a regular dose of beach and sun.

---

address The Ice Hotel, Marknadsvägen 63, S-981 91 Jukkasjärvi, Sweden

t (46) 980 66 800 **f** (46) 980 66 890 **e** info@icehotel.com

room rates from SEK 2,800 (including snow-mobile overall, shoes, hat, gloves, sauna and breakfast)

Tropique du Cancer

I. Teger
I. Fuerteventura
C. Bojador
I. Canar
I. Juby
Hamâda
Ain Salah
Agably
Sebka
d'Amadgor
Hoch.
FEZZAN
Ghat
Traghan
Kebi
Haut Mgnes Noires
Mtes Cintra
Dj. Hogar
Idélés
Ahaggar
Bîr Msegguem
Idélés
Djanet
Mesrou
Mourzouk
Gatrone
Dj. Akrouf
S A H A R A

C. Blanc
Mgnes Blanches
Ouadan
OU GRAND DÉSERT
Banc d'Arguin
Adrar
Chinguêtí
Tlîgh
AHIR
Asouthy
Oasis de Seggedem
TI
C. Miruk
Tagant
Taghent
Mabrouk
Bilma
Portendick
Forêts de Gommiers
Tombouctou
Aghadez
Damergou
du Aghadem
Pays de

Iles du Cap Vert
I. S. Antonio I. S. Nicolas
I. de Sel
I. Bravista
Daqana
Podor
Diri
Kabra
Kouarra
Limite Septentrionale
Lori
Kanem
OU TAKI
St Louis
L. Cajor
Quallo
Sedo
Koumakary
Kemnou
L. Dibbie
Massina
Adafudia
Haoussa
Kachenah
Zirmie
Kano
Engornou
Kauka
R. Yeou
Tangalia
Fogo
I. S. Yago
C. Vert I. Goree
Albreda
Saloum
Bambouk
Satadou
Ségo
Djenny
Fellatahs
Gouba
Sakatou
Yaouri
Boussa
Zariya
Mandara
Mora
Begharm
Loogoun
Beghar
Bathurst
Sedhiou
Gambie R.
Geba
Niger
Bamakou
Bouré
Toumane
Kombori
Dagoumba
Zogha
Katunga
Egga
Niffé
Djaeoba
Adamowa
Musfeia
Dar Kull
Cacheo
R. Grande
Kakondy
Fouta Diallon
Ouassoulo
Tangrera
Banda
Yandi
Le Kong
Tchadda
Calabar
Vouanga
Ungwa
Maggou
I. Bissagos
S. Domingo
Kotlo
Rakelle
Mt. Loma
Timé
Bagoe
Dagoumba
GUINÉE SEPTEN. OU OUANKARAH
S. Felton
Freetown
Sierra Leone
Coumassie
Achanti
Abomey
Bénin
Biafra
Bisou
I. Sherboro
Bafia
Fanti
Quitta
Ouaddah
Wari
Kona
Kalabar
Monrovia
Liberia
Lahou
Acra
Ouaddah
Côte de Bénin
I. Fernando Po
Biafra
C. des Palmes
Cote d'Ivoire
Côte d'Or
G. de Bénin
G. de Benin
C. de Calabar
Mongo
C. des trois Pointes
I. du Prince
G. de Biafra
Gabon

A T L A N T I Q U E

Equateur
GOLFE DE GUINÉE
I. S. Thomas
C. Lopez
Camma
Matimbas
Mani-Seat
I. Annobon
R. Camma
Setté
Monsol
R. Setté
Mtes du St Esprit
Anzico
MOUNDONGO
Ma-yumba
Loango
Cango
Bouali ou Loango
Kingele
Loango
Cacongo
Cabinde
En-Goyo
Banza Congo
Basamba
Fl. Loire ou Congo
Banana
ou St Salvador
Bamba
Kabas
Ambriz
Matami
Dande R.
Dande
I. Ascension
Coënza Fl.
Massangano
Polongo
St Paul de Loanda
Tamba
ANGOLA NORD. ET DIONNE
Monten
Cuvo R.
Biallundo
Ganguellas
Novo Redondo
Inhandunha
Sto Felipe de Benguela
Bike
BENGUELA
Caconda
C. Martha
I. Ste Hélène
Mossamedes (Angra Negros)
C. Negro
Presqu'île des Tigres
R. Nourses
Cimbeba ou
Boschema
Mucuixes et Macasses
C. Prio
Otchikoto
Man
Bo de St Ambroise
CIMBEBA
Bo Walwich
Damaras R. Swakop
Mtes Murray
BOSCHOTTE
I. Itchaboe
Angra Pequena
Herus Namaqua
Orange ou Gariep Fl.
Mt. Kamus
R. Eléphant
Bo Ste Hélène
Pte Pater Noster
Malmesbury
Bo de la Table
C. de Bonne Espérance

Brod.
Schroeder sculp.

AFRICA

For the traveller, first and foremost, cliché or not, Africa is a game reserve; a vast slice of the planet where nature in all its glory and fury still reigns supreme. Who can imagine Africa and not think of its wildlife? Sure, most of us have witnessed some of the continent's magnificent animals in captivity, but what is that compared with the opportunity to encounter them in the wild?

Despite setbacks such as encroaching suburbs, poachers and illegal trading, the wildlife still thrives, and so too does the safari experience. Except these days, instead of shooting with a gun, you'll be using a camera. A safari of experience has replaced a safari of bloodshed. And the camp, too, has changed. 'Roughing it' in a few hastily pitched canvas tents is definitely no longer part of the package. The new-generation camps are as glamorous and luxurious as a maharaja's palace, and these days the thrill of the wild is combined with the thrill of a *fab* wine list.

But then there's another Africa, which is completely different. It has no exotic wildlife, but it's just as compelling for other reasons. Egypt and Morocco do not immediately spring to mind when Africa is mentioned, but they are very much part of the continent. Marrakesh, in particular, is the current fashionable favourite. Just lately it has become the hottest little city on the planet. Art directors, designers, brokers, savvy bankers and trendy tycoons are all lining up to buy a *riad* (palace) in Marrakesh's medina. One of the world's most intact medieval cities is, apparently, an adult thrill impossible to resist.

The food, the nightclubs, the shopping…. Sounds like any other city? Not quite. The enduring appeal of Marrakesh is that you can still have one foot in the groovy present and the other in a biblical past: donkeys and Dolce & Gabbana, jellabas and jeroboams. Spend a morning sipping *thé à la menthe* on a grand boulevard; spend the afternoon in a village of the Atlas foothills that is still without roads or electricity.

There are few places in the world that continue to offer such a duality of history. Morocco is one; Egypt is another. Despite all the package tourism and the plethora of tour buses and Ost-bloc-style cruise ships, the Nile remains evocatively exotic and romantically rewarding. You can even duplicate Hercule Poirot's cruise down the river – in the very same boat. And if you want to experience an escape to a completely other world, head to the fabled oasis of Siwa – just as Alexander the Great did more than two thousand years ago.

adrère amellal

Before marching his troops eastwards to Persia, in 331 BC Alexander the Great made a little known detour to the distant oasis of Siwa. It had long been whispered that Alexander was the son of the god Amun, and he came to Siwa to consult the legendary Oracle of Amun and discover whether this was true. Though we'll never know exactly what happened there, it seems that Alexander left Siwa with the answer he was looking for. He returned from the desert to embark upon some of the greatest conquests in the history of civilization.

The most extraordinary thing about Siwa today is that the place is not so different from the time of the Macedonian conqueror's visit. Its inhabitants still speak a Berber language, Siwi, and their customs and traditions have changed little. Islam may have replaced animism as the mainstay of their beliefs, but the people's way of life remains the same: there's no industry, there are more donkeys than cars, and most of them still make a living from growing and selling dates and olives.

If you stay at Adrère Amellal, the impression that time has passed by this niche of the North African Sahara is even more pronounced. The architecture, decoration and building materials (salt, timber from palm trees and baked mud) are

just as they would have been more than two thousand years ago. Add to this the fact that there are no telephones or electricity and the time warp is complete.

Adrère Amellal offers the most complete escape imaginable, not just from daily routine but from the world as we know it. Set beside an enormous saltwater lake, it's hard to believe that you're sixty feet below sea level, bang in the middle of the world's largest sand deposit. But, you may ask (as most people do), how comfortable is it to live without electricity or modern telecommunications? The answer, surprisingly perhaps, is that it's not only comfortable; it's actually quite luxurious. With the exception of being on a commercial flight, it's one of the few opportunities to exist without being telephoned, e-mailed or text-messaged. No one needs to be convinced of the romance of dining by candlelight, but the experience of a bedroom and bathroom illuminated solely by dozens of candles (all in natural beeswax) is something few of us have encountered. Suddenly your skin looks radiant and you can forget about make-up. In other words, it's conducive to total relaxation.

As an intelligent concession to the expectations of Western travellers, there are bathrooms galore (with plenty of hot water and water pressure), but the real luxury of this

hotel is not in the bathrooms or the bedrooms. It's in the experience. I defy anyone to come here and not return home with at least a handful of dinner party stories. Take, for instance, the lake: unlikely as it may be, your room is on the shore of a massive body of water that dominates the scenery in every direction. More unusual still, it is completely without water traffic. None. No boats, no fishing craft, not even the odd felucca so common on the Nile. This emptiness only adds to the spare machismo of the landscape. And then there's the unexpected plus that the lake is brilliant for swimming – or rather floating. With similar remedial properties to the Dead Sea, it's so salty that it's almost impossible to submerge.

And then there's the Sahara. Think of a celluloid fantasy set in the desert: *Lawrence of Arabia*, *The Mummy*, *The Scorpion King*, *Beau Geste* or even the sci-fi film *Dune* – any of these could have been shot in the area around Siwa.

It's a vast expanse of rippling dunes straight out of *The English Patient*. Even if you've been to countless other deserts (which I have), nothing can prepare you for what you'll encounter here. Alone and surrounded by endless mountains of talcum-powder-quality sand, a guide will take you on a 'Sahara rollercoaster', where you drive with tyres deflated at breathtaking speed. And just when you think you've seen it all, you hurtle down the side of yet another mammoth dune and find yourself at a different lake. You're free to dive straight into the water, which is surprisingly cold and deep. Swimming in the middle of the Sahara's sand dunes is an experience you're not likely to forget.

Neither is staying at the Adrère Amellal. With its countless candles, myriad of torches and spectacular open fires lit in ever-changing locations, it's like the title of Mr Hemingway's book, a moveable feast – a feast framed by the magic of Aladdin's one thousand and one Arabian nights.

---

address Adrère Amellal Oasis, Sidi al-Ja'afar, Siwa, Egypt
t (20) 02 738 1327 **f** (20) 02 735 5489 **e** info@eqi.com.eg
room rates from US $300

shompole

Take the organic minimalism of legendary Japanese-American sculptor Isamu Noguchi, mix in the exotic and capacious *palapa* architecture of Mexico, pop the whole package on a steep and lofty position in Kenya, with sweeping views of a mighty volcano opposite and the dusty plains of a conservation area below, and you have your Shompole (pronounced Shum-*bow*-lay) soundbite.

In terms of looks and experience, there's nothing like it in Africa. Shompole combines a previously unvisited and uniquely unexploited part of East Africa (it has marshes, mountains and salt flats) with an equally unique approach to accommodation.

Until quite recently, this vast stretch of southern Kenya, framed by the massive mountain ridge known as the Nguruman escarpment, was home only to the odd traditional Maasai village and its cows, as well as herds of zebra, wildebeest, impala, buffalo, kudu and onyx, packs of baboons, parties of giraffe, and the more elusive lion and leopard. Just on the other side of the escarpment is the Maasai Mara, site of massive annual migrations of zebra and wildebeest, and less than an hour away by four-wheel-drive is Tanzania's fabled Lake Natron, home to one of the world's largest and most photogenic flamingo populations.

Clearly, this is not an area short on potential wildlife experience. And yet, part of the motivation for building this exquisitely beautiful lodge in such a remote location was to have a place in the bush where you could lie around and do nothing, in complete privacy. With the exception of Shompole's organic bungalows, nothing here has changed. The Maasai still live as they've always done, tending their livestock, dressed in their red loincloths and tribal blankets, adorned with beaded jewelry and armed with a swordlike knife. And the wild animals are still uncomfortable around humans because there are so few of us. In fact, it would be safe to say that the only cars in the entire Shompole conservation park belong to Anthony Russell, the brains and brawn (financially speaking) behind Shompole.

A seasoned safari camp entrepreneur, Russell recognized the extraordinary beauty of the area and responded accordingly. The architecture and design of the lodge are his inspired three-dimensional reaction. Utilizing the earthy traditions of Africa, such as roofs of thatch, walls rendered with mud, and timber used in its found state, Russell set about building a collection of bungalows that are completely minimal in their absence of decoration, but bewitchingly in tune with their environment. They are vast

bush platforms, completely dedicated to allowing the visitor to enjoy the surroundings in as hedonistic and laid-back a fashion as possible.

Most importantly, disturbing the environment with intrusive 'mod cons', such as air-conditioning, glass or concrete, was not an option. Practical matters, such as keeping cool in what can be one of the most blisteringly hot parts of Africa, for instance, were addressed in a completely natural way. Fresh spring water runs down gullies flanking the entrance to each bungalow, cascades down the back of the bed, continues running along the base of the bed, and eventually empties into a personal plunge pool. Because the water keeps moving, there is no need to add chlorine, nor does it present a hazard vis-à-vis mosquitoes, and the presence of the water, in conjunction with a slight breeze, acts as a natural air-conditioner, without that annoying humming.

As for sleeping at night, the open pavilions sport enormous mesh tents, which are zipped shut to keep out bugs and creepy-crawlies. It's a clever combination: you maintain the sensation of sleeping in the great outdoors, with only a roof of thatch over your head, while you are in fact neatly cocooned in a mosquito-net marquee.

Shompole is unique because it offers a very stylish, 'back to nature' experience in a completely untouched part of Africa. The experience is further enhanced by the proximity of big herds of wild beasts and by the authenticity of being in Maasai country. Most of the staff are Maasai and still wear traditional dress and, if you insist, they can tell stories about lions, leopards and hyenas that will make you feel very silly about being afraid of spiders and snakes.

If you dream of having Africa to yourself, of being vastly outnumbered by the wild and with no other *bwana* for hundreds of miles, Shompole is the place.

---

address Shompole, c/o The Art of Ventures, PO Box 10665, Nairobi 00100, Kenya

t (254) 20 884135 **f** (254) 20 883280 **e** info@shompole.com

room rates from US $365 (including activities) + $25 conservation fee

caravanserai

A caravanserai was where camel trains would stop to rest and stock up on supplies as they worked their slow way up the oasis route through the Sahara to Marrakesh; it makes a good name for a hotel. Marrakesh was a town mixing cultures centuries before this became a style trend. Traders exchanged African slaves, gold, jewelry and nuts for cloth, oil, and manufactured goods from Europe.

Mixing cultures, or, more accurately, the design signatures of different cultures, was exactly what Max Lawrence and Mathieu Boccara had in mind when they first came up with the idea of this hotel. As the son of parents who travelled for a living, Max had seen quite a bit of the world and, as could perhaps be expected, a place in England was not for him. He came to Morocco after completing school and never left. One of the first friends he made here was Mathieu Boccara, son of one of Morocco's best-known architects, Charles Boccara. Mathieu went off to Paris to study architecture, but on his return opted *not* to follow in his father's footsteps. Instead he decided to become a client, choosing to get involved in property development, and in particular in the design and development of hotels. Max Lawrence by then had considerable experience in renovating riads in the old medina of Marrakesh. With

complementary skills – creative and practical – they decided to join forces.

What they wanted to create was a place grounded in ethnic character but not necessarily purely Moroccan. It was to mix the whitewashed aesthetic of Greece, the colours of India and the courtyard architecture of the Mediterranean. The furnishings were to have the seductive appeal of handcraft, whether Rajasthani, Nepalese or Moroccan.

As it happened, Boccara senior had just the venue for this ethno-chic project. Long before Marrakesh began its recent expansion (the city now counts more than a million inhabitants) he had purchased practically an entire village on the fringe of the city's palm-studded hinterland. Architecturally, it was nothing much: just a cluster of small huts built in the traditional way out of compacted mud. But this Berber village had a great location and real ethnic credentials. It was perfect as the starting point for Caravanserai. Max and Mathieu negotiated to acquire the site and their multicultural dream started to take shape.

Architecturally, their vision was clear. People staying here would not just get a room. Guests at Caravanserai would each get their own small house equipped with a collection of spaces every bit as eclectic and unexpected

Antique Moroccan painted bridal chests are part of the multicultural assemblage that defines Caravanserai

Countless carved Moroccan doors continually lead from one hidden space to another

The roof terrace, which borrows from a Greek tradition, overlooks the Palmerai and the Atlas mountains

In converting this old Berber village into a hotel, tremendous care was taken to preserve texture and character

One of the guest suites has a mini-Majorelle garden painted in the distinctive Majorelle shade of blue

Another suite with a private pool (below) also comes with a spacious hammam or steam room

as the ethno-artifacts decorating them. Thus you might find yourself in a suite (for want of a more suitable word) featuring a private garden painted Majorelle blue, an expansive bathroom opening onto the garden, and a series of other discrete spaces including a small bedroom and a study. Another suite has a small private pool in a small private courtyard, off which lie a bedroom and separate study, an entrance hall, and a bathroom that happens to be equipped with an enormous private hammam (the traditional Moroccan steam room). The bedroom has beautiful vaulted ceilings and a traditional fireplace.

While the design approach is authentically multicultural, the ingredients of Caravanserai are in fact largely Moroccan. Its architectural concept owes a lot to the Berber village, which is traditionally full of unexpected courtyards, terraces and hidden spaces. And its building techniques and materials have been used in southern Morocco for centuries.

Wooden frames are constructed on either side of an existing wall, and then damp earth stamped on top of it, compacted and allowed to dry. This is a system that offers great insulation as well as aesthetic character. It doesn't fare well in heavy rain, but that's not too much of a problem in Morocco.

Extraordinarily, each collection of rooms and spaces still costs less than an average hotel room. From the very beginning, the intention was to make this particular Moroccan experience affordable. Now that it's finished, it's a pleasure to be able to announce that they have achieved all their aims. Caravanserai really lives up to its name. The look is a seductive tribal blend, the spaces are at once generous yet mysterious and contained, the variety of accommodation is amazing, and the location is romantic and unspoiled. All in all, it creates the powerful impression that time here has stood still – even if you know it's not true.

---

address Caravanserai, 264 Douar Ouled Ben Rahmoun, Marrakesh, Morocco

t (212) 44 30 03 02 **f** (212) 44 30 02 62 **e** contact@caravanserai.com

room rates from DH 1,150 (including breakfast)

la gazelle d'or

The 'Golden Gazelle' is a hunting lodge deep in the south of Morocco. Located outside the old city of Taroudant, an hour inland from Agadir, La Gazelle d'Or lies in the valleys between the Atlas mountains and the sea.

It might be a hunting lodge, but it looks more like a hacienda on the plains of southern Spain than an Alpine hideaway. The entrance is reached by a very long and elegant driveway entirely screened by bamboo, a first indication of the lush oasis you are about to come upon. Surrounded by acres of green and gardens filled with towering bougainvillaea and neat rows of cypress trees, the property itself is a complex of spacious stone buildings and a collection of twenty-odd cottages. These are arranged around two huge semi-circular expanses of lawn that would look at home in the heart of Oxfordshire. Exotic clusters of oleander, jasmine, hibiscus, cactus and north African palms between the guest cottages create the impression of a verdant Eden and provide the privacy that makes this such a delightfully romantic hideaway. Outside the gates the landscape is rugged and dusty, bleached and beaten into submission by the unrelenting sun. Inside, the oasis that is La Gazelle d'Or is so luxuriously planted and cultivated that the climate is transformed. The overbearing heat of the sun

is diffused by the gardens, which provide a permanent canopy of shelter and create a refreshing breeze that gradually cools further as it travels across the numerous pools, canals and water gardens. This natural form of air-conditioning was originally discovered by the Persians, and it helps to explain how the garden came to acquire mythical status in Arabic culture – so much so that their word for heaven translates as 'garden of paradise'.

Simply walking through the gardens is a profoundly calming and soothing experience. The estate is equipped with stables, tennis courts, and a large and immaculate swimming pool – yet it seems singularly ill-suited to sport. The atmosphere and ambience are more conducive to the languid pace of life of desert peoples. I'm normally not much good at doing nothing, and if anyone had suggested I'd be happy to sit and listen to two toads in a lily pond croaking at the sunset I would have laughed. But such is the seductive magic of this oasis in Morocco's deep south.

Apart from doing nothing, the day is taken up with eating. This, however, is eating not as essential nourishment but as elaborate theatre. Breakfast begins when you push a button on your bedside telephone to signal your readiness for the first act. In no time, a tall Moroccan in jellaba and fez

arrives with a huge tray balanced on one shoulder. Croissants, pastries, traditional Moroccan pancakes and home-made marmalades are laid out on a linen tablecloth on your private terrace.

Act two, lunch, is in a different location. Consisting of grilled fish and meat combined with a wide variety of salads grown on the property, it is served under the shade of the poolside olive trees. Bathing suits and towels are the correct attire. Dinner, the final act, is worthy of *A Thousand and One Nights*. It is served on the garden patio illuminated by candlelight from lanterns artfully arranged along the mosaic floor. Guests dress for dinner in the old-fashioned sense – dinner jackets and evening gowns – and the pace of the evening is equally dignified. Dinner lasts for hours, and the succession of courses is seemingly endless.

La Gazelle offers a taste of a Morocco that supposedly no longer exists: the Morocco of the 1920s and '30s, when Europeans came here to live like pashas, to be intrigued by the mysterious and exotic culture, and to marvel at the extraordinary gardens such a hot and dry country could produce.

If you cannot stomach quite so much indulgence, then a simple remedy is to hire a four-wheel drive and explore the surrounding area. This is the untamed south, a rugged landscape of spectacular canyons, palm-tree-filled gorges and idyllic, time-forgotten villages. But what about the hunting? This is, after all, a very popular destination for shooting holidays. Some even travel with their own loaders. They leave before daybreak and, with the help of beaters, shoot partridges (a plague according to locals, because they steal all the wheat). Some enthusiasts have been coming here for almost two decades, though personally I can't fathom how shooting can possibly compete with the pure indulgence of doing nothing.

---

address La Gazelle d'Or, BP 260, Taroudant, Morocco

t (212) 48 852039 **f** (212) 48 852737 **e** reservations@gazelledor.com

room rates from UK £150 (including breakfast and dinner)

auberge tangaro

Painted in a simple palette of white, blue and ochre, the colours of Morocco's Atlantic coast, Auberge Tangaro is a cluster of whitewashed buildings assembled on a wind-blown point a few miles outside the town of Essaouira. Furnished simply with hand-woven rugs from the local souks and furniture made by the town's craftsmen, this former brothel was given a new lease of life by an Italian tourist who liked the area so much he decided to stay.

Being a typically style-conscious Italian, he couldn't resist doing the place up. His approach to the interiors was a combination of restraint and authenticity. Blue and white Moroccan tiles line the walls of the bathrooms and terracotta tiles cover the floors throughout. Most rooms feature little more than a bed, a table and a couple of chairs – an elegant simplicity that is most welcome in the whitewashed heat of North Africa. The very last thing you want in these sweltering temperatures is lots of fabrics and furniture. The bathrooms are spacious, with hot and cold running water and Western-style plumbing. There is no electricity, but this only adds to the charm – it means that the candlesticks in every room are more than decorative. The atmosphere, particularly at night, is reminiscent of Paul Bowles's *The Sheltering Sky*. Even the dining room is entirely illuminated by candlelight, and what it lacks in convenience is more than compensated for in romance. Auberge Tangaro is a return to the sense of Oriental mystique and intrique that has always been such a drawcard for Morocco.

With camels grazing outside the front gate and a long dusty road leading to deserted beaches, Tangaro's biggest plus is its location. Situated on the highest point of a promontory that looks back towards the town of Essaouira, it has sweeping views of the rugged wind-blown shore that makes this part of Morocco's Atlantic coast so popular with windsurfers. It is close enough to be able to dart into Essaouira for a quick coffee or an expedition to the markets, but far enough out of town to offer the beauty and seclusion of an out-of-the-way spot. Essaouira, formerly known as Mogador, was once a Portuguese trading town and is a well-known centre in Morocco for traditional crafts such as woodworking. Its appearance is so well preserved that Orson Welles chose it as a primary location for his film *Othello*. In his opinion, it resembled more closely a typical Mediterranean trading town of the seventeenth century than any other in existence.

This part of Morocco has its share of colourful history. Under the Romans, who took Essaouira after a tough

Whitewashed and sunburned, Auberge Tangaro is typical of the style of the nearby town of Essaouira

Traditional Moroccan furniture made from the branches of the oleander tree is used throughout

Situated on a windswept promontory of the African Atlantic coast, Auberge Tangaro is a favourite with windsurfers

Fireplaces and candlesticks are not
merely decorative – there is no electricity

The terrace is where breakfast and lunch
are served under the shade
of eucalyptus trees

Pristine and uncomplicated, the interiors
are perfectly suited to the barefoot lifestyle
and to the heat

campaign against the nomadic mountain Berbers, it became an important little trading town. A small island just off the coast was used to manufacture the rare and precious purple dye made from ground mollusc shells that denoted high rank in Roman times. So prized was this that its value was equal to that of the finest precious metals or gems.

In more recent times it was more the attraction of 'purple haze' than a purple cloak that drew visitors to this sleepy fishing village. Everyone in town, not least the fast-talking stall holders in the local souks, will tell you that Jim Morrison once spent an entire summer in Essaouira – although no one seems to remember exactly where he stayed (apparently neither did he). But those were the wild sixties and times have changed some. The new tourists come for the waves, the wind and the weather (or so they say), but they still tend to stay for weeks if not months. A lot of this has to do with the cost of living (Auberge Tangaro for example is only £50 a night including dinner and breakfast). But mainly they are seduced by the ambience. As in Bali, Byron Bay in Australia and Kerala in southern India, the lifestyle here is 'hippy-luxe'. People are laid-back and friendly, and there's a real café scene in town. The waves are ideal for surfing (when there's no wind) or windsurfing (when there's plenty, which is often).

But the best advertisement for Essaouira has to be the story of a couple I met briefly in Marrakesh. I saw them again, weeks later, at the airport and commented on how souvenir-less they were. They grinned and admitted their souvenir was too big to carry on board. It was their first time in Morocco but one week in Essaouira was enough to convince them that they had to have a house there. So they bought one, then and there, a two-storey Portuguese-style town house in the medina, the old centre, for just £14,000 sterling.

---

address Auberge Tangaro, Quartier Diabat, BP8 Essaouira, Morocco

t & f (212) 44 78 47 84

room rates from DH 800

kasbah ben moro

It's known as the road of a thousand kasbahs: a long thin sliver that starts in the frontier town of Ouarzazate and extends into the seemingly infinite desert of Morocco's southern Sahara. Just twenty miles along the way you reach the ancient oasis town of Skoura. Here the famous caravanserai, the trading camel trains, would stop for supplies and one final rest before embarking on the arduous crossing of the mighty Atlas mountains en route to their destination of Marrakesh.

Skoura is remote, hot and exotic. By day it's blanketed in a crystal-clear, purple-blue sky; by night in a deep black star-studded sky. Its lush palm oasis contains many examples of the mud castles, or kasbahs, of southern Morocco that have inspired countless artists, writers and travellers. Most of these structures, with their distinctively shaped towers and graphic chiselled detailing, are in a state of ruin: impressive, enthralling, like nothing else you have ever seen, but sadly uninhabitable. All, that is, except one. The Kasbah Ben Moro, in the middle of the Skoura Palmerai, has been restored to the condition it was in when first built by a Spaniard in the late eighteenth century.

By a twist of fate, the resurrection of this splendid Moroccan fantasy has come about by the energy and enthusiasm of another Spaniard, Don Juan de Dios Romero Muños. Juan used to visit Morocco regularly. A passionate off-road motorcyclist, he was well acquainted with the striking landscape that begins on the far side of the Atlas mountains from Marrakesh. But I doubt he believed that he would one day live here, much less that he would rescue a piece of the region's extraordinary architectural history. He worked as a bank manager in Cadiz and, although he has Andalusian blood in his veins, he was an unlikely candidate to say goodbye to his day job and embark on a Sahara adventure. Yet that's exactly what he did. Fed up with modern Spain, in the late 1990s he upped stakes and moved to Ouarzazate.

He had found and fallen hopelessly in love with the dilapidated ruin of a once proud kasbah, and he was determined to restore it. All that stood in his way were the fifty-four relatives who owned the property. Undeterred, he decided to stay in Ouarzazate for as long as necessary to get all of them to agree to sell. It took six months for the eleven representatives of all the clans to sign an official document. Then finally Kasbah Ben Moro was his – or at least what was left of it was. Its elegant, noble outline was still discernible, but that was about all. None of the internal

Simple details like this wall lamp set
the atmosphere – dark, exotic
and very Moroccan

This is the traditional territory of Berbers,
the fiercely proud and independent
nomads of North Africa

Every detail, right down to the carved
wooden door hinges, was remade
to authentic patterns

The restored Kasbah Ben Moro is one
of the finest examples of Morocco's
famous fortress architecture

In the pitch black of night, the labyrinthine
mud architecture has a
spooky atmosphere

Such massive and imposing kasbahs were
meant to impress friends and enemies –
but especially enemies

At the very core of the courtyards
is a multi-storey lightwell with
numerous arched openings

The landscape is the same colour as the
kasbah itself – not surprising, given that
they are both of the same material

Dark, mysterious, even a bit scary,
this is the Morocco of Paul Bowles's
The Sheltering Sky

Inside, Kasbah Ben Moro is an Escher-like
structure of courtyards within courtyards
within courtyards

The symbols, shapes and building materials
define a centuries-old architectural tradition

The bleak and unforgiving landscape
en route to the kasbah makes the lush
Skoura Palmerai even more inviting

The bedrooms are simple but handsome.
Furniture, accessories and detailing are
all authentically Berber

The oasis of Skoura is a vast expanse of
palm trees framed by the snow-capped
Atlas mountains and the Sahara desert

Even the twisting staircase is an exotic experience,
complete with handcrafted bronze balustrade
and hidden spaces

Despite its remoteness, the restaurant,
in the yellow and maroon colours of
southern Morocco, is surprisingly good

The four-hundred-year-old kasbah was
restored with minute attention
to original detail

Once upon a time, a constant lookout
was kept from the watchtowers for the
arrival of travelling camel trains

structure, which once housed the first Spaniard, plus wives, children and livestock, survived. It was clear that Juan had not just purchased a monumental building but a monumental project.

For two years he slept on site in a mud hut while he and his workmen set about rebuilding the kasbah exactly as it once was. Although the techniques of building in mud are slowly dying out, he managed to find enough tradesmen in the south of Morocco who were skilled in the traditional ways. His architectural blueprint and manifesto was the work of a photographer friend who had documented the most important kasbahs still standing in Morocco in a book filled with invaluable detail of everything from the construction of wooden hinges to the layout of spaces. This enabled Juan to achieve his goal of authenticity. As he enthusiastically points out, what he has created – or rather recreated – is a vivid insight into ancient Morocco. Instead of exploring

scattered ruins, here you eat and sleep in the real thing.

So what's it like to stay in a four-hundred-year-old mud castle? The word that comes to mind is quiet – dead quiet. Set in the middle of the Skoura oasis, framed by the snow-capped Atlas in the distance, the absolute absence of noise is a continual reminder of the proximity of the Sahara and the remoteness of everything else. At night it can feel a little spooky to be so gloriously situated in the middle of nowhere. The nearest town is Ouarzazate (an hour's drive) and Marrakesh is six hours away through the mountains. In designing the interiors, Juan focused on what was important and left out what was not. Rooms are simple but impressive and bathrooms are spacious and efficient. The food too is rather good – a surprise in such a remote setting. But above all, he didn't turn the place into something it never was. It really is again as it was when the camel trains pulled in four centuries ago. It's not plush, it's real.

---

address Kasbah Ben Moro, 45500 Skoura, Ouarzazate, Morocco
t (212) 44 85 21 16   **f** (212) 44 85 21 16   **e** hotelbenmoro@yahoo.fr
room rates from DH 500

riad kaiss

Not so long ago staying in the medina of Marrakesh – the medieval heart of Morocco's most exotic city – was not something a visitor could or probably would do. There were a few exceptions: riads, or inner city palaces, were acquired by the odd wealthy Western eccentric or Eurotrash aristocrat, but for most it was a strictly daytime thrill, and definitely not a real estate proposition.

When Morocco became a French protectorate in 1912, its first governor Marshal Lyautey laid down the policy of the future colonial regime. The French, he specified, were 'not to touch a Moroccan hair or disturb a single Moroccan custom'. French settlers and the colonial bureaucracy were thus established in new neighbourhoods built outside the old city walls, and the medinas of Fez, Rabat, Meknès and Marrakesh were left undisturbed. Their inner networks of lanes, bazaars, workshops and hidden courtyards remained as some of the most authentic medieval survivals in the world. Morocco had, after all, turned its back on the rest of the world for more than four hundred years after the collapse of Islamic rule in Andalusia. When the French took over, the country had no railways, no electricity, no sewerage, and no running water. Self-imposed isolation had preserved a way of life unchanged since the Middle Ages.

By the second half of the twentieth century this timewarp, complete with all the sounds, smells, and bustling activity of the medina experience, had become an irresistible lure to the adventurous, West-weary traveller. It was (and still is) a journey back to a pre-sanitized way of life. And in the case of Marrakesh, it is a journey into a city that since the thirteenth century has had a reputation as one of the most exotic on earth. This was where Europe and Africa met to trade in gold, spices and slaves. Even now that Morocco has cars, televisions, supermarkets, mobile phones, Pizza Huts and the Internet, the Marrakesh medina still tempts and often overwhelms the unsuspecting Western visitor. It's a daily piece of fascinating urban theatre, a maze of shady alleys lined with tiny butchers' shops, carpenters' workshops, reeking dye works, shoemakers set up in impossibly small closet-like spaces, donkeys pulling carts that are only a few inches narrower than the streets, old men in hooded jellabas, modestly veiled women, and carpet merchants awaiting their next customer with fresh mint tea.

As the contrast between the old Morocco and the modern world becomes ever more pronounced, the attraction has only magnified. And these days visitors can't get enough of the intoxicating atmosphere of the medina.

Whereas once a tourist would venture in only during the day with a guide (essential, by the way, because even the average local doesn't know his way around this huge labyrinth, which contains some 26,000 houses), now they also come for dinner to places like Yacout, a palace converted into an extraordinary restaurant. Many go one step further, turning traditional Moroccan tourism on its head by staying in the medina and taking the odd daytrip beyond the confines of the old walled city. Not so long ago this wasn't possible – the option of staying in the medina, other than with friends, was simply unavailable. But in the past few years many Europeans have quite logically concluded that if an old riad can make a spectacular restaurant then it would probably work just as well or better as a hotel.

Moroccans themselves can't work it out. Why would anybody, let alone wealthy foreigners, choose to stay in the medina? It's cramped, there are no street signs, everybody gets lost, one dark laneway looks like the next, and it's aromatic (to put it most politely). Many medina residents dream of the suburban life they see on TV – but most of the arrivistes have had enough of exactly that.

There are riads and there are spectacular riads, but few are as palatial as Riad Kaiss. Situated at the end of a typically dark, typically narrow laneway, Kaiss is owned by French architect Christian Ferre, who used to design hotels in Asia. After early retirement, he too could not resist the pull of the medina's medieval mystique. Riad Kaiss has a grand tiled courtyard with fountains and mature trees, and beautifully ornate rooms with fireplaces and authentic decorative detail, all restored with the sure hand of a professional. You may even find yourself wishing they didn't have guides – then you'd have an excuse never to leave.

---

address Riad Kaiss, 65 Derb Jdid, Riad Zitoune Kedim, Marrakesh 40000, Morocco
t (212) 44 44 01 41   **f** (212) 44 44 01 41   **e** riad@riadkaiss.com
room rates from DH 1,530 (including breakfast)

lebombo lodge

Since its opening in late 2003, Lebombo Lodge has quickly captured the attention and imagination of the world's travel press. It has been voted Hotel of the Year by UK-based *Tatler* magazine, as well as US-based *Condé Nast Traveler* magazine, and the texts devoted to this – the third of Singita's lodges located in and around Kruger National Park – have sought to employ the full lexicon of admiring adjectives: delicious, fab, luxurious, exciting, sublime, minimal, magical, adorable, striking, pure, vigorous, sensational, etc, etc. If it's in the dictionary, it's probably been used to describe Lebombo. And yet none of these words truly conveys the essence of the place.

To understand the power of Lebombo, you have to go back to its roots, which are firmly grounded in the ideals of originality, sensitivity and authenticity. It's fine to talk about Lebombo as a groovy environment in the bush, with a view of a river with hippos and crocodiles from your bathtub, and a glimpse of giraffes from your designer desk, but this soon starts to seem rather superficial. What has been achieved with Lebombo is nothing less than a complete reinvention of the safari camp genre.

Originally, of course, no thought of architecture was attached to the idea of the safari at all: it was purely a transitory experience, with tents as the only overnight option. But ever since 'the camp' started to take on more permanent connotations, the accepted format has been some derivative of the thatch-roofed mud hut. As Lebombo architects Andrew Makin and Joy Brassler of the Durban-based design group OMM readily admit, the impulse to 'dig in' – to build in thatch and mud, with screed flooring – has, until now, been the legitimate response to a three-dimensional approach to the safari. With Lebombo, however, the designers and Singita entrepreneur Luke Bailes have thrown the rule book out of the window, abandoning historical precedence in favour of architectural innovation. The guiding principle, 'touch the earth lightly', takes a leaf from legendary Australian architect Glenn Murcutt.

In order to make the most of the hotel's setting in unusually steep and undulating terrain, accentuated by enormous boulders, in one of the most remote but picturesque corners of Kruger Park, the design philosophy has been to represent the more abstract qualities of these 15,000 hectares of African bush – the beautiful light, the infinite horizon, the vast emptiness.

Structures were fabricated in lightweight steel and bolted directly to the rockface, from which they are

215

suspended, creating, in the architects' words, 'platforms floating between the earth and the sky, roofed to keep the rain out, glazed to keep the animals and extreme heat out, and veiled in screens to integrate them into the surrounding topography'. To reflect the notion of endlessness, walls were constructed in glass, and both the furnishings and the furniture were chosen to enhance a continuing and consistent concern for lightness.

The result is a tour de force, both in terms of originality and appropriateness. The South African bush, which is vast, bright and seemingly infinite, appears to pass almost uninterrupted through the ethereal cantilevered structures of the camp.

The point of all this innovation is the experience. By way of originality and creativity, Lebombo has conceived a new way to experience Africa's wildlife. It's as if everything – the views, the sounds, the visitor's awareness of the animals – has been amplified; as if you're floating above the bush on your own cloud, all-seeing and all-hearing, while remaining undetected and unthreatened. For the guest, it's an almost surreal experience. But much as the whole design concept is all about openness, the one thing you can't do is leave your door open, because the naughty baboons at Lebombo know exactly where your mini-bar is....

Of all the adjectives that have been used to describe Lebombo, the word 'pure' comes closest to describing the sensation of being there. It is odd, yet simultaneously liberating, to be unprotected and unreinforced – no solid walls, no fences, no gates. Just you on your cloud above, and Africa, stretched out below. The impression is one of nature untouched and unaltered, as it was meant to be. For once the land has not been subjected to man's will – and therein, surely, lies the future of our interaction with natural beauty.

address Lebombo Lodge, c/o Singita Head Office, PO Box 23367, Claremont 7735, Cape Town, South Africa
t (27) 21 683 3424 **f** (27) 21 683 3502 **e** reservations@singita.co.za
room rates from ZAR 7140 (including meals and activities)

sweni lodge

Safari…. In Swahili the word means 'journey'. But for most of us, it conjures up a much more evocative and powerful image. For more than a century, ever since the world discovered the exotic beauty of eastern and southern Africa, a safari has promised the expansive beauty of the African *veldt* (bush) with the adrenaline rush of coming face to face with the planet's most charismatic and fascinating wild beasts.

The first traveller to embark on a safari as we know it today – a quest to encounter Africa's wildlife for no other reason than pleasure – was a convalescing officer in the British army: Sir William Cornwallis Harris. To recover from an illness contracted in India, Harris arrived in East Africa and, with a veritable army of porters, he embarked on an extended stay (six months) in the bush. Apart from sixty-odd books, he also brought along silverware, porcelain plates, crystal glasses and tents large enough to furnish in a manner not lacking in domestic comforts. Unknowingly, his expedition launched the tradition, now almost taken for granted, of combining luxury and style with the rugged remoteness of untamed wilderness.

Interestingly, more than a hundred and fifty years later, not much has changed. True, the rifle with a scope has been replaced by the camera with a long lens, but now, as then, the aim is to see as many animals as possible, both in terms of diversity and sheer numbers. More, in safari terms, is definitely better. And a successful game drive is still rewarded, in the manner of the British colonials, by drinks and dinner in refined style. The only casualties of progress, it seems, are the porters. Safari camps are, by and large, no longer a collection of tents; they are permanent sites, established in areas chosen for their beauty and their proximity to game, and dedicated to continuing the tradition of combining luxury with adventure.

It's a tradition that Singita lodges are particularly good at. With over 4,500 bush lodges to choose from in Africa, you have to be very special to stand out. And Sweni, the newest of the four Singita lodges (there are two in Sabi Sands and two in a remote corner of the Kruger National Park), gives you all the ingredients that have made the name famous worldwide: the flawless logistics, the knowledgeable rangers, the abundant wildlife, the sophisticated food, more luxury than a five-star city hotel, plus an eye for design and architecture that is simultaneously innovative and eco-sensitive – a daring approach that has taken the safari camp to the next level.

223

In terms of location, Sweni is not far from Lebombo, but in terms of ambience and atmosphere, it is vastly different. Where Lebombo is light, open and bright, Sweni is dark, cool and sexy.

Nestled at the bottom of a verdant ridge, overhanging the banks of the Sweni River, it is a green strip of subdued light, polished black shapes, khaki and olive tones, and a feeling that you are in the belly of Mother Africa. It is a retreat from the heat and the harsh light of the bush – a natural cool that you share only with the hippos who live on the river.

In creating Sweni, the Singita group wanted to retain the architectural philosophy of Lebombo, but on a smaller, more exclusive, more secluded scale. With only six guest bungalows, it is possible to book the whole place – your own svelte pad in the bush, for just you and your mates; the ultimate in hedonistic privacy.

But no matter how happily, luxuriously and snugly tucked away you may be, people still come for the game … and in that department Sweni offers the same extraordinary opportunities as Lebombo. Because this property – a vast concession in the far north-eastern corner of Kruger – was previously undeveloped, the animals are still completely wild; as in, they are not accustomed to humans. On the one hand, this means you have to work harder to spot them, but on the other hand, the resulting experience is more rewarding and adventurous. Tracking a leopard at night, just after it has feasted on a kill, produces the kind of body chemicals you would never generate in an area where you know the animals are comfortable with humans.

Thus, style and luxury aside, the real immeasurable plus of Sweni, like Lebombo, is that you can experience the kind of Africa that Sir William Cornwallis Harris experienced: an authentic, unspoiled, raw spectacle.

---

address Sweni Lodge, c/o Singita Head Office, PO Box 23367, Claremont 7735, Cape Town, South Africa
t (27) 21 683 3424 **f** (27) 21 683 3502 **e** reservations@singita.co.za
room rates from ZAR 7140 (including meals and activities)

ASIA

Ever since Marco Polo dictated the stories of his travels to a cellmate while imprisoned in Genoa – resulting in *The Travels of Marco Polo*, a bestseller for 300 years – the Far East has captured popular imagination. The 'Orient' has long been a synonym for anywhere exotic and unknown, and China, Japan, Siam, Burma, Java, Ceylon and Indochina were considered the most 'Oriental' of all.

With the advent of direct flights from London, New York, Paris, Amsterdam, Frankfurt and other major international airports, Asia is no longer as far away as it used to be. But if, as a destination, it has become far more convenient, thankfully it has become no less exotic. Despite having entered the modern world of digital telecommunications and high-speed Internet access, Asia has not done so at the expense of its cultural heritage. Throughout the continent there are more than enough places that still immerse the traveller in a spellbinding setting without resorting to clumsy clichés or themed fantasies.

From the temple-like architecture of Borobudur's Amanjiwo, to the divine crumbling decadence of a former maharaja's city palace in Jaipur, to the sophisticated Zen discipline of a 300-year-old traditional inn in old Kyoto, Asia serves up a menu of extraordinary variety. But these are tantalising travel experiences with a difference. They are authentic experiences that you, the traveller, can inhabit rather than merely visit.

If anything, today's Asia offers too much choice. The way to deal with it is to focus on personal preference. If your taste is for idyllic beaches and turquoise waters, opt for Goa. If the architectural legacy is what motivates you, then you will not be disappointed by the ruins of Angkor Wat or the Mughal palaces of Rajasthan. If you're swayed by the splendour of Dynasty-era China portrayed in films such as *Raise the Red Lantern* or *Crouching Tiger, Hidden Dragon*, then head for Beijing's China Club or Hangzhou's Fuchun.

Whether it's the spiritual forests of Bali's Ubud that appeal or the colonial remains of Penang, the intricate handcraft that survives in Nepal or the unspoilt luminescent green of Luang Prabang's jungle setting, the Dutch style of an old admiral's mansion in Sri Lanka or the pared-down brutality of a series of beachside bunkers on a forgotten stretch of Thai coast, the Orient offers the discerning traveller the most amazing plethora of persuasive possibilities.

begawan giri estate

Begawan Giri Estate is not a hotel. It's a dream. It's everything the first-time visitor wants Bali to be, and everything the person who knows the island is hoping to find. It's a mystical, spiritual, exotic, immaculate, architectural and unashamedly luxurious retreat.

Begawan Giri was never intended as a hotel. What it is today is the result of the original owners' total commitment to a property. Bradley Gardner was a British expat who had established a successful chain of fashion jewelry shops all over Asia. When he and his wife Debbie stumbled upon the Begawan Giri site in 1989 while on a mountain walk, they had a revelation – they simply understood the magic of the spot. Bit by bit they acquired small parcels of land, until eventually their acquisitions grew to an expanse of eight hectares, which encompasses a small plateau that drops away, ravine-like, to the Ayung River below. But it wasn't yet clear to the owners what to do with this dramatic terrain. As Bradley Gardner put it, 'It was not until some time had passed before we were sure what we wanted from the land – or, more accurately, what the land wanted from us.'

Long before they erected a building of any kind, the Gardners commenced an ambitious landscaping project. Over a period of nine years, they deployed a small army of gardeners to plant more than 2,500 trees; carve countless terraces into the steep hillside leading down to the river; build scores of footpaths cut from blocks of black volcanic stone; excavate a series of terracotta-paved roads; and cover acre after acre with a dense, verdant carpet of *alang alang* grass. No detail was left unattended. Like a cleverly crafted film, the gardens of Begawan Giri reveal themselves slowly. Inspired by legendary Sri Lankan architect Geoffrey Bawa's gardens at his Lunuganga estate, the Gardners have created the same carefully cultivated sense of natural wilderness. As a guest, you make a new discovery with every excursion from your room, whether it's a discreetly placed balé, a stone wall covered in green moss, or one of several natural springs. It's a visual theatre of botanical art direction.

The Gardners' appreciation of the property was enriched by local legend. Once upon a time ordinary villagers were loath to venture into the dense, steeply declining jungle. The only people who dared to enter it were three wise men who invested the land with a powerful spiritual energy, and it became known among the villagers as *begawan giri* or 'wise man's mountain'. Folklore aside, a plan emerged as to what to build on this magical site.

The Gardners envisaged an estate, a retreat in the old-fashioned sense where you come to recover from the stress and toll of daily life, and your personal butler takes care of the day-to-day tediums of packing, unpacking, laundering, pressing and arranging flights. What's more, they wanted to build a house, or a series of houses – not a large box with a series of identical rooms.

Though the idea behind Begawan Giri was fuelled by a longing for the old-fashioned, the form this would take was anything but. Together with Malaysian architect Cheong Yew Kuan, the Gardners set out to create a dynamic Asian architecture with a strong Balinese flavour. Where a less adventurous client and architect would opt for the logical simplicity of building on the flatness of a plateau, Gardner and Cheong chose to build their first project on land a shade short of vertical. The engineering required was formidable, but the result is all drama and privacy. The structure overhangs the horseshoe-shaped gorge that defines the property, and the waterfalls below provide a soothing, permanent acoustic backdrop. What's more, its position renders it virtually invisible from the road leading through the property. This formula provided the blueprint for four more residences, which vary in style but all share in the property's extraordinary beauty as a focal point.

With time, Begawan Giri grew beyond anything the Gardners had ever imagined. Their baby was starting to demand more and more time and even more money. With two restaurants, two shops, a fully fledged spa and another seven private villas, it was clear that Begawan Giri needed more than the Gardners could give; in 2004, the property transferred into the capable hands of hotel impresario Christina Ong. Now, at last, the Gardners themselves are able to enjoy the estate, in exactly the way they intended their guests to.

---

address Begawan Giri Estate, PO Box 54, Ubud, 80571 Bali, Indonesia
t (62) 0361 978 888 **f** (62) 0361 978 889 **e** res.begawan@begawangiri.como.bz
room rates from US $495

the balé

A *balé* is a traditional Balinese structure: a house on stilts, a timber platform with an overhanging roof usually thatched in *alang alang* grass. But you will find no such structure at the Balé. The name is an abstract reference to the age-old raised shelter. In the same way, the design refers to Balinese tradition, but not obviously so.

Bali has its own form of Hinduism, Agama Tirtha, which literally means the religion of holy water; every well, waterfall and fountainhead possesses spiritual significance. Indonesian architects Anthony Liu and Ferry Ridwan took this aspect of Balinese culture to heart when they designed the Balé. There are more than seventy individual pools on this multi-terraced property, twenty-two of which are dedicated to swimming, two to bathing (in the spa) and the remaining forty-eight to ornamentation. Not bad for a hotel that only has twenty rooms. Then again, the word 'room' is hardly an adequate description. At the Balé, every guest is accommodated in their own individual bungalow – a sleek and streamlined pavilion – complete with a private swimming pool (which you access directly from your bathroom), an outdoor living room/entertainment area and a magnificent sweeping view of the crescent-shaped beaches of Nusa Dua below.

For the lucky few who stay here as guests, it's a magnificently luxurious experience, to be sure – one international architecture magazine described the Balé as having 'a majestic quality, like a modern Persepolis'. And yet it's hard to find someone in Bali who has a kind word to say about it. 'It's so minimal and so pale you need your sunglasses all the time,' is one comment; 'It has nothing to do with Bali,' is another; 'It looks OK now but what will happen in a few years' time?' is still another. It's clear that the place is misunderstood, but none of this general mudslinging has had any effect on occupancy: the Balé is the most booked-out hotel on the entire island. That's because consumers recognize a good deal when they see one. Privacy, luxury and modernity – the Balé has it all. What's more, aesthetically speaking, the creative team of Liu, Ridwan and Bali-based American landscape architect Karl Princic have proven that a design does not have to rely on ornamentation in order to be Balinese.

Critics of the Balé have clearly missed the point. The design, in all its monochrome, minimalist modernism, is still very much a response to the site. Unlike the lush tropical vegetation that defines most of Bali, the Bukit Peninsula on which the hotel is situated is starker and more severe.

It's also more desert-like in its dominant shades of bleached browns and sand. This rugged, neutral-toned landscape is reflected in the architects' choice of pebble-washed, sand-coloured terrazzo floors, and the retaining walls in local limestone. The idea was to emphasize the beauty of the surroundings and the view of the ocean below, rather than the local culture. Just down the road is Seminyak, the epicentre of Balinese tourism and home to some of the island's trendiest restaurants and nightclubs including Ku De Ta, which regularly features guest DJs such as Paris's legendary Claude Challe. In short, this is the most cosmopolitan part of Bali, and the Balé is its most cosmopolitan overnight address. Interestingly, such a place would have been inconceivable even a decade ago. But the rise of inter-Asian travel has changed all that. Bali is easily accessible from Singapore, Jakarta, Bangkok, Hong Kong and even Sydney and Tokyo, and hotels such as the Balé

reflect the emerging Asian taste for minimalism as opposed to the preference of Europeans and Americans for 'ethnic' decorativeness. Released from Western cultural vanities, designers in Asia are free to create, tapping into influences irrespective of origin. Liu's inspiration is typical: his designs draw from John Pawson's minimalism, from the spare poetry of Japan's Tadao Ando and from the pristine precision of Switzerland's Peter Zumthor.

It's doubtful that the young Asian couples who choose the Balé as their honeymoon destination give much thought to the intellectual *raison d'être* of the property's design, nor would they lose sleep over the question of whether the place is Balinese enough. For them it's a simple matter of staying at a beautiful place in a beautiful setting. And surely therein lies the new ethos of Asian design: less dependent on tradition and so-called authenticity, and more concerned with quality and modernity.

address The Balé, Jalan Raya Nusa Dua Selatan, PO Box 76, Nusa Dua, 80363 Bali, Indonesia
t (62) 0361 775 111 **f** (62) 0361 775 222 **e** bliss@thebale.com
room rates from US $480

la résidence d'angkor

The most puzzling thing about the ruins of Angkor is how little survives of the day-to-day existence of the people of the Khmer Empire, which flourished for over five hundred years and at its height covered the whole of present-day Cambodia and most of Thailand. There's nothing: not a house, book, jewel, domestic implement or single item of clothing. Most of what we know about everyday Khmer culture comes from the carvings and inscriptions in the temples it left behind. It's a bit like learning the culture of Europeans solely from a few surviving cathedrals (a scary thought indeed).

A Khmer temple was not a meeting place for the faithful like a church, mosque or synagogue: it was the palace of a god. A god such as Vishnu had the power of beneficence, both here and in the hereafter, and the more beautiful his palace, the happier (and more generous) he would be. Gods took the form of statues in the temples, and it was the duty of devotees to tend to them: for instance, they would dress them, adorn them with jewelry and bring them offerings of food, flowers and incense at least three times a day. At Angkor, the scale of this work was in line with the scale of the temples, i.e. huge. From an inscription in the ruins of Ta Prohm (featured in the movie

Tomb Raider), we learn that in the twelfth century this temple complex was serviced by almost thirteen thousand monks, and its maintenance required the toil and produce of another eighty thousand people in the various villages that belonged to it.

Whereas today the temples are impressive but austere, in their heyday they would have been lively and crowded. The area between the outer wall and the temple would have been packed with small wooden structures on stilts; the statues would have been covered in the finest silks; and the corridors would have been filled with the smell of incense and the to-ing and fro-ing of shaven-headed, saffron-clad monks. The most colourful player in Angkor life would have been the king, whose every movement was accompanied by tremendous pageantry. Zhou Daguan, a Chinese envoy who visited Angkor in 1296, wrote a unique eyewitness account of the spectacle of the Khmer king's entourage in his *Memoirs on the Customs of Cambodia*: 'When the King leaves his palace the procession is headed by cavalry – then come the flags, the banners and the music. Three to five hundred gaily dressed palace girls, with flowers in their hair and tapers in their hands, are massed together in a separate group…. Following them come chariots drawn by goats and

245

Stone murals at La Résidence d'Angkor
mimic the carved galleries of nearby
Angkor Wat

La Résidence is in Siem Reap, the town adjacent
to Angkor Wat, which hosts a large
population of Buddhist monks

Vast expanses of teak are punctuated by walls
of carved stone at one of Southeast Asia's
most handsome hotels

Angkor's monumental treasures were built
by Hindus – the Khmer converted to
Buddhism many centuries later

At the peak of the Khmer Empire, even kings
lived in wooden palaces; stone structures
were reserved for the gods

Buddhist monks look after the statues
in the temple – they are the valets
of the gods

horses, all adorned with gold.... Finally the Sovereign appears, standing erect on an elephant....'

Apart from the temples made of stone (a material reserved exclusively for the dwellings of gods), all Khmer architecture was built in wood. Even the king lived in a wooden palace, albeit a very grand one with a tiled roof. It's therefore appropriate that the Pansea Orient-Express Hotels group opted for wood when choosing a stylistic approach for their Angkor property. La Résidence d'Angkor, in the heart of the small but pretty tree-lined town of Siem Reap, is an exotic, dark-wooden-panelled escape from the heat and bustle of outdoors. The minute you enter the building, you feel the soothing effects of your surroundings. Although La Résidence is very affordable, it certainly doesn't look it. For starters, there's the pool, a sumptuous 130-foot-long stretch of emerald-green tiles with two Hindu-inspired fountains. The guest rooms continue the theme of both

dark wood – for the floors and the furniture – and the luxury of space, with bathrooms the size of an average hotel room in Paris. The decor combines an earthy Asian signature with a contemporary flourish: dark timber and white walls are punctuated by splashes of vividly coloured Cambodian silks used as tablecloths and pillows throughout the hotel.

Without fail, most newcomers to Angkor are impressed by La Résidence's two-storey teak lobby and the moat you cross to get to it. But don't forget, they haven't been to the temples yet. And that's the point of Angkor. You go there to marvel at the engineering feats of the Khmer Empire, to consider the sheer number of magnificent temples they constructed and the complexity of the waterworks they created on such a monumental scale. The beauty of La Résidence is in its architectural continuity. Then and now, people visiting stone temples dedicated to Vishnu return to houses built entirely in wood.

---

address La Résidence d'Angkor, River Road, Siem Reap, Cambodia
t (855) 063 963 390   **f** (855) 063 963 391   **e** angkor@pansea.com
room rates from US $205

amansara

When visiting dignitaries such as Brezhnev, Ho Chi Minh or Jackie Kennedy were invited to Siem Reap in the early 1960s for a private tour of the temples of Angkor, they would be put up in the guest villa of Prince Norodom Sihanouk (later the King of Cambodia). Architecturally speaking, the two worlds couldn't have been more opposite. Known then as the Villa Princière, Prince Sihanouk's pad was a white-walled compound of modernist reinforced concrete. Designed by French architect Laurent Mondet and completed in 1962, it was and still is a sleek collection of low horizontal lines and capacious circular domes. Angkor, on the other hand, is a riot of Hindu shapes, figures and carvings, executed in acre after acre of solid sandstone.

On a pragmatic level, Prince Sihanouk had understood that there was no competing with Angkor Wat's exotic grandeur. He had also guessed, quite wisely, that after a day spent visiting the area's temples and monuments, guests might welcome a retreat into a soothing absence of decorativeness. And though nowadays he no longer owns or runs it, his villa continues to operate in the same contrast-rich style. Amansara's clean, sixties-inspired lines have more in common with Frank Sinatra's Palm Springs than with Jayavarman's VII's great capital of the mighty Khmer Empire. Exploring the monumental remains left behind by a succession of Khmer kings is a strenuous pastime, and the hotel's groovy modernist aesthetic hasn't lost its appeal as a haven from Angkor's Hindu hype.

Angkor Wat is a Caligula-style feast of statistics, covering over five hundred acres of land – the surrounding moat alone is over six hundred feet wide and nearly four miles long. Built during the reign of King Suryavarman II in the first half of the twelfth century, the great complex was originally dedicated to the god Vishnu, striving through its architecture to create a microcosm of the Hindu universe (although it has since been converted to Buddhist practice). Its quintet of conical towers mimics the five heavenly peaks of Mount Meru and, to emphasize the rewards of heavenly life, the structure is adorned with carvings of over 1,800 *apsaras* (celestial maidens). But the most remarkable artistry lies in the galleries that run around the whole temple. These seemingly never-ending 'tapestries' of beautifully executed, intricately detailed bas-reliefs depict scenes from Hindu mythology and civic lore, covering the gambit of human experience.

To take in all the stories told by these figurative visual feasts would take many, many days – more time than most

visitors have. That said, the greatest mistake that many travellers to Angkor make is not allowing enough time. It's impossible to visit Siem Reap successfully in just two days, no matter how determined or dedicated you are to the task. That's because Angkor Wat is only part of the picture. There are also – to name just a few – Bantheai Srei, Preah Khan, Ta Prohm and Neak Pean, not to mention Angkor Thom, the great town within whose walls the Khmer kings resided. And central to Angkor Thom is one of the most striking structures in the religious world, the temple of Bayon, composed of a collection of fifty-four massive stone towers, each carved in the shape of the smiling face of Buddha.

Simply put, Angkor is overwhelming, and Amansara's pristine sixties-inspired modernism with an Asian twist is just what you need after the carved cacophony of the Khmer temples. Architect Kerry Hill's renovation of the Villa Princière is comfortable, clever and appropriate. He has taken the 1960s as a starting point and introduced furniture inspired by Jean Prouvé, executed in the distinctly Asian materials of teak and raffia. But it's the scale of Amansara that makes it so comfortable: it retains the feel of staying in someone's villa, without the occasional headache of having to be nice to the host. And yet because it's an Aman, the level of service creates the impression that you're the only one there.

From black-and-white snapshots taken when it first opened, it's clear that not all that much has changed since the Prince welcomed visitors here; the round dining room, for instance, is the same space used in the same way. But the place benefits hugely from the Aman group's commitment to aesthetic perfection. Guests lounge by the pool in Californian Palm Springs fashion; it's just that here the golf courses are (thankfully) replaced by the world's most captivating temples.

---

address Amansara, Road to Angkor, Siem Reap, Cambodia
t (855) 063 760 333 **f** (855) 063 760 335 **e** amansara@amanresorts.com
room rates from US $700

china club

Crouching Tiger, Hidden Dragon. These were the first words a friend in Hong Kong used to describe the China Club in Beijing. 'You'll love it,' she said. 'It's just like staying in the film but with great food.' And she was right.

Situated down a quiet *hutong* (typical Beijing lane) not far from the Forbidden City and Tiananmen Square, this former palace has changed very little since it was built in the seventeenth century for a son of Emperor Kang Xi of the Qing Dynasty. Remarkably, virtually all of its architectural features have survived intact. This no doubt has a lot to do with the fact that for four decades it housed one of the best restaurants in Beijing – it was the favourite Szechuan kitchen of Deng Xiao Ping, the Chairman of the Communist Party post-Mao. Eventually, however, despite the restaurant's reputation and stellar clientele, at one hundred thousand-plus square feet (divided into countless smaller dining rooms), it was too large to sustain, particularly in the newly competitive post-Communism Beijing. Even the patronage of the country's number one leader was no longer enough.

When the opportunity arose a decade ago to take over this historic property, Hong Kong-based tycoon, art collector and fashion entrepreneur David Tang didn't hesitate. An extensive but sensitive renovation project was embarked upon and completed so successfully that it's impossible to spot such giveaways of modernity as air-conditioning units, even though there's one in every dining room.

The true beauty of the place is the way it's divided into pavilions. Everywhere you go, there's another hidden courtyard, private dining room or secret bar. Design-wise, Tang has nonetheless adhered to the idea of a club, a supper club that also happens to have some very smart overnight accommodation. Best of all, if you stay here there's really not much reason to go out because the China Club plays host to one of Beijing's most successful 'scenes'. Every evening at around 7pm, an entire convoy of shiny black limousines with tinted windows pulls into the cramped first courtyard. Elegantly dressed ladies of leisure, fat captains of industry and the odd media glamour puss step out into the almost film-set environment of the Beijing China Club. Even though the surrounding towers of glass and steel serve as a reminder of the new dimensions of China's capital, there's still something distinctly nostalgic about the whole experience. The China Club is chic, cosmopolitan and decadent, in a 1920s Shanghai sort

of way; it's a place for long, silk *cheongsam* dresses split at the side and sober black suits.

What is perhaps most impressive about the China Club, apart from the fact that it has managed to survive both the Communist and Cultural Revolutions, is its seductive use of colour. We always associate China with the colour red, but traditional Chinese interiors are far more multicoloured than you'd expect. At the China Club, yellow, purple, royal blue, light blue, cream, black, orange and green – chartreuse, olive and lime – all feature as part of the decorative palette, along with plenty of gilding. Yet despite the profusion of colour, it has been used in a deliberate and systematic manner. Colour guides you from one space to the next, and distinguishes one room from another. Within the private dining rooms, the chromatic schemes are pared down to two or three hues. There is, for instance, a yellow dining room accented with purple silk and dark timber, just

as there is a cream-coloured private dining room with black furniture and splashes of green and orange.

In the guestrooms, colour has been limited to dark red or chartreuse green Chairman Mao-style club seats in bouclé velvet with white lace armrests. These rooms are unlike any you're likely to have been in before. The bed is hidden in its own alcove in the centre of the space, divided from the living room and the bathroom by corridors created with Chinese-patterned timber trellis panels that also provide a decorative focus. The effect is reminiscent of the film *Raise the Red Lantern*. There is nothing vaguely 'hotel room' about these suites, and even the towels break vividly with tradition. Hotel towels are almost always white or cream. At the China Club they're bright pink. Never did I think I'd be walking around in a pink bathrobe, but such is the power of a mysterious and seductive environment.

---

address The China Club Beijing, 51 Xi Rong Xian Lane, Xi Dan, Beijing, China
t (86) 010 6603 8855 **f** (86) 010 6603 9594 **e** tccbadmn@public.bta.net.cn
room rates from US $108

fuchun

Set in the verdant, uniquely Chinese landscape of Hangzhou, the traditional retreat destination of mainland China, Fuchun looks just like a Chinese watercolour. As it turns out, I wasn't the first to think so. The hotel is built on the exact location that inspired the legendary Yuan Dynasty painter Huang Gongwang to focus on a handscroll that took over ten years to complete. Although he didn't start painting until the age of fifty-one, Huang is credited with the reinvention of Chinese landscape painting. From the Tang to the Sung and then the Yuan Dynasties, painting in China was so grounded in tradition that it became stagnant. Huang was a revolutionary: bored of strictly imitating the masters, he began to paint what he *felt* rather than what he saw. Together with Ni Zan, Wu Zhen and Wang Meng, he became known as one of the Four Masters of the Yuan, regarded by some as China's first Impressionists.

At the ripe old age of seventy-four, Huang moved to the Fuchun region and started work on *Dwelling in the Fuchun Mountains*, the scroll that would seal his fame and many centuries later serve as inspiration for the extraordinary Fuchun Resort. Most days he would wander the mountains with his paper, brushes and ink, and paint still lifes of whatever inspired him. On his return home he would painstakingly transfer his creative efforts to the scroll. Finally, in the year he turned eighty-four, he finished his now famous painting.

It's a good story, worthy of a slow-moving, beautifully filmed Chinese movie, and one that caught the imagination of a driven Taiwanese industrialist. Bengo Cheng is a successful paper producer with factories all over mainland China as well as on the island of Taiwan. His success has allowed him to pursue his passions, one of which is traditional Chinese culture. He imagined a retreat that would celebrate rather than ignore Chinese history, and so he set about the ambitious project of Fuchun Resort. Stage one was a golf course, a clubhouse and some residential villas. Normally, at this point, my eyes would glaze over, not because I don't like golf but because I don't find golf courses very interesting. Fuchun, however, is the first place I've seen where the natural beauty of the surroundings is actually enhanced by a golf course, all entirely thanks to landscape design. The course's eighteen holes follow the contour of the land, while the clubhouse is built in Taoist style on an island in a spectacular manmade lake. But the creative tour de force was the decision to surround the course with the boldly architectural terraces of a working tea

Set in the middle of a lake, the architecture and design of Fuchun is inspired by Taoist tradition

Bedrooms are decorated in a modern take on 1920s Chinese Art Deco and arranged along elaborate courtyards

Fuchun's landscape is straight out of a Chinese scroll painting; the terraces of a tea plantation adds a geometric edge

Fuchun is the result of the proprietor's
passion for Chinese history
and culture

The lobby is an immense hall,
a virtual forest of towering
teak pillars

Architecturally, the most inspiring space
is the soaring, temple-like structure that
houses the indoor swimming pool

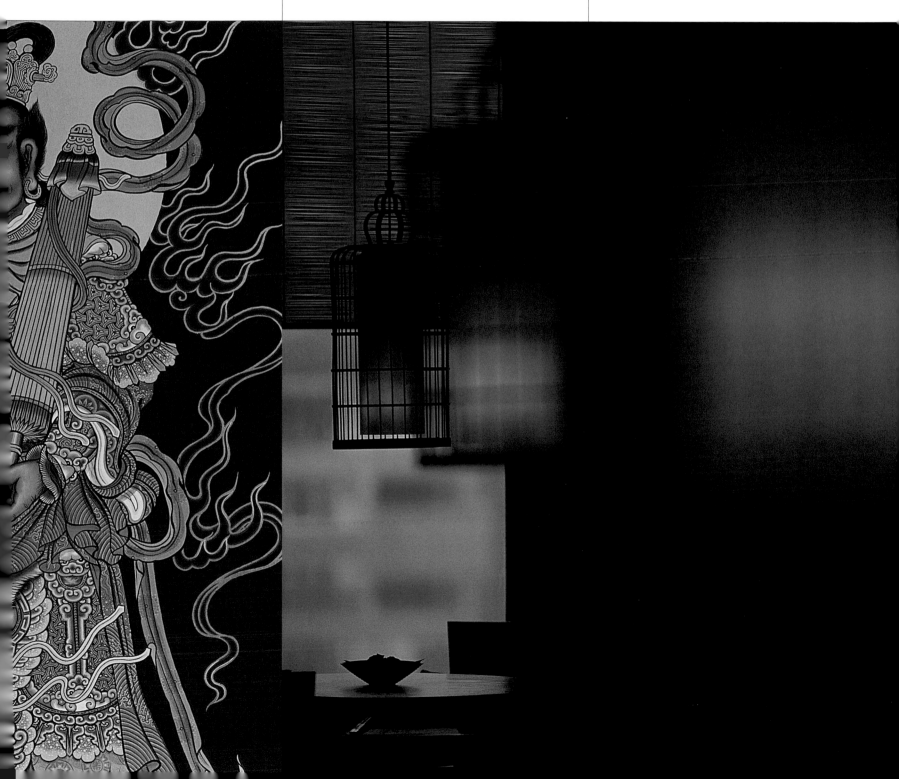

plantation. In many places the tea grows all the way up to the fairway.

When the course and the clubhouse were completed in 2000, they caused quite a stir around the world. *Golf Digest* named Fuchun the best course in Asia, and *Condé Nast Traveller* voted T8, the club's restaurant, one of the fifty best in the world. Even Giorgio Armani came to see what all the fuss was about. It was one of those rare design success stories, a hit with locals and foreigners alike. But the best was still to come.

The hotel, which opened in 2004, rises like a modern version of a Taoist temple in the middle of the lake opposite the clubhouse. With its traditional roof tiles and sloping walls of light grey granite, Fuchun has a distinctly Chinese aesthetic without being a pastiche. The same holds true for the interior. The granite floors, the China red carpet, the occasional strip of copper-coloured silk, the rows of massive columns and the bronze lanterns that line the corridors all pay tribute to the history of China and to the talent of Kuala Lumpur-based French architect Jean-Michel Gathy. And I haven't even mentioned the pool; you're not likely to find another one like it anywhere in the world. At over 250 square feet and entirely clad in copper- and gold-coloured mosaic glass tiles, it's located in a soaring structure defined by giant pillars and a typically Chinese interlocking beamed roof. If you can imagine swimming in a temple, then this comes close. And then there are the rooms. Arranged along a series of water gardens, they are vast apartments of oiled teak, copper silk, black stone and grey granite equipped to the highest standards of any Asian hotel (think Aman).

With a surrounding landscape straight out of a painting, the luxury of a princely palace, and the privacy and privilege only afforded to China's feudal warlords, Fuchun offers the China of myth – even if you don't play golf.

address Fuchun Resort, Hua Shu Village, Fuyang, Hangzhou, Zhejiang, China
t (86) 0571 6346 1111 **f** (86) 0571 6346 1222 **e** fuchunresort@lcpc.biz
room rates from US $250

devi garh

India's historical legacy is second to none. Few people realize that the culture of this vast subcontinent predates that of the Ancient Egyptians, or that the Indus Valley was home to the largest of the four ancient urban civilizations of India, Egypt, Mesopotamia and China. India was top on Alexander the Great's conquest list, and even the classical civilizations of the Mediterranean such as Greece and Rome coveted the region's beautiful silks.

It's because of all this history that India's architectural heritage is hard to match. In the northern state of Rajasthan, where the hot, dry weather has been particularly kind to buildings of substance, there is a wealth of awe-inspiring historical reminders of the fact that India was home to an aesthetically sophisticated culture long before the Brits arrived. Far ahead of Alexander the Great's ill-fated attempt to reach this fabled land of silk and tigers, Indian civilization invented the number system we now take for granted in mathematics (among many other contributions that seem to be forgotten, at least by the rest of the world).

As in France, India's many rulers (the subcontinent was divided into hundreds of tiny fiefdoms) built magnificent palaces, grand follies endowed with marble, stone and wood carving, inlaid jewels, fountains, gardens and even swimming pools in the form of stepwells (upside-down four-storey structures burrowed into the ground). Eventually the same fate befell India's aristocratic residences as the châteaux of France: the nobility could no longer afford to keep them. Following Independence in 1947, the country's former ruling classes had to find new ways of making ends meet, and one of the few options open to them was to convert their palatial properties into hotels. That's how Udaipur's fabulous Lake Palace came to be a hotel; the same goes for Jaipur's Rambagh Palace and many others. The trouble was, there weren't enough visitors to justify the restoration of India's myriad of (so-called) lesser palaces and forts. Or so everyone thought, until a small creative team with lots of zeal, plenty of imagination and the necessary financial means tackled the renovation of Neemrana Fort Palace near Delhi. Looking like a Rajasthani palace while feeling nothing like a hotel, Neemrana set a new benchmark. The response was immediate, and it's as hip today as it was when it first opened.

The success of Neemrana inspired a dream to renovate another Rajasthani palace. Taking care to retain the original external architecture, the interior was to be reinvented in a style that could best be described as funky Indian

minimalism: a traditional palace on the outside and a pared-down, monochromatic series of spaces on the inside. Nestled in the Aravalli hills about an hour's drive from Udaipur, the eighteenth-century Devi Garh Fort Palace had been abandoned in the 1960s. By the time the Poddar family found it a couple of decades later it was a total wreck. Photographs taken at the start of the project reveal a ruin, an almost unrecognizable pile of rubble and stone – little wonder that it took over a decade to bring to fruition. Undeterred, Lekha Poddar's vision was of a soothingly spacious interior environment. With minimal decorative detail, Devi Garh was to be luxurious in a thoroughly contemporary yet unmistakably Indian manner.

The result is a model for all future historical projects in India. The palace is inspiringly beautiful, and the contrast between antique authenticity and minimalist modernity is nothing less than striking. What I couldn't help noticing, especially after having visited many other palaces, is how the hotel's reductivist approach amplifies its Indianness: the Mughal arches, the stone carving and all its other distinctive architectural signatures end up both clearer and stronger. In a sense, there's a parallel with the Taj Mahal. Up close this emblematic edifice is a highly ornate collection of niches, carvings and inlaid jewelry. From a distance, though, it's an immaculate fairy-tale structure, perfect in its whiteness. Its real visual strength lies not in its details but in the abstraction of its form.

With Devi Garh, the Poddars have struck just the right balance between a passion for history and a lust for contemporary luxury. Instead of relying on gold taps and fluffy towels, they have used sophisticated architecture and interior design to create a timeless blend of culture, history and space. It's a powerfully attractive combination.

---

address Devi Garh, Village Delwara, Tehsil Nathdwara, District Rajsamand, Rajasthan, India
t (91) 029 53 289 211   **f** (91) 029 53 289 357   **e** devigarh@deviresorts.com
room rates from US $150

nilaya hermitage

Nilaya, roughly translated, means 'blue heaven' in Sanskrit. It's an appropriate name. Perched on top of a jungle peak in tropical Goa, the Nilaya Hermitage is an exquisite blue sanctuary with spectacular views of swaying palms and the Arabian Sea below. Its architectural signature is incredibly eclectic: there are Indian, Mexican, Balinese, New Age and organic influences, as well as borrowings from Gaudí and the styles of colonial Goa. And that's just the architecture: the interior detailing is an even more exotic mix of cosy French, minimal Mexican, and streamlined Rajasthani.

This ethno-eclecticism makes perfect sense when you consider the lives of its proprietors, Claudia Derain and Hari Ajwani. Hari was born in India, educated in Germany, and worked in Europe as an engineer before returning to his native Goa. Claudia, the creative engine of the project, is even more international: with a German mother and a French diplomat father, she has lived in more countries than most people visit in a lifetime.

But if part of Nilaya's charm owes to its creators being citizens of the world, it is also due to the spontaneity of the project. Claudia and Hari never intended to build a portion of paradise from scratch. They already had a colonial house in Goa, and by all accounts it was a very beautiful one: it had

the high ceilings, wooden floors, and all the style of Goa's four centuries of Portuguese heritage. They operated it as a successful upmarket *maison d'hôte*. There was only one snag. Although they had completely renovated the place, they didn't legally own it. The proprietor had promised to sell it to them (eventually), but no more than that. Then an old Portuguese law cropped up prohibiting the sale of a family property without written agreement from every single living member of the family. When an aunt in Mumbai refused point blank, that was that.

Feeling devastated, frustrated, and decidedly ripped off, they set out to find somewhere new. The first and most logical place to look was the coast, but the right property failed to turn up. In any case, given the rate tourism was developing in Goa, they feared being rapidly swallowed up by hideous development. Then a substantial plot on a hilltop in the hinterland became available. At first they both dismissed it outright – what would they do there? It would be too difficult to get to, too hot, and it was not exactly walking distance from the beaches, Goa's key attraction. Even so, Hari suggested hiring a team with machetes to chop their way to the top and at least peek at what was on offer. There they discovered not just a vista of swaying palms and distant beaches, but also a cool breeze wafting up the mountain – much cooler than by the sea. Their decision was swift. With no plan clearer than a determination to create another exceptional guest house, they got started. The work took three years in all. First they had to build access roads, and then clear the site – this was, after all, a patch of jungle. When they finally started building there was still no masterplan. As Claudia tells it, things evolved on a daily basis – which explains why Nilaya gives the impression of having been nurtured, not manufactured; grown, not designed.

With the exception of the odd gold dome and the mosaic-tiled swimming pool, the exterior is rugged rather than pretty, its porous brown volcanic stone blending perfectly with the verdant natural setting. It sets up a dramatic contrast with the interior, where all is blue: light blue terrazzo; washed blue walls accented by silver and gold paint; aquamarine surfaces contrasted by traditional pots in copper and gold. The colours, the Rajasthani antiques, the undulating surfaces and carefully arranged objects create a multi-ethnic melange. So distinctive is Claudia and Hari's approach that guests' constant inquiries of 'where did you get this' and 'where did you get that' eventually led to a shop. No half-measures for these two, though. In a step that brought them full circle, they acquired a beautiful dilapidated colonial building by the coast and created not just a shop but an entire complex dedicated to the Nilaya look and the Nilaya lifestyle. This is no run-of-the-mill showroom. It's a spectacular space, designed to highlight Claudia and Hari's particular blend of Indian and Western aesthetics and values. Here, as at Nilaya, you feel at once relaxed and inspired, happy to be immersed in a style the likes of which you will probably not have experienced before.

address Nilaya Hermitage, Arpora Bhati, Goa 403518, India

t (91) 0832 227 6793   **f** (91) 0832 227 6792   **e** nilaya@sancharnet.in

room rates from US $140 (including half board and transfers)

samode haveli

As India changes at extraordinary speed, cultural authenticity is fast becoming one of the country's most sought-after commodities. Let's face it – none of us travels to India in order to drive Japanese cars, eat at McDonald's or drink Coca-Cola. The fact that India now has all of these, when only a decade ago it had none, is testament to the speed and scale of change. But with this unrelenting drive towards modernity has come an ironic turnaround for tourism. Whereas discerning visitors once searched for an oasis of Western comfort, now they seek the real India.

But what is the real India? The answer to that is as manifold as India itself. For many visitors, however, especially first-time visitors, the real India is Rajasthan. This is the India of maharajas and their intricate palaces, of men with bright turbans and women with equally vivid saris – bolts of gem-like colour in a land of heat and dust. Rajasthan is the India made famous by E.M. Forster's *A Passage to India*. And despite progress the good news is that the beauty and the spectacle that inspired books and films is still there to see and experience.

The declaration of independence in 1947 brought an abrupt end to the privileges and the income of India's famous princes. The maharajas no longer enjoyed the tax revenues that the British had allowed them to raise. Although they still had their palaces and properties, in most cases they had no way of maintaining them. Many highnesses had no choice but to become hoteliers. Of the 800-odd palaces that still stand in Rajasthan today, about 150 have been converted to hotels, some with more success than others. Many former maharajas went to great lengths to ensure the comfort of their Western guests – with the result that numerous palaces have been effectively ruined. The famous palace that stands majestically in the middle of Udaipur Lake, for instance, still looks splendid from the outside, but the interior is a cross between a Middle Eastern Hilton and a Bollywood filmset. Many more have suffered the same fate.

Fortunately, some of the Rajput aristocracy realized before it was too late that the best way to convert their former homes into successful hotels was to change nothing. Who cares about minibars, plastic hair dryers and cable TV when you can spend the night in a room once reserved for the conduct of a maharaja's amorous liaisons? What we want above all else is fantasy, and a maharaja's palace, preferably an *unconverted* one, fits the bill perfectly.

Given that there are so many palaces in Rajasthan, where does one start? The simple answer is in Jaipur –

or, more accurately, within the old city walls of the famed pink city. Jaipur is the heart of Rajasthan, and for many centuries it was the seat of the state's ruling dynasty. Granted, the city has been modernized quite considerably, but from within the old walls, it's still possible to glimpse the magic and romance of days gone by – especially if you are staying at the Samode Haveli. Until quite recently, this was the townhouse of the Singhji family of Samode. The family's title came from the principality and palace of Samode, and dates back more than four centuries to the seventeenth-century prince Prithviraj Singhji of Amber. Samode is a beautiful, remote and mountainous stretch of Rajasthan, and the Samode palace is as impressive as its surroundings. But in more recent times, the family lived in their Jaipur *haveli*, using the palace in Samode mainly for holidays and special events. Eventually, in 1985, they made the inevitable decision to convert it to a hotel. Meanwhile, the family

continued to occupy their city residence within the walls of old Jaipur. But even this in time proved too cumbersome to maintain – *haveli* may literally mean townhouse, but city palace is a far better description. Thus in 1994 they decided to convert it too into a hotel. By that time, visitors' desire for authenticity was an unmistakable trend, and thus the original rooms were hardly touched, with the exception, where necessary, of updating the electrics, plumbing and telecommunications.

The result is a style that may be summed up as 'maharaja-shabby-chic': slightly frayed but wonderfully authentic. Samode Haveli ranks as the perfect introduction to Jaipur. From the dining room, with its extraordinary blue-painted walls that have clearly inspired a textile designer or two, to the popular mirrored romantic fantasy of suite 114, this city palace gives the visitor the most precious experience of all: direct access to the legend of India.

address Samode Haveli, Gangapole, Jaipur, 302 002 Rajasthan, India
t (91) 141 2632 407 / 370 **f** (91) 141 2631 397 **e** reservations@samode.com
room rates from US $52 (including breakfast)

surya samudra beach garden

This Kerala beach retreat was the unlikely brainchild of two German adventurers. One, Karl Damschen, is an architect who originally drove all the way to India from Switzerland in the last days that this was safely possible. The other is Klaus Schleusener, a German professor who used to teach at the famous Indian Institute of Technology in Madras, now source of one-third of the brain bank of Silicon Valley, California. In those days, the government of India had closer ties with the USSR than with the USA, and by law foreigners were forbidden from owning real estate. But there were ways around this, and both Karl and Klaus (unbeknown to each other) were looking for the same thing: a choice piece of land on the then virtually undiscovered Kerala coast.

Karl made his way to Kerala from Bombay on a motorbike. Following the coast, he parked his bike not far from where the hotel entrance is today, and proceeded on foot. He had barely stepped onto the secluded beach, empty save for a Christian convent in the adjacent forest of palm trees, when he was informed by locals that a German had just bought the rocky promontory he had been admiring. 'Well, he's a brave man,' was Karl's response. 'It will be very difficult to grow anything on this pile of rocks.'

But fate was cast that day. The two expats met and got along well enough for the professor Klaus to commission a house from architect Karl. And no ordinary house. 'He absolutely wanted an octagon,' says Karl. 'I don't know why, but he was obsessed.' In those days Karl divided his time each year between Bern in Switzerland and Cochin in Kerala. So he produced detailed plans and drawings, with instructions as to materials and methods, and departed for Europe. When he returned to India six months later he was delighted to find the octagon built just as he had envisaged it. The adjacent bathroom, however, was another story. It was huge, almost three times as big as it was supposed to be. Damschen was baffled. How could the same builders get the octagon almost exactly right and yet be so far out on the bathroom? Only when he happened to pick up the tape measure did it finally click. On one side were centimetres (the side used for the octagon), on the other were inches (the side used for the bathroom). The bathroom part was knocked down and done again, and both client and architect learned a lesson in working and building in India's deep south.

The house proved a big hit, as did the idyllic location, and within a short period of time, Klaus went back to Karl to

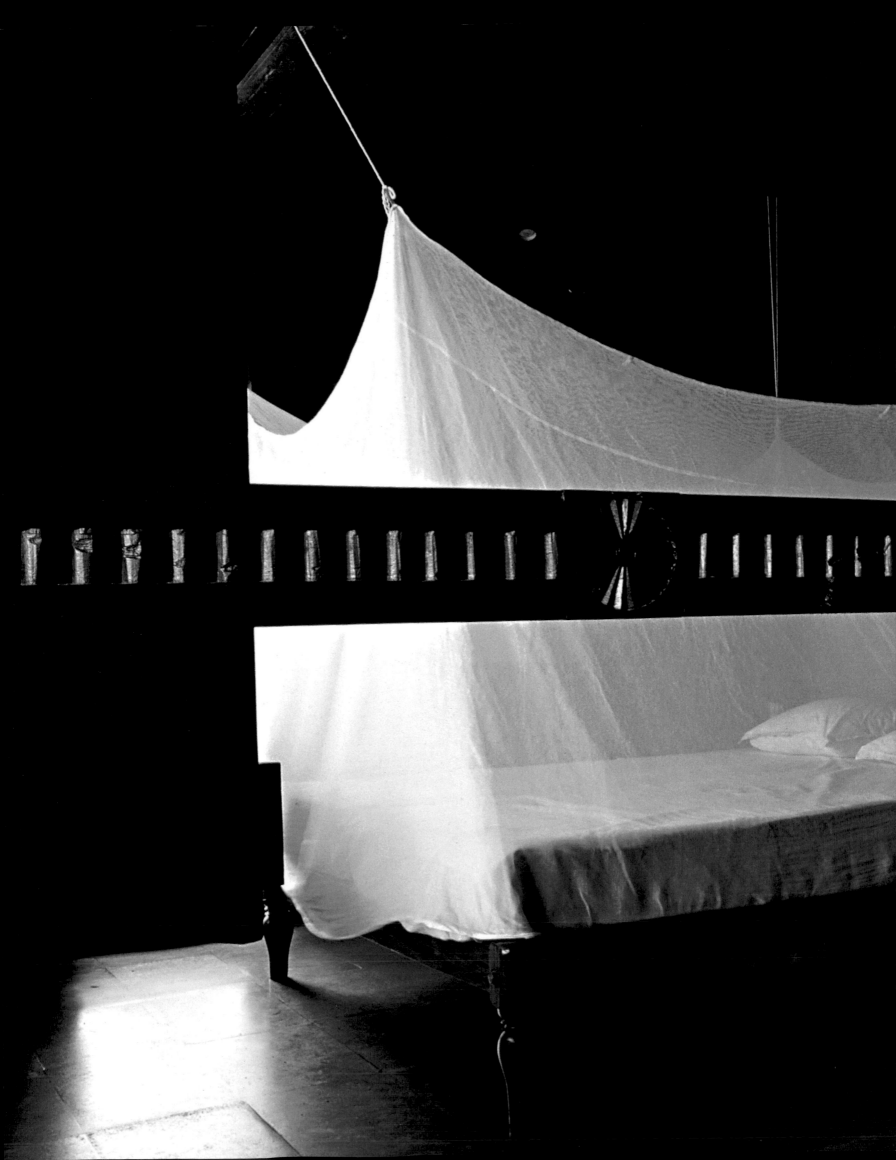

ask for another house, a place to deposit his many guests. It was an opportunity both of them had been waiting for. Karl Damschen in particular was a great enthusiast for the traditional Kerala teak house, the *tharawad*. It was killing him that these exquisite constructions were being dismantled and sold off as a source of furniture timber. Karl's advice to Klaus was, 'See if you can buy a traditional Kerala home, and we will work out a way to re-erect it on the property.'

The next time he visited, he was met by Klaus bearing a large grin. 'Look at that pile of timbers,' said Klaus. Neatly numbered and sequentially packaged, there were not just one but several teak houses awaiting resurrection. And that was not the end of it. More houses followed, accompanied by more landscaping, until the decision to turn the private compound into a small exclusive hotel became a natural next step. Facilities were basic compared to what they are today. There was no pool, no phones in the rooms, no water

filtration system and no real restaurant. But none of it mattered. It was (and still is) a place of tremendous charm – a magnificently secluded hideaway.

Surya Samudra has changed a lot since then. There's a beautiful new elephant-shaped pool carved into the rocks, an Ayurvedic spa, and the garden has matured almost beyond recognition. Klaus has moved on, though Karl remains involved as an architectural adviser. But the most dramatic change has neither to do with progress nor new management. Years ago, Surya Samudra had one big sandy beach to the left and a tiny one to the right. Today the tiny beach is far bigger even than the one on the left. Locals see it as a divine omen: the gods are happy. But for me it's a wonderful example of the fleeting nature of beauty. A couple of years ago, the beach didn't exist, until a particularly persistent monsoon brought it here – but another monsoon could just as easily take it away again.

---

address Surya Samudra Beach Garden, Pulinkudi, Mullur P.O., Trivandrum 695 521, Kerala, India
t (91) 471 2267 333 **f** (91) 471 2267 124 **e** info@suryasamudra.com
room rates from € 110 (including breakfast)

the tawaraya

Kyoto's Tawaraya is a national treasure: a supremely, sublimely Japanese *ryokan* (traditional inn) that has entertained household names such as Marlon Brando, James Michener, Leonard Bernstein, Jack Nicholson, Isaac Stern, Pierre Trudeau, Alfred Hitchcock, Richard Avedon, Jean-Paul Sartre, Peter Ustinov and Willem de Kooning, to list but a few.

Of the eighty thousand-odd ryokans spread around Japan, the Tawaraya is one of the oldest and definitely the most famous. Even though all the inn's components – the bamboo, the paper screens, the dark wood floors, the *tatami* mats, the cedar bathtubs and the precisely art-directed garden – are cultural staples, the exquisitely beautiful rooms somehow don't feel traditional in a backward-looking way. Instead, they feel modern and contemporary. The guest has the extremely rare privilege of experiencing an internal environment arranged entirely according to the guiding principles of *wabi*, the Zen notion of reducing something to the point where nothing further can be taken away. You live in a space where all that's left is sublimely simple perfection: not an empty room but a perfect space made up only of essentials (two very different things). It's the kind of environment that makes you want to throw out the family silver and heirlooms when you get back home. True, the gardens are immaculate and the rooms are splendid in their refined Zen simplicity, but the Tawaraya experience is not just a visual one. It involves all the senses. For your ears, there's the silence: no muzak, no televisions in the background, no clatter of plates, no ding when elevator doors open, no electronic noises made by electronic doorlocks … there is an almost complete absence of noise. The only sound you hear is the soft swish made by the kimono-clad hostesses as they glide across the tatami and wood in their socks. For your tastebuds, there's the ten-course traditional *kaiseki* dinner served on a low table in your room. There is no dining room, restaurant, bar or breakfast nook at the Tawaraya; the emphasis is on total privacy and personal experience – like a monk, albeit a spoiled one. And for your feet, there's the smooth transition of textures as the floors change from tatami to polished wood to bamboo and back again in a tactile rhythm dedicated to your bare foot.

Beauty, simplicity, silence, texture, taste, tradition – these are the key words of the Tawaraya experience. And yet they are terribly inadequate. They mention nothing, for instance, of the legendary level of service – the kind of

service that happens all by itself, that relies on anticipation and intuition, not suggestion or command. The *nakai* (ryokan staff) don't speak fluent English, which is wonderful – what they say and how they say it fits perfectly with the experience (what a pity it would be if someone blurted out, 'Have a nice day'). Perhaps the most revealing testimonial comes from Baron Hilton himself, who described the Tawaraya as 'a lesson to hotel men on what service is all about'.

Admittedly, the Okazaki family has had a long time to get it right. The founding of the inn originally goes back to the first decade of the eighteenth century by Wasuke Okazaki, a successful textile merchant from the county of Tawara. He sent his son to open a trading post in Kyoto which also took in travelling merchants. Word spread that the Tawaraya was a comfortable and familiar place to stay in what was then the slightly forbidding imperial city. The establishment slowly gained a reputation, and by 1904 the Tawaraya had been singled out in a guidebook to Kyoto as the best and most distinguished inn in town.

Today, Mrs Toshi Okazaki Satow is the eleventh generation of Okazakis to operate this historic inn, and she is evidently not one to rest on her ancestral laurels. Widow of the late Ernest Satow, a half-American professor of fine art at Kyoto City University of Arts and accomplished photographer in his own right, Mrs Satow continues to update and refine the interiors – not because the Tawaraya needs it, but because of a personal conviction that the inn must remain vibrant and contemporary.

And therein lies perhaps the most telling message of this enchanting ryokan: it's not a case of transporting the guest back into Japanese history but more of bringing Japan's past into a contemporary context. It's inspiring to see age-old tradition translated into modern experience. The Tawaraya may be small, but its message is big.

---

address Tawaraya, Anenokoji-agaru, Fuya-cho, Nakagyo-ku, Kyoto 604-8094, Japan
t (81) 075 211 5566 **f** (81) 075 211 2204
room rates from Yen 35,000

three sisters inn

I'd come to Kyoto, old Kyoto, to experience a bit of Japanese authenticity; to eat in a noodle bar with taxi drivers and spend the night in a traditional Japanese inn – preferably one with an aesthetic of paper screens, wooden floors and straw tatami mats. It's a place where you sleep on a futon, where you eat on the floor with your legs crossed and your knees bang against a low lacquered table. All of which begs the question: why submit to what is essentially a disorienting experience, when even the Japanese themselves opted for Western-style beds and tables long ago?

The answer is because it's a chance to experience something different. Most people would be disappointed, for instance, to discover how little Japan resembles the land of *The Last Samurai*. As one of the most densely populated places on earth, Japan on the surface seems like urban clutter from one prefecture to the next. In the train from Osaka to Kyoto you see no countryside at all, just buildings and more buildings. Unlike in Europe, where there is normally some discernible trace of a unifying style, here there is none – you have the impression that people build whatever, wherever. Yet the culture depicted in countless films still exists in many less obvious aspects of day-to-day life.

Zen is still very much alive in contemporary Japan. You can see it in the meticulous preparation and presentation of sushi; in the takeaway *bento* boxes so beautifully arranged and packaged that they're more like an anniversary present than a snack to be eaten on the train; in the spotless white gloves of the policemen; and in the linen and lace seat-covers in the taxis.

For the visitor to Japan, a stay at a ryokan is a must, and the Three Sisters Inn is one of the most enduring, charming and affordable of those that still exist in the former imperial city of Kyoto. It is also, without a doubt, the best located. Situated a stone's throw from two of Kyoto's most important monuments, the Kuradani Temple and the Heian Shrine, the inn is hidden in an idyllic residential part of the city, away from the bustle of downtown Kyoto. In fact, at night it's so devastatingly quiet that you can hear the traffic lights change from red to green from a block away.

The house that now operates as Three Sisters has been in the Yamada sisters' family for fourteen generations. Since 1957, Kikue, Sadako and Terumi (also known as Kay, Sandy and Terry) Yamada have been running their ancestral family home as an inn – and have become famous for doing so. It's hard to find a guidebook that doesn't give them a

glowing testimonial, and the walls of the reception are decorated with photos of the sisters with such luminaries as Senator Ted Kennedy, among others. All the thank-you letters are consistent: in essence, 'Thank you for the experience'. And just what is that experience? It's a personal glimpse into Japanese culture. No matter how many things you see, museums you go to, shrines you visit or books you read, nothing will give you the insight that one night at a ryokan will provide. Your room looks as if the ceiling has been lowered and the furniture has been removed, and one glance at the thin futon on the floor of your room and at first you're convinced that you'll never get a good night's sleep. Yet after one night, as most guests will confirm, you'll have slept better than you can remember. What's more, the clarity and precision of the space makes a normal hotel room seem clumsy and cluttered. A guestroom at Three Sisters is a carefully considered box, executed only in natural materials such as wood, paper and tatami. It doesn't matter that there's no phone; in fact, I wished there had been no television.

Three Sisters is a perfect platform from which to explore Kyoto. It establishes a link between you and the city's past by accommodating you in its history. I've seldom been in a place where the guests have been on such on a mission to explore. Some were intent on shopping for antiques; others were researching textile traditions; others had a shopping list of temples to visit. But the common ingredient was a passion for Kyoto's treasures – a passion amplified by staying in this ryokan.

The sisters who run this unique inn are certainly old Japan. They belong to an era of kimonos and deep bows, but their Western training and impeccable English are there to soothe Western nerves, especially when it comes to scary things such as getting a taxi.

---

address The Three Sisters, Main Inn, Okazaki, Sakyo-ku, Kyoto 606-8321, Japan
t (81) 75 761 6336 **f** (81) 75 761 6338
room rates from Yen 13,000

amanjiwo

It's difficult to convey the experience of staying at Amanjiwo. Sure, it's luxurious: many guest bungalows have their own swimming pool. It's also undeniably beautiful with its circular, temple-like forms that mimic the stupas of Borobudur, the monumental Buddhist sanctuary nearby. And then there are the silver-leaf ceilings, the copper tabourets, the teak furniture and the blue-and-white batik cushions scattered along the sandstone steps of the restaurant; not to mention the immaculately dressed staff or the idyllic location, perched as it is against a dramatic hillside that looks like a Chinese watercolour landscape. But these are all tangible qualities, and it's the intangibles that make it so unique. There's a subtle mysticism to Amanjiwo: at the risk of sounding New Age, the place has a powerful spiritual energy.

One thing is certain: there's a link between Amanjiwo and Borobudur, and it's not just that they share visual consistencies. Borobudur is, after all, 'the mountain of a thousand statues', one of the most important archaeological and religious sites in Asia. Yet if it hadn't been for the curiosity of Thomas Stamford Raffles, governor general of Java (1811–1816), it might never have been found. Erected in around AD 800, Borobudur was largely forgotten on the island by 1700: most people had converted to Islam, and the remains of an abandoned religion hardly merited attention. But Raffles was fascinated by Asia's antique cultures and made it known that he was interested in any artifacts of Hindu or Buddhist provenance. Imagine his surprise when, in 1814, a villager handing over some bronze figurines mentioned that he knew of a vast but long-abandoned ruin that might be of interest. Intrigued, Raffles dispatched Dutch engineer H.C. Cornelius to investigate the site. Located deep within the island's interior, it had been so long neglected that it took two hundred men six weeks just to cut away the surrounding jungle.

But what they found was worth it. Predating Henri Mouhot's 'discovery' of Angkor in Cambodia by forty-six years, Borobudur's rediscovery opened Western eyes to the level of sophistication achieved by Southeast Asian civilizations. While it was a shock to witness the extent to which India's spiritual teachings had travelled, even more surprising was the fact that the world's largest and most magnificent Buddhist structure had been built on a remote island three thousand miles from India, rather than at the birthplace of Siddharta Gautama (Buddha) at the foot of the Himalayas.

Ironically, Borobudur tells us far more about the ancient Javanese than Javanese history can tell us about Borobudur.

Without any kind of documentary records, which would have been kept on perishable material such as dried palm fronds, all theories concerning this monumental structure and the culture behind it are derived from its architecture. From the size of Borobudur, for instance, we know for certain that the Javanese had not only skilled craftsmen, but plenty of them. On this basis, historians suggest that many farmers in ancient Java were also part-time artisans, as they are in Bali today. From the number of stones (more than a million blocks weighing over two hundred pounds each) and the amount of carving (over five hundred life-size statues and 1,460 bas-reliefs) at Borobudur, construction is estimated to have taken seventy-odd years, assuming that almost none of the workers would have been able to work full-time.

The history of Borobudur is fascinating and complex, full of unsolved mysteries. But when all's said and done, compelling as it is, Borobudur is a relic of a lost culture.

Amanjiwo brings it back to life. Architect Ed Tuttle has sensitively managed to distil the style of the temple in the design of the hotel. The construction of the stone screens leading to the massive circular dining room, the columns supporting the roof and the form of the central building – all of these evoke the distinctive shapes and details of the nearby monument. But the connection is deeper than that. Thanks to clever planning, Amanjiwo functions as an observatory: everywhere you look from the hotel, the vista ends with Borobudur. The temple is omnipresent; it's no accident that the entire orientation of the hotel hinges on the view of the mountain of a thousand statues.

As Amanjiwo's staff move silently around the stone buildings preparing guestrooms for the night, so do their saffron-clad counterparts attend to the statues in the Buddhist sanctuary across the valley. It's the closest you'll ever get to sleeping in a temple.

address Amanjiwo, Borobudur, Central Java, Indonesia
t (62) 293 788 333 **f** (62) 293 788 355 **e** amanjiwo@amanresorts.com
room rates from US $650

the apsara

Luang Prabang was a mystery to me. I knew next to nothing about Laos, and even less about this historic town on the mighty Mekong River. It was curiosity that compelled me to get on the flight from Bangkok. There was a daily flight to Luang Prabang, which meant that there must be enough people wanting to go to northern Laos to justify the frequency. Why, I wondered, are all these people going to this exotic-sounding destination, and what do they do when they get there?

The answer, I discovered, is quite straightforward: the attraction of Luang Prabang is the town itself. Protected in its entirety by a UNESCO heritage listing since 1995, it is exactly how one might imagine the traveller's fantasy of a perfect town in the tropics of the Far East, an exemplary piece of unspoilt Southeast Asia. Ten years ago, it had no electricity, running water or roads to speak of. It had been abandoned by the government, left to its own devices to crumble away slowly as a decaying symbol of the previous regime. But Luang Prabang was too important to ignore for long. After all, this had been the traditional seat of Laos's royal family; they had their palaces here and there were more temples than houses. What's more, when the French became the resident colonial power, they built many

impressive villas, most of which have survived intact because they were mothballed from lack of interest. It's not completely clear which came first, the tourists or UNESCO, but most people will agree on the date: whereas in the early 1990s the town was looking rather forlorn, by 1996 restoration work had begun.

From a traveller's point of view, it's hard to think of a destination with more to offer. Flanked by mountainous limestone cliffs shrouded in mist, Luang Prabang is built on a peninsula defined by the Mekong River on the one side and its tributary the Khan River on the other. The surrounding area is still pristine in its sparsely inhabited agrarian purity, and just outside of town you will come across Lao hill tribes in all their traditional finery. For those with enough time on their hands, the six- to eight-hour journey by car to Vientiane takes you through a slice of Asia most people will never see: a countryside of waterfalls, rice paddies and customs unchanged by the march of modernity. It was by way of such a drive that Ivan Scholte first ended up in Luang Prabang. A British expat who has been living in Asia for almost two decades, he has been, among other things, a Hong Kong-based wine importer and an organizer of guided antique-hunting expeditions through

the backwaters of Southeast Asia. His real ambition was, however, to own and operate a hotel and restaurant, and it was his discovery of Luang Prabang in 2000 that finally cemented his resolve. At the time there were no direct flights, and visitors consisted mainly of Lonely Planet backpackers. There were only two upmarket hotels in town and just one upmarket restaurant (serving French cuisine). Attracted by Luang Prabang's size, sensuality and sophistication, Scholte took over an existing guesthouse and proceeded to transform it into a hotel to match his vision.

The result is the Apsara, named after the heavenly maidens carved into the gallery walls of Cambodia's Angkor Wat in their thousands. The hotel has introduced a simple but street-wise sophistication to the town's accommodation options. Scholte brought interior designer Niki Fairchild in from Bangkok to assist him with the design, and what they've come up with, most visitors will agree, ranks as the most chic place in town. Both the restaurant and the rooms reflect a refined sense of taste. The restaurant, for instance, features a polished concrete floor, Chinese-style lanterns hung in multicoloured clusters, a pair of sculptural Burmese offering boxes and a handful of specially commissioned Thai paintings. Aside from the fact that it's one of the best places to eat in town, that the rooms all have views of the river below from their colonial terraces and that it's extremely affordable, the best thing about the Apsara is that it is smack bang in the middle of town. All the cafés, temples and shops are within easy walking distance, and if you're up at 6am you can witness Luang Prabang's thousand-odd monks form a snaking, mile-long, saffron-coloured queue as they go about collecting their daily alms. It's one of the few places in Asia, if not the world, where the town in which you're staying is the reason for spending time there. Simply being in Luang Prabang is all the itinerary you need.

address The Apsara, Kingkitsarath Street, Ban Wat Sene, Luang Prabang, Laos
t (856) 71 212 420 f (856) 71 254 252 e info@theapsara.com
room rates from US $55

cheong fatt tze

He was known as the Rockefeller of the East. When Cheong Fatt Tze arrived in the Straits from Guandong province in China in 1856, he was barely sixteen and penniless. By the time he passed away in 1916 at the age of seventy-six, he had amassed one of the greatest fortunes in the Orient. Such was his stature that on his death, British and Dutch colonial authorities ordered their flags to be flown at half-mast.

Cheong Fatt Tze's ascent from rags to riches began with his first job in Batavia (now Jakarta), the old colonial capital of the Dutch East Indies. He soon came to the notice of his employer, and not only did he rise through the ranks but he ended up marrying the boss's daughter. At the height of his career in the 1890s, he was Consul General for China in Singapore, adviser to the Manchu Dowager Empress Cixi and a director of China's railways and first modern bank. Dubbed 'China's last Mandarin and first capitalist', Cheong's cultural duality was an asset. Completely Oriental in his dress and mannerisms, he could be convincingly Occidental when he needed to be. But, first and foremost, he was a trader, dealing in the most valued goods of the era, from spices and rubber to the illicit but lucrative commodity of opium.

With great wealth came great spoils. Cheong had eight wives and many more houses, but his favourite residence was the mansion he built on the island of Penang, in the bustling trading port of George Town. It was here that he chose to bring up his sons and spend most of his time. The so-called Blue House (due to its distinctive indigo-painted exterior) was purpose-built to show off his financial prowess. It was flamboyantly extravagant, with thirty-eight rooms, five courtyards, seven staircases and – to counter the heat – two hundred and twenty windows. It also reflected Cheong's multicultural personality. The layout was essentially Chinese, with strict adherence to the discipline of *feng shui*; but the detail was engagingly eclectic, with English Stoke-on-Trent ceramic floor tiles, Scottish cast-iron balustrading, French Art Nouveau stained glass windows, Chinese cut-and-paste porcelain, and Gothic louvred teak windows. Not only is it one of the largest Chinese houses ever built outside of China, but it's a formidable example of nineteenth-century Straits Settlement architecture.

Cheong left behind a will dedicated to protecting his legacy, with care taken to ensure that his favourite mansion would be preserved and not sold until the death of his youngest son, then a baby. But even Asia's most brilliant turn-of-the-century capitalist couldn't have foreseen the ineptitude of his trustees, whose disastrous investments

led to a dramatic dwindling of the Cheong family fortune. The house's contents were sold for income, and by the early 1960s it stood as an empty shadow of its former self. It was then rented out room by room, and by the time local architect Laurence Loh and his wife Lim discovered it, a total of thirty-five different families were living in the once magnificent mansion. Six decades after the Rockefeller of the East had passed away, Cheong Fatt Tze's beautiful house had become a lowly tenement.

Luckily for Penang, the story of the Blue House has a happy ending. When the last of Cheong's sons passed away, Loh and a small syndicate were able to buy what was left of the house, and set about the monumental task of restoring it to its former glory. The cut-and-paste porcelain, the Art Nouveau stained glass, the intricately carved and gilded Chinese screens, even the distinctive blue wash of the exterior walls, were all reinstated. Their labour of love was convincing enough to win it a UNESCO Asia Pacific Heritage Award in 2000.

But the best thing about the restoration is that, as a guest, you can once more admire the flair and extravagance of one of the Orient's most flamboyant houses, and you don't need an invitation to stay here. Better still, you pay a lot less than Cheong Fatt Tze would have been happy with. His mansion is, without a doubt, the most extravagant 'bed and breakfast' in Asia, and a perfect, affordable base from which to explore the beaches and history of Penang. Rooms are large and comfortable with soaring ceiling height, bathrooms are white and pristine the way architects like them, and breakfast is served adjacent to the mansion's main courtyard. These days the rickshaws parked out front are just for decoration, but there's enough authenticity left to stimulate even the most accidental of tourists.

address Cheong Fatt Tze Mansion, 14 Leith Street, 10200 George Town, Penang, Malaysia
t (60) 4262 5006 f (60) 4262 5289 e cftm@tm.net.my
room rates from Ringgit 250

dwarika's

It's the hotel of a thousand nooks and crannies. Hidden behind an extraordinary array of intricate wooden screens, spread out among half a dozen irregularly laid-out traditional Nepalese buildings and connected by a series of walkways, bridges and carved pillars, Dwarika's is a place for people who appreciate authenticity with a dash of eccentricity. It's more than a hotel; it's an environment, and it is without question the best place to stay in Kathmandu. Dwarika's cleverly introduces you to Nepalese culture and traditions without sacrificing creature comforts. Staying here, you will learn more about Nepalese food, craft and architecture than you ever would at the Hyatt or the Hilton, or even backpacking around the Himalayas for a couple of months.

It all started, strangely enough, in 1952 when Dwarika Das Shrestha, a Nepali tour operator, was taking his morning exercise in Kathmandu. He was jogging by the ruins of an old building torn down to make way for a modern structure, and came across some workers taking apart an exquisitely carved wooden pillar. They were trying to salvage the wood and regarded the carving as nothing more than a hindrance. On sheer impulse, Shrestha gave the men new timber in exchange for the carved artifact, with no idea of what he would do with it. So began a lifetime

quest to preserve Kathmandu's Newari heritage, a once rich artistic legacy of bronze, woodcarving and terracotta in what was not long ago a forgotten medieval Hindu kingdom. Whenever an ancient building was about to be torn down, he would rush in and purchase all the rescuable decorative art, and before long his collection was scattered in makeshift sheds all over his garden. The most logical thing to do with his finds was to construct a building, and he decided to combine tourism and building conservation for the greater good of the Kathmandu Valley by opening a guesthouse. He argued, reasonably, that visitors to Nepal would prefer to stay somewhere authentic – and he was right. Sure enough, the hotel quickly expanded from one small building into the village-like compound it is today.

As Dwarika's developed, so did Shrestha's conservation efforts. No longer satisfied with simply saving historical relics, he set up a school that would train craftsmen in the near-extinct Newari tradition of woodcarving. The same dedication was applied to architecture. Traditional Nepalese terracotta structures are distinguished not just by their unique shape but by their apparently mortarless brickwork; in fact, the bricks are tapered to hide their cement. As these bricks were no longer being manufactured, Shrestha had

Bronze details such as this door handle reflect a regard for authentic style not found in any other Nepalese hotel

Saving traditional Nepalese carved doorways and windows from destruction is how Dwarika's started

Red, black and white: the colours of the Nepalese flag are used throughout the hotel, from fabrics to staff uniforms

With spectacular fountains and quiet hidden courtyards, Dwarika's feels more like an enchanted village than a hotel

Bedrooms are light and spacious; Nepalese decor is limited to fabrics and the odd piece of furniture

The power of Dwarika's is the way history and tradition are integrated into a cultural experience

them made just outside the Kathmandu Valley. At the same time, he developed a manufacturing process that used moulds to mimic woodcarving motifs, thus making it possible to create a traditional building facade at a much lower cost.

If all of this sounds dry and overly technical, the result is anything but. Dwarika's is primarily a place to enjoy Nepal's unique culture (even if construction detail isn't high on your things-to-see list). For example, its restaurant Krishnarpan transports you all over Nepal by serving dishes from various parts of the country. *Momo* (steamed dumplings) are from a region near the Chinese border and hence are reminiscent of dim sum. By contrast, *roti* (unleavened bread) and *palungo ko saag* (sautéed spinach) come from the southeast, near the border with India, and bear a strong similarity to Indian dishes. Everything in the restaurant is in accordance with Nepalese custom: no shoes on the oiled teak floor, low tables and floor cushions designed for eating cross-legged, and staff dressed in traditional Nepalese clothes that correspond to the regions from which the different dishes originate. It's a sophisticated and engaging way to sample the surprisingly complex and subtle local cuisine.

If you talk to people who are lucky enough to have visited Kathmandu twenty-odd years ago, they will tell you about a tantalizingly exotic medieval Hindu town. Alas, the Kathmandu of today is modernizing at breakneck speed. That said, it's still a very beautiful place, and the surrounding Himalayas, with their rural villages, have changed far less. Many adventurers who arrive in Nepal will confess that they are drawn to the exotic nature of the country more than the trekking, and in that respect Dwarika's has embarked upon exactly the right approach: it allows the guest to soak in the authentic charm of Nepal, without a hint of a blister.

---

address Dwarika's, PO Box 459, Battisputali, Kathmandu, Nepal
t (977) 1 447 0770 **f** (977) 1 447 1379 **e** info@dwarikas.com
room rates from US $110

doornberg

Doornberg, or Dutch House as it is also known, used to be the residence of an admiral of the Galle-based Dutch East India Company's merchant navy. Built in 1712, the mansion is a relic of Holland's Golden Age, when trade with the East produced unheard-of riches: at its zenith, the Company counted more than three thousand ships in its fleet, and just one of these laden with spices could generate enough profit for a middle-class *burger* to retire for life.

The key word was trade, and the Dutch were masters at it. The secret was knowing what to trade. The Dutch coveted the spices grown by the people of Java and Sumatra, but what could they offer in return? The traditional European currencies of silver, gold or even linen or velvet were of no interest to the Indonesians, but the *ikat* textiles of India were. Thus the Dutch ships rounding the Cape of Good Hope would head for the Indian region of Hyderabad, load as much ikat as they could carry and then journey down India's coast towards the southern tip of Sri Lanka to the Dutch colonial stronghold of Galle. From there, after a brief stop to reload supplies and rest the crew, they would continue to Batavia (now Jakarta). Full to the brim with spices, they would once again sail to Galle. Unlike most colonial powers, it was never Holland's intention to colonize Sri Lanka; its aim was just to capitalize on the strategic position of one of its ports. Thus the Dutch invested major time and money into boosting the city's defences.

The remains of Holland's fort-buildings are still to be found in Galle, one of which is Doornberg. Set high on a hillside with an idyllic view of the Bay of Galle, the admiral's former house is a particularly attractive example of Dutch colonial architecture in the tropics: a combination of pared-down, neoclassical columns supporting a series of overhanging verandas with lofty ceilings, long elegant spaces and stately period furniture. The effect, contrary perhaps to what one might expect, is at once terribly grand and surprisingly comfortable – almost cosy. Aside from Doornberg's architectural pedigree and second-to-none location, the added plus here is the fact that the building has survived as a house. Various rooms and spaces are use much as they would have been originally, and the guest at Doornberg experiences something not dissimilar to staying with the admiral himself. All too often, the temptation with hotels is to use existing structures – in this case the main house – as a reception–lobby–office, meaning bedrooms have to be built elsewhere. At Doornberg there is no lobby or office and, in fact, all

Long, tall and spacious – Doornberg's elegant
guestrooms are generous in size
and colonial in shape

A pair of wooden clogs in the entrance hall
is a gentle reminder of the building's
Dutch colonial legacy

More like an apartment than a hotel room,
Doornberg's guest suites feature both
a living room and bedroom

Details such as frangipani flowers in
earthenware bowls are casually
placed around the property

Bathrooms are exquisite – probably some
of the most refined and spacious
in all of Sri Lanka

Doornberg was once the residence of an
admiral of the Dutch East India Company;
the car is a new addition

discernible traces of its function as a hotel have been removed.

This suits Hong-Kong-based English proprietor Geoffrey Dobbs very well indeed. Dobbs's approach to hotels and tourism is to keep things small and sophisticated; his other Galle property, Sun House, has made quite a name worldwide, even though it only has seven rooms. It too is a historic colonial house, but that's where the similarity ends. Where Sun House is fresh, bright and affordable, Doornberg is darker, more chic and somewhat less affordable – you might even say expensive, but it's well worth every penny. The refined furniture and fabrics create the ambience of stately colonial grandeur without the clichés. And not only is each of the staterooms immense, but so are the bathrooms. Doornberg also has beautiful gardens, just as you would expect of a house that once belonged to an admiral. What with the recent addition of an infinity pool discreetly tucked

away on one side of the estate, it's easy to forget that the place you're staying in is actually a hotel.

It's difficult to describe the unique atmosphere of this place, but I vaguely recognize it: it reminded me of being at my grandmother's townhouse in the Hague. Doornberg's clever combination of formality and informality, of precious antiques combined with simple rattan, sets it apart in terms of interior design and charm. There's simply nothing else like it in the Orient, and that in itself is reason enough to stay here. But Doornberg's real drawcard is the seductive pace of the place. Doing nothing, very slowly, is the order of the day. No one here seems to be a slave to itineraries, nor is there a continual gathering of people about to depart on sightseeing trips. At Doornberg, you're left with the impression that all the guests have been here for so long that they have completely adjusted to the Sri Lankan way of life – even if they only arrived yesterday.

address Doornberg, c/o Sun House, 18 Upper Dickson Road, Galle, Sri Lanka
t (94) 91 4380275 f (94) 91 2222624 e sunhouse@sri.lanka.net
room rates from US $330

taru villas

A completely private getaway by the sea, on a beach with perfect weather … it's an archetypal dream destination. If it also happens to be inspiringly stylish and blessed with great service, it becomes somewhere you're tempted *not* to tell your friends about.

Taru Villas is exactly that. Located just outside the town of Bentota and a three-hour drive from Colombo's international airport, it's the kind of place you can imagine staying for long enough to write a book. Apart from the very tangible benefit of being affordable, Taru's convincing combination of style, sand and service make it worth the flight to Sri Lanka.

Years ago, the pleasures of this tropical island – a milder, gentler, less frenetic version of India – were compromised by the threat of terrorism and violence associated with the independence campaign of the northern Tamil-speaking minority. Now there's a truce. Hostilities between the Hindu Tamils and the Buddhist Sinhalese are confined to the negotiating table, and Sri Lanka's economy is free to get back to marketing the country's remarkable coastline.

Taru Villas was discovered not by visiting sunseekers but by a cosmopolitan crowd from Colombo. Nayantara Fonseka (better known as Taru) is a flamboyant creative figure in the Sri Lankan fashion world, who, by the strength of her personality, has become synonymous with her own clothes label. For years, she and a few carloads of friends would make the two-and-a-half-hour trek from the city on a Friday evening to spend a relaxed, idyllic weekend on the coast. This became such a fixture in Taru's life that she pledged to take any opportunity she could to pursue her passion for the property and its location. One day it went up for lease – and that's how Taru got into the hotel business.

The place had good bones. Even though the site itself was awkwardly long and narrow, the original architect had been clever with the use of space, and the buildings were arranged to avoid giving the impression of being in a tunnel. The villas, set along a single wall, are subtly oriented so that all of them face different directions. This ensures total privacy, and for guests it's like having your own house.

To this already successful establishment, Taru has brought her sense of style and hospitality. Taru Villas now has the colour, warmth and character that is so often lacking from an architect's disciplined vision. Walls painted a musty shade of pink are juxtaposed with plenty of white, and bright saffron yellow is combined with black and white (a traditional colonial Portuguese combination). More than anything, though, Taru Villas is a triumph of simplicity. It's not easy to make a place look good with very little, but that's exactly what Taru has done to distinguish this little bolthole on the beach. It's a blend of good choice of colour, interesting selection of furniture and the omnipresent avoidance of clutter.

One of Taru Villas' most unconventional attractions is the train that runs straight through the property. It may not sound like the most desirable feature in a hotel, but it's not as obtrusive as you'd think: the last train stops well before bedtime, and during the day the noise is a gentle reminder of a different age. You have to cross the single railway track to get to the beach – 'cross' not in the sense of pedestrian crossing, but actually stepping over rails and sleepers – and most guests find this both quirky and fun. Running all the way along the coast, the train from Colombo to Galle claims the best view and location here – something the Sri Lankans may have picked up from the British, whose train routes are also often spectacular.

What surprised me more than the train was the beach. Having been many times to Kerala – the very south of India – as well as the nearby Maldives, I was expecting to find small stretches of sand and calm waters in Bentota. Instead, the beach here reminded me more of Australia than Asia. At Taru Villas it goes on for miles, and the water is wild and woolly enough for some decent bodysurfing. While the sea is not dangerous – certainly not by Australian standards – most locals refrain from going in. But visitors shouldn't be deterred. Compared with Bondi it's tame, and the hotel can even lend you a boogie-board.

At Taru Villas you can escape to one of Sri Lanka's best beaches. And at this price you can go barefoot in the sand for as long as you like. Before you know it, you'll be signing your postcards 'Bentota Beach Bum'.

---

address Taru Villas, 146/4 Galle Road, Robolgoda, Bentota, Sri Lanka
t (94) 34 2275618 **f** (94) 11 4724632 **e** taprobana@taruvillas.com
room rates from US $91

amanpuri

More than sixteen years after it first opened, this extraordinary complex on Phuket's Sanui Beach is still the most mesmerizing hotel in Thailand. It's not just because of its idyllic location on a private crescent of white sand framed by a verdant amphitheatre of palm tree-clad hills; or its super-chic, all-black horizon pool; or the food, which is easily the best of all the Amans. Amanpuri has something that's difficult to put into words. It has to do with the fact that it's very unusual and yet very Thai, a thoroughly contemporary place with a vernacular aesthetic that doesn't resort to or rely on cliché.

Often design, at least the quality of design, is judged by time. It's not so much about something aging well; it's about not aging at all, which is the category Amanpuri falls in. If anything, it looks better than when it first opened in 1988 because the landscaping has had a chance to mature. Apart from the increased height of the palm trees, the only evidence that years have passed is perhaps the fact that the bathrooms are not as spectacular as those of more recently completed Amans. Over the past decade and a half, bathrooms have been getting larger and sleeker, and while Amanpuri's bathrooms are by no means small, they are no longer as groundbreaking as they were when the

hotel first opened. But surely that's part of Amanpuri's contribution. All the things we now take for granted in luxury accommodation were pioneered by this first Aman: no reception desk, bellboys or lobby; no checking in or out; the idea of a private bungalow; a well-stocked library; and the notion of space, plenty of space, to allow the guest to experience a real escape. All of these are Aman inventions, and Amanpuri was the first. Judging by the present-day state of Phuket, few people have taken a leaf from Aman's book. Phuket property development is in overdrive with very little regard for quality, integrity, cultural consistency or ecology. Not many lessons have been learnt.

Still, despite unattractive prospects by the dozen, Amanpuri preserves the dream of Phuket as an escape destination, largely because it's isolated within its own bay with its own beach. For better or for worse, Phuket, formerly known as Junk Ceylon (a Western corruption of the Malay 'Tanjung Salong' or Cape Salong), has changed beyond recognition. In light of Amanpuri's distinct brand of 'barefoot in the sand' luxury, you could be forgiven for thinking that Phuket was only a recently discovered beach destination. Yet for centuries the island has been of strategic importance to the rulers of Siam. From early times, Arab traders came Junk Ceylon for its abundance of tin. The mining of tin was considered the exclusive province of the king of Siam, and its extraction, refinement and sale were subject to substantial royal taxation. But despite these hefty levies, tin was a lucrative trade and Junk Ceylon's mines attracted the business of Chinese immigrants. The island's southern port of Bukit became the main hub for the shipping of the much-coveted metal. Thus, a remote part of Siam came to the simultaneous attention of the Thai royal family, Arab traders, Indian merchants and seafaring European entrepreneurs. Within Asia, the island has been swapped back and forth several times between the mighty Khmer Empire of Cambodia based in Angkor and the Mon Empire based at Sukhothai, later known as the kingdom of Siam. The only thing that hasn't changed is the descriptions of the island's beauty. From French sea captains to British journalists and even Swedish scientists, there are numerous records that testify to the island's natural endowment, and, almost without exception, each and every writer refers to its exquisite beaches framed by the dense green of rainforest immediately beyond. There's even a specific reference to the Bay of Patong, though no one who knew it then would recognize this current victim of overdevelopment. As it turns out, the beauty of Junk Ceylon has ultimately become more exportable than tin. Blessed with a climate conducive to beach life year-round, Phuket, as the island eventually came to be known, has developed into one of the most famous resort destinations in the world.

The appeal of Amanpuri is best summed up by a guest. 'I haven't been to any other Amans,' he volunteered. 'Why should I? I can't imagine it would be better than here – how could it be? Every time I leave the property, even for a few hours, I always end up regretting it.'

---

address Amanpuri, Pansea Beach, Phuket 83000, Thailand

t (66) 76 324 333 **f** (66) 76 76 324 100 **e** amanpuri@amanresorts.com

room rates from US $675

costa lanta

Koh Lanta is a different slice of Thailand. Located a few hours' drive south of the resort town of Krabi, its two islands of Lanta Noi (the smaller one) and Lanta Yai are a peaceful alternative to the flashier, better known Thai beach destinations of Koh Samui or Phuket. It takes two ferries and two dirt roads to get here. There's no nearby airport, no designer Italian restaurants on the beach, no busy shopping streets and absolutely no nightlife … unless you count geckoes and mosquitoes.

Until relatively recently, Koh Lanta was a thoroughly undiscovered part of Thailand. Five years ago, the island had no electricity and no telecommunications, and to this day there is an unhurried, agrarian pace of life. It was exactly this pristine wildness that attracted the family of Kasma Kantavanich, who would holiday here when she was growing up, before it became known as the new Hua Hin or Phuket. Enchanted by the area's natural forest, sandy beaches, exceptional diving and signature clumps of rock sticking into the Andaman Sea, they even bought their own piece of bush on the beach on the northwestern edge of Lanta Yai. It was a purchase based more on emotional impulse than logical reasoning. They had no idea at the time what to do with it, and for many years the family would simply go there

and camp out. Then in 2000 everything changed. All of a sudden the area had electricity, telecommunications and … hotels. Lanta Yai had been 'discovered'. Kasma and her family were at a crossroads. What were they to do? Should they sell the land and look for an unspoilt Eden somewhere else? Or should they join in with the local development steadily gaining momentum? Though the arrival of tourists marked the end of an era, it was bound to provide a much-needed source of income and employment for the area. At least in opting to develop their own land, they would also be able to have an influence on the direction that tourism would take.

Thus, without any previous experience in the hotel industry, Kasma dived in. She assembled a group of investors and took on board Thai architect Duangrit Bunnag to tackle the question of aesthetics. Bunnag was full of ideas from his first visit and, according to Kasma, he was already sketching schemes for the property on his flight back to Bangkok. At first no particular design approach was ruled out, including traditional architecture featuring peaked roofs and lots of gilding. Ultimately, though, it was agreed to proceed in a modern, open direction.

Design-wise, it's a triumph of the box – the concrete box. Costa Lanta is not a hotel in the conventional sense. There are no rooms as such, only a collection of stand-alone houses arranged along a natural forest immediately behind the beach. The trees were the only inflexible part of the design brief, and the architect has used them as a way of providing each box with maximum privacy. The concrete bungalows are connected by a wooden walkway that snakes its way through the property and eventually ends at the dining bar and living pavilion located on the beach. As a design statement, it's both inventively original and pragmatically clever. The best view and location are reserved for the space that you're likely to spend the most time in: the dining and living area, which also happens to be the place closest to the water.

Ironically, the concrete box is more authentically Thai than you might expect. The fact is that throughout contemporary Asia, whether it's Cambodia, Malaysia, Myanmar or Indonesia, the simple concrete box is the people's choice. Some will lament the gradual extinction of traditional forms and shapes, but convenience, comfort and efficiency have overtaken convention and formality.

That said, the boxes at Costa Lanta are particularly comfortable and well designed. Divided into a sleeping area and a bathroom space, the box can be as open or as enclosed as you like: two of the four walls fold out completely, so during the day your box is open and at night it's closed. The bathroom, a monastic expanse of polished concrete, is surprisingly spacious with a smart translucent canopy-roof that floats above the walls, eliminating the need for extractor fans. The sleeping part is a box within a box within a box (a mosquito net enclosure inside the sleeping room box inside the outer concrete box). What you get is life-size Russian doll architecture with a Thai twist.

---

address Costa Lanta, 212 Moo 1, Saladan, Amphur Koh Lanta, Krabi Province, Thailand
t (66) 2 660 3550 **f** (66) 2 260 9067 **e** info@costalanta.com
room rates from Baht 2,750

evason hideaway

It's the perfect name. Situated on a hidden beach on a lush, mountainous peninsula overlooking a series of overlapping bays, the Evason Hideaway is exactly that – you would never even know it's there. From a distance, the enclave of thatched huts on the beach and wooden houses suspended on the rocks is completely invisible. And even as you approach it by boat – the only way to get there – you still need binoculars to pick out the houses nestling in the dense foliage just behind the pristine sands.

With fifty-four individual villas, a spa complex and two restaurants, the Hideaway is clearly more than a few rudimentary beach huts. Yet that's exactly the impression it creates. It's the kind of destination that immediately makes you wonder how it was found in the first place. For many years, this was a secret picnic spot for guests of Ana Mandara. Sheltered from prevailing winds and tucked away from all traces of civilization, it's the ultimate beach fantasy. The possibility of building a retreat in such a place must have occurred to proprietors Eva and Sonu Shivdasani (hence Evason) many times, but it didn't come into being until General Ha Van Dung (pronounced Zoong) entered the picture. A war hero from the North, the general is also a civil engineer who is now mainly busy with public works for the Socialist Republic of Vietnam in the South: he built Nha Trang's new airport as well as the brand new four-lane concrete highway that leads to it, both to commemorate the late Ho Chi Minh's birthday. Without General Dung, the Hideaway would still be a dream because the land is leased from the military. What's more, the logistical challenge of building on what is essentially an inaccessible site (with no roads whatsoever) falls more within a description of a military exercise than a building project. The military analogy goes even further than one might imagine. Despite the laid-back, Robinson Crusoe ambience of the place, it has taken an army of workers to bring the fantasy to life. More than six hundred labourers have toiled here for almost two years to bring power, sewerage, running water and telecommunications to a completely virgin piece of jungle on the coast. Everything – from the trucks and machinery to the pipes and cables – was brought in by boat, D-Day style. The general and his 'troops' considered building a jetty, but in order to preserve the integrity of the crystalline bay ultimately decided against it. Likewise, everything about the design – the architecture, the building materials, the manner of construction using interlocking wood with no nails or glue – was chosen with the aim of creating the ultimate

escape. The result is a series of huts and houses that represent a new style of luxury: more rugged, raw and natural, with space and privacy as primary considerations.

I've not come across an environment that delivers these ingredients more convincingly than the Hideaway's water villas. Built into and onto the massive boulders scattered along the shore, they are the three-dimensional realization of the ultimate barefoot beach shack. Architecturally they are particularly clever because they are at once completely open and completely private. Constructed entirely in timber – wooden beams, wooden floors, wood-panelled floors, even wooden baths – they are exposed to the elements in every direction, with huge doors that slide back and lead to surrounding decks and verandas, which in turn offer sweeping views of the crescent-shaped beach. But privacy is ensured by the giant rocks that form an integral part of each villa's construction.

The boulders are both sculpture and screen, an organic feature and focal point but also a means of naturally separating one villa from the next. Like gigantic organic ornaments, they simultaneously dominate and decorate the cutout views created by the hand-assembled, interlocking timber architecture.

The sublime irony of this extraordinary place is that General Dung himself has little idea how special it is because he has nothing to compare it to. As part of a peculiar hangover from the previously embattled Socialist regime, he is unable to travel overseas; the government refuses to give him a passport, ostensibly because as a war hero he holds many state secrets. Thus Dung has never had a chance to visit other countries or indeed resorts, so he's probably not aware that staying here is an experience akin to residing in an Isamu Noguchi art installation.

---

address Evason Hideaway at Ana Mandara, Beachside Tran Phu Blvd, Nha Trang, Vietnam

t (84) 58 829 829 **f** (84) 58 829 629 **e** resvana@dng.vnn.vn

room rates from US $400

CHINE

A

I. Kiusiu   Sikokf   EMPIRE

I. Crespo

I. Morell

Nan-king

J. Moor

Ile

Femme de Loth

I. Byers ou Patroca

Groupe de Parry

Fou-tcheou

E. Margaret

Bonin-Sima

Ec Liou-Tchou

I. Peel

Ec Grampus

Ile Sébastien Lobos
Ile

Tropique du Cancer

Es Madjico-sima

Es Volcanos

Canton

Dionisio

Macao

I. Rasa

I. Peart?

Es Bashees

Réc Douglas

P

Urracas

I. Marshall

I. Camira?

I.Wake ou Alcyon

I. Formose

Hainan

Manille

I.Mindoro

I.Panay

I. Crigan

I. Sariquan

Es Spanish

I. Tinian

I. Guam

Es St Bartholomé

Es Rimsley Korsakoff

I. Gaspar Rico

Es Brown

Es de la Providence

Bigar

Calvert

Andaman

EMPE BIRMAN

ROY. DE SIAM

EMPIRE D'ANAM

Martaban

Bangkok

Huc

MER DE CHINE

I.LUÇON

ILES PHILIPPINES

Samar

I.Negros

Es Sequiera

Es Coulou

I.Lidia

I. St Augustin

Rouk Hogoleu

Es Andema

Es Bonham

Mulgrave

I. Oualan

C. Negrais

Andaman

I. Palawan

Dét. de Balabac

I. Pelew

I.Babeltouap

Es St André

Es Yelenk

Kouripigue

GRAND

I. Labouan

Es Sooloo

Bornéo

I. Sangir

I. Morty

Es Pitt

Es du Scarbor

Es Simpson

I. Atlantique

ILES Carolines

Ralick

Mortlock

I. Ngark

Pounipet

I. Naturas

I.Lorian

I.Sedang

Mer de Célèbes

Es Piguiram

I. Pleasant

I. Océan

Es Bischop

Pondianak

BORNEO

I. Gilolo

I.Waigou

I.Jobie

C. de l'Amirauté

Es Fra

Banjarmassin

I. Billiton

MOLUQUES

Es Bouton

NOUVELLE GUINÉE

I. Dampier

Ile Nle Irlande

I. Bougainville

I. S. Augu

MER DES INDES

Mer de Java

Mer de Banda

Papous

I.Choiseul

Es Ellice

I.Ysabel

I. Peystor

Batavia

JAVA

SONDE

Timor

Mr Aird

Es Salomon

I. Malayta

I. Kennedy

ILE DE SUMATRA

I. Engano

I.Madura

I.Sorwatty

Iles

I. Kennell

Es de Sta Cruz

I. Varikoro ou mourut Lape

C. Londonderry

Baie de Carpentarie

Woodlack

Dét. de Torres

York

I. Rotumah

C. Léveque

AUSTRALIE Septentrionale

I. Melville

Es Farquhar

I. du St Esprit

I. Mallicollo

I. Vaivau Lebo

Es Roebuck

C. Nord-Ouest

AUSTRALIE

ou NOUVELLE HOLLANDE

Queensland

Brisbane

I. Koromanga

I. Viti Lebu

I. Tanna

Chabrot

T

Australie Méridionale

L. Eyre

C. Byron

Es Solitary

Loyalty

Nle Calédonie

E. des Pins

Tropique

Perth

Australie Occidentale

Terre de Flinders

Bathurst

Pt Macquarie

Es Norfolk

A

Adélaïde

Sydney et Pt Jackson

Es Mangsa Fawi

Cut

C. Lecuwin

L. Kanguron

Victoria

Melbourne

Port Philip

Dét. de Bass

NOUVELLE ZELANDE

Es King

Tre de Van Diemen ou Tasmanie

Christchurch

Tavai-Pounamou

Hobart Town

Péninsule Tasman

Dunedin

I. Stewart

I. de la Cie Royale

Rienzi

Es Auckland

Division de Rienzi

Le Juge et son Clerc

I. Macquarie

I. Campbell

Polynésiens.

Banquise (1840)

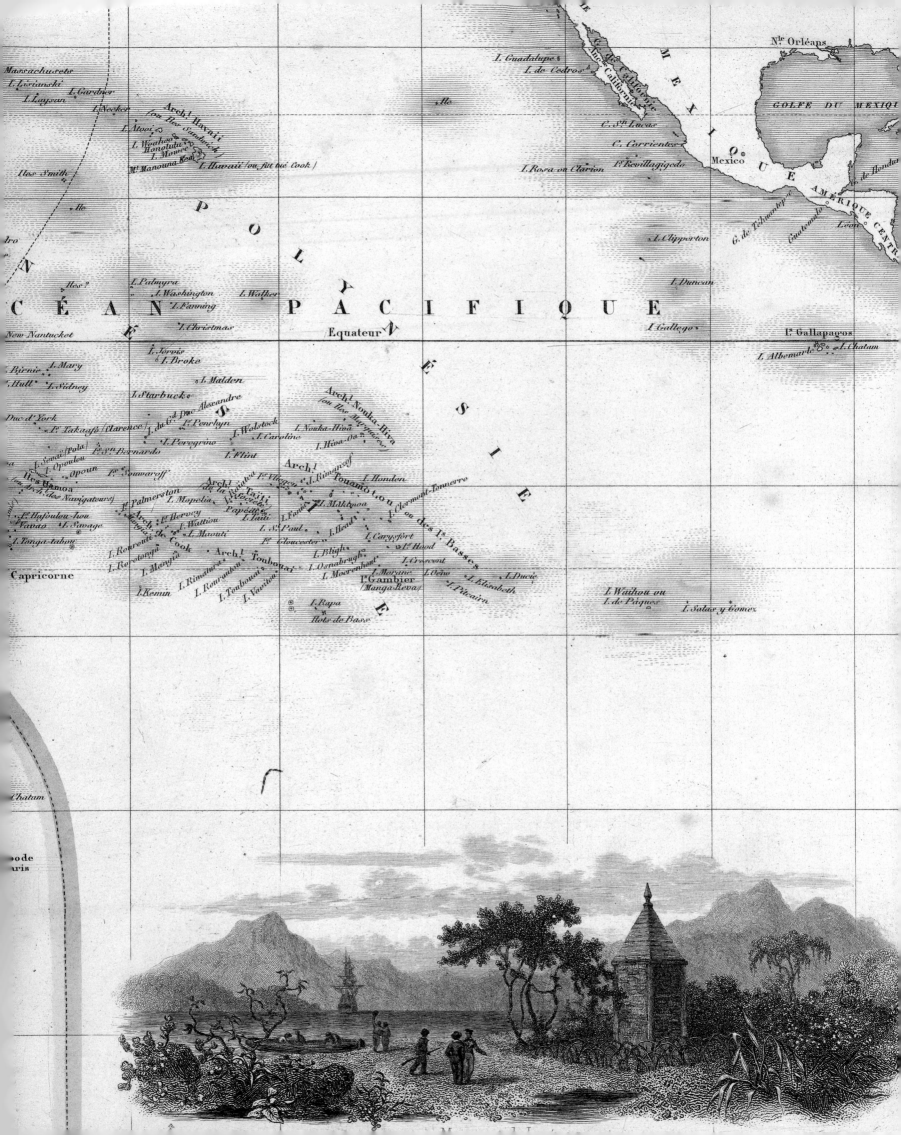

AUSTRALIA

It used to be known as the Antipodes. That's because Australia was about as far away as one could get. It was, literally, the other side of the world – a disadvantage as far as travellers were concerned. Unless one had half a year to spare – twenty weeks at least to simply get there and back – it just wasn't worth it … that, plus an overwhelming sense of isolation that made it difficult to stay too long.

How things have changed. Today there are daily direct flights from London to Sydney (with just one stop in Singapore). You can leave Europe on a Tuesday night and arrive in Australia early Thursday morning. More to the point, a sense of isolation, of being away from it all, is now exactly what people are after.

Australia is what the world was like before it got too crowded. The cities are, admittedly, not that different from their American or European counterparts – except for warmer weather and surf beaches in the middle of town. But just beyond the cities the difference is awe-inspiringly spectacular. This really is the empty continent. Across vast expanses you're likely to find only the odd house or village – if that. And contrary to the clichéd image, exaggerated by Australian beer advertising, the outback is not all flat, red, dusty and swarming with flies. Australia has snow-capped mountains, green rolling hills, tropical rainforests, plenty of prairie, forests of gigantic trees like those in California, rocky canyons and not inconsiderable wine country.

Wildwater rafting, surfing, trekking, cross-country skiing and visits to wineries are just some of the activities that await the visitor who is prepared to explore … with the big difference being that the nature that serves as a backdrop is hardly ever compromised by pollution or property development. Nature in Australia is served *pure*. As such, you're often likely to be one of only a handful of humans on location. It's a unique experience. In Australia, unlike anywhere else, there are still stretches of powdery white beach that go on for hundreds of miles with not a person, boat, building or even surfboard to be seen.

It's always been like this. What's changed is that straight-talking, uncomplicated Aussies are now equally straightforward about their lifestyle. They take their wine, food, coffee … and wine … very seriously. The corner pub has changed into the corner brasserie, and even the most remote watering hole has a kitchen that would put many a chi chi city restaurant to shame. The country's unmatched beauty is now there to be enjoyed with a glass of Margaret River Chardonnay and a slice of King Island Brie.

bay of fires lodge

I had a friend who moved to Melbourne from France. Every weekend he'd jump into his Range Rover and drive. 'Where do you go?' I once asked him. 'Nowhere in particular,' he replied. 'I just pick a direction and keep driving.' 'But why?' 'Because,' he explained, with almost childlike enthusiasm, 'I can drive for hours, sometimes days, without seeing a single person or any sign of civilization – no buildings, no road signs, no power lines, no telegraph poles.' He just couldn't get enough of the emptiness of this continent.

Going to the beach in Oz is not so different. Here you really can achieve the ultimate – a beach entirely to yourself, maybe even several. This vast island, a continent unto itself, is one of the few places in the world where such extravagant solitude is still possible. The Bay of Fires is on the far northeastern tip of Tasmania, on the edge of Mount William National Park. A magnificent succession of fine, white, crescent-shaped beaches interrupted by rounded granite headlands coloured bright red by lichens, this is an area of potent natural theatre: the reddest rock, the bluest water and the whitest sand, framed by rolling hills and densely verdant shrub. It is home to all sorts of indigenous fauna: wallabies, echidnas, brush-tail possums, wombats and Tasmanian devils, to name but a few. And the only building

in this almost untouched coastal wilderness is the Bay of Fires Lodge. From a distance you would be hard-pressed even to spot it. Designed by Sydney architect Ken Latona, it's a thoroughly modern, almost transparent pavilion that respects Glen Murcutt's dictum that buildings should 'touch the earth lightly'. Scarcely a boulder or rock was disturbed in erecting this long wood and glass box that juts out of the surrounding bush like a spear to claim a sweeping view of the coast's extraordinary beaches.

The lodge's discreetly hidden structure houses ten double guest rooms, a library, a loft-style glass-sided dining room that seats twenty-four, a living room complete with an enormous contemporary cast-iron fireplace, a huge deck that doubles as an outdoor breakfast area, and another deck surrounded by bush. Electricity is solar-generated, the dunnies are organic compost toilets (which don't smell – not even a tiny bit), and the stainless steel showers are powered by pressure you provide by putting some old-fashioned elbow grease into a handpump beforehand. That said, the lodge has none of the woollen socks and sandals atmosphere often associated with 'green' places. It's no crime to be a city-based capitalist here; just don't chuck your ciggy in the organic dunny.

One guest summed up the place with characteristic Australian understatement: 'Pretty good lodge, mate,' he volunteered in a distinctly Queensland twang. 'Would have been fun and games building this in the middle of nowhere.' So it was. Most of the materials were flown in by helicopter. The only road is a muddy, sandy goat path strictly limited to four-wheel-drive vehicles, and then only when the weather is reasonably dry. But that's the whole point of the Bay of Fires Lodge. It is meant to be inaccessible. All guests arrive on foot, complete with backpack and hiking boots. The lodge is the culmination of the second day of a guided walk that starts at a spot called Boulder Point and passes along the deserted beaches of Stumpy's Bay, Cobler Rocks, Cod Bay, Purdon Bay, Picnic Rocks, Deep Creek, Eddyston Point, Shell Coves, and finally to Abbotsbury Peninsula, location of the Bay of Fires Lodge. The first night is spent at a camp on Forester Beach, where your local guides prepare dinner using fresh local produce and seafood. You reach the Lodge at the end of the second day's trek; day three is spent sea-kayaking across nearby Ansons Bay. Midway through day four, guests depart on foot with their packs.

This is one hotel where the question 'What do you do there?' is totally redundant. But just as importantly, the Bay of Fires Lodge is no boot camp. It's what the most individual hotels in the world all are: an experience you will remember forever. For four days you don't just have a beach to yourself, you have an entire national park. (Well almost, but excursion groups are never bigger than ten.) And you stay in a place that effortlessly and stylishly combines the most compelling qualities of this extraordinary continent, namely virgin nature, stylish modern architecture and sophisticated new-style Mediterranean food – and of course those easy-going Aussies, who think it's the most natural thing in the world to be on a beach all by yourself.

address Bay of Fires Lodge, c/o 'Pleasant Banks', 170 Leighlands Rd, Evandale, PO Box 1879, Launceston, Tasmania 7250, Australia
t (61) 3 6391 9339 f (61) 3 6391 9338 e bookings@cradlehuts.com.au
rates from AU $1,495 (for all-inclusive four-day walk)

the prairie hotel

They call it the back of beyond. This is the real outback, where everything is surrealistically distorted, where farms of 200,000 acres are considered to be on the smallish side, yet towns such as Parachilna count an official population of seven. Cattle are distributed one cow per square kilometre and the stockmen rely on planes, helicopters and motorbikes to keep track of their herds. A four-wheel drive is the most essential social tool (how else are you going to get to the pub?), and air-conditioning is the equivalent of heating in Scandinavia: life would be impossible without it.

There may be no more illustrative example of the back-of-beyond experience than the Prairie Hotel, or the Parachilna Pub as the locals know it. Parachilna is situated at the foot of South Australia's Flinders Ranges, the last geographical barrier en route to the middle of the continent. This is a vast empty land of red sand dunes, spectacular gorges, forests of dead trees, sparkling white salt beds that stretch to infinity, mountains that turn purple in the afternoon sun, and endless flat red plains punctuated by nothing more than the odd shrub. Almost every outback visual cliché exists within a thirty-minute drive. This is where they filmed *Holy Smoke* (Kate Winslet and Harvey Keitel stayed in rooms 11 and 12), while big-name director Philip Noyce of

Patriot Games fame headed here to shoot his first film back in Australia, *Follow the Rabbit Proof Fence*. Using Parachilna as a base, every outback adventure is possible, from a picnic in a dry creek bed to a cattle drive on the prairie or a scenic flight over the Flinders Ranges. The fact that the hotel's own plane uses the road in front as a landing strip makes it even more convenient.

All in all, therefore, Parachilna is the last place you would expect to find fine cuisine. Yet the Prairie Hotel has earned an international reputation for its innovative use of bush tucker – or what they call 'Flinders Feral Food'. Where else in the world can you get an antipasto of camel mettwurst, smoked kangaroo, emu prosciutto, and emu liver pâté with wild goat curd and bush tomato chutney? Or how about the feral mixed grill, with a goat chop, kangaroo fillet, camel sausages and emu pattie served on a bed of mashed potatoes with home-made gravy? The front bar even serves a roo burger for lunch. Skippy on a bun? Try it and you will get over your reservations. Kangaroo tastes like a cross between venison and beef, smoked camel is almost the same as pastrami, and emu is like fillet of beef.

The unusual cuisine is not a gimmick – far from it. The fact is that Australia has wild camels (too many),

It wouldn't be the outback without at least
one dry creek bed. Parachilna is a place
straight out of a Slim Dusty song

Things aren't thrown away in the outback,
they are recycled. Old biscuit tins get
a new life as *objets d'art*

The Anchor of Hope sign is a filmset
leftover from *Holy Smoke*, shot here
with Kate Winslet and Harvey Keitel

Emu-egg omelette is occasionally on the menu.
One egg feeds a dozen people –
that's a big omelette

The most popular item on the front bar menu
is the roo burger – minced skippy on a bun

Wattle leaf, gum nut, dried rooberries –
wild bush food for those who wouldn't
know how to find it for themselves

The intense summer heat produces
mini-tornadoes that send the ubiquitous
red dust swirling upwards

Owners Ross and Jane Fargher created
a comfortable lobby in the space between
the old pub and the new extension

The trains no longer stop in Parachilna,
so the old station now houses
the electricity generator

The outback is full of distortions of scale:
for a town of seven, the Parachilna
mail box is huge

Guest rooms at the Prairie Hotel are
built partially below ground level
for natural temperature control

Propping up the pub with a 'stubby'
of beer in hand is a popular
pastime in Parachilna

The stark Flinders landscape of red sand
dunes makes it a favourite location
with film makers

The severe terrain of the outback is the source
of place names like Dead Horse Gap
and No Name Creek

The galah, a beautifully colourful type
of cockatoo, is a distinctively
Australian bird

'Flinders Feral Food' – including wallaby,
camel and emu – tastes surprisingly
like continental charcuterie

The accommodation block to the rear of the
pub seamlessly blends eco-modern
design with outback vernacular

With its verandah and corrugated roof,
almost nothing has changed at the Prairie Hotel
since it was built in 1874

kangaroos (too many), wallabies (too many) and emus (too many). And these animals need to be culled on a regular basis. Common sense says that if they are going to be killed they might as well be eaten. That's certainly what Jane Fargher thought, when she and her station-owning husband Ross took over the Parachilna Pub some ten years ago. And there is the added bonus that the meat of these animals is very low in fat and cholesterol.

But to dwell too much on the ingredients served at the Prairie Hotel is an injustice to the chef. The menu has great diversity, and there are many dishes that don't feature Australia's more graphic fauna. In any case, fascinating food and spectacular scenery were only part of Ross and Jane's agenda for their outback establishment. They were also intent on creating an architectural experience. Modern architecture is not exactly commonplace in the bush – which for Jane was all the more reason to pursue it.

The accommodation, lying behind the typical stone facade, corrugated roof and lace ironwork of the old pub, is a fine piece of eco-modern design. It was devised to provide a cooling system that would not consume vast amounts of energy. The solution was to dig the rooms into the ground. The surrounding earth acts as insulation while the interior space is made much more interesting. Each room is on two levels, a balcony where you enter and a cool, shady lower sleeping area. Bathroom and corridor are at ground-floor height, bedroom half a floor lower.

Still, few people spend much time in their rooms – not when there is the ever-changing spectacle of 'bush life' in the front bar. During the day it is frequented by local characters: stockmen, bushies, rangers, truckies, mineworkers and flying doctors. All afternoon they sit in the front bar looking out at the fence, and when it cools down, they sit on the fence and look back at the bar....

---

address The Prairie Hotel, CMB 109, High Street Parachilna, SA 5730, Australia

t (61) 8 8648 4844 **f** (61) 8 8648 4606 **e** info@prairiehotel.com.au

room rates from AU $170

G R A N D

O C É A N

P A C I F I Q U E

Tropique du Cancer

Iles Aléutiennes

Presq.ᵉ Alaska

Pᵗᵉ aux Renards

I. Kodiak

Arch.ᵗ du R. Georges

Sitcha

Arch.ᵗ du Pce de Galles

Dét. de Vancouver

I. de la Reine
Charlotte

Dét. de la Reine Charlotte

I. Quadra et Vancouver

Dét. de Juan de Fuca

C. Flattery Victoria

Olympia
Astoria
Oregon
Salem

I.ᵗ Umpqua
C. Blanco
Pt S.ᵗ Georges

C. Mendocino

Bodega
Bᵉ et V. de S.ᵗ Francisco

Monterey

S.ᵗ Luis Obispo
C. Conception
I. S.ᵗ Cruz
I. S. Nicolas
I. S.ᵗ Clémente

C. S. Quintin

I. Guadalupe

I. de Cedros

C. S.ᵗ Lazaro
Bᵉ de la Magdalena
I. S.ᵗ Margarita

C. S.ᵗ Lucas

I. Las Tres Marias
C. Corrientes
I. Revillagigedo
Pt Natividad

NOUVELLE

STEKIN
Norfolk

Washington
M. Rainier
M. Hood
M. Jefferson
Klamet

Ind.ⁿ Serpents
Fᵗ Boisé
Boisé

Nevada
Carson
Sacramento
Fillmore City

Arizona
Prescott
Pimeria-Alta
Arispe
Sonora
Pitic
Guaymas
I. Naqui

Montana
Virginia
Wyoming
Mᵗ Bighorn

Colorado
Denver
Pic James

Santa Fe
Albuquerque
Socorro

Chihuahua

Villa del Fuerte
Cinaloa
Culiacan

Durango

Mazatlan
S.ᵗ Blas
Guadalaxara
L. Chapala
Colima
Guanaxuato

Acapulco

Frédéric Legrip del.

Schoeder sculp.

NORTH AMERICA

Caribbean beaches, Canadian mountains, Mexican ruins, American deserts, Alaskan glaciers…. If you include the Caribbean and Mexico in North America, which this atlas does, then it's understandable why so few citizens of the USA have passports. With majestic forests, awe-inspiring canyons, some of the world's largest freshwater lakes, and much much more on your doorstep, it seems reasonable not to feel compelled to travel further, at least until you've experienced the natural beauty of your own nation.

In terms of incredible sights, North America is the queen of the beauty pageant; a contestant blessed with an abundance of variety and plenty of pure knock-you-out wow factor. But what makes this continent different and special is how it lends itself to intrepid discovery without a guide. Rent a car and go – that's the American way. The road trip, particularly without a set itinerary, is a Stars and Stripes invention. When Europeans get in a car, it's almost always with a specific destination in mind: the trip takes as long as it takes – to get there. In North America, because of an extraordinary network of roads, and because people tend not to have much vacation time, and because they don't all take their holiday simultaneously (unlike, say, in Italy), the trip takes as long as it takes. Period.

There's something compellingly adventurous about stepping into an automobile, turning the key and driving off without knowing exactly where you'll end up and when. Added to which, deciding what direction to head off in is largely a matter of which particular 'fantasy lifestyle' appeals most. The East Coast of New England gives you WASP summers straight out of a Ralph Lauren advertising campaign – all boat shoes, clam bakes, varnished sailing boats and whitewashed colonial clapboard houses. Further north, in Canada and along the Great Lakes, you travel into lumberjack territory – check shirts, log cabins, canoes and leaves that change colour in spectacular fashion. Down Texas way you'll find the rugged, big-hat, big-country ambience of the cowboy 'dude' ranch – all Navajo blankets, adobe walls and days spent in the saddle.

But all this travelling can take it out of you, and that's where North America is blessed with two idyllic escape venues: Mexico's Pacific coast and the Caribbean. If you want to lie on a beach, interrupted only by the odd dip in clear water, the fantasy is available all year round. And it's convenient, too, because most islands of the Caribbean are no more than a three-hour flight from New York City. Variety, convenience, value – how all-American is that?

carlisle bay

It's hard to believe, but there was a time when Antigua's abundance of sandy beaches was anything but a blessing. While other Caribbean islands were protected by rocky inhospitable shores, Antigua's countless coves made it an easy target for marauding bands of the predatory and much-feared Carib Indians. Long before Columbus reached the Americas, the island of Antigua had been inhabited by peaceful agrarian tribes who had made their way here from South America via Trinidad. That was roughly 4,000 years ago, when the world's oceans were about 275 feet lower, making inter-island journeys that much easier.

I confess I knew nothing about Antigua's pre-Columbian history until I read a handbook on the subject at Carlisle Bay. Like many people, my knowledge of the West Indies started with the plantation era, the days of the so-called evil triangle of trade. Ships transported African slaves to the Caribbean to work the plantations, and returned to mother England laden with the sugar, tobacco, cotton, etc., produced by their backbreaking labour. They completed the triangle by heading back to the coasts of West Africa. The truth is, culturally and historically, these islands are far more intricate and old than we imagine. And though they are evocatively grouped together as Caribbean, they are each as distinct in geography, topography and anthropology as the various nations of Europe.

You could say that Antigua is the Ireland of the Caribbean. It's a colourful place, both in terms of its houses, painted a rainbow of bright tints, and in terms of its people, who have a fun-loving, feisty nature. Antigua is also surprisingly green. Away from the beaches, the island is a verdant vision of rolling pastures and the odd craggy peak. With a population of just 66,000, the majority of whom live in and around the capital, St John's, most of the island is sparsely inhabited. Tourism has only really reached Antigua's outer perimeter. And even then, there are still plenty of stretches that remain undeveloped. Unlike chic St Barths or cosmopolitan Barbados, Antigua is remarkably untouched by the massive tourism that the Caribbean generates.

The lush countryside, the colour, the warm disposition of the people – these might be what distinguish Antigua from other Caribbean islands, but for Gordon Campbell Gray, the very successful proprietor of London's One Aldwych, the decision to invest in Antigua was swayed by the special beauty of Carlisle Bay. This natural harbour in the most remote corner of the island, defined by a fine crescent of sand, is straight out of an ideal Caribbean press release.

Its emerald-green, crystal-clear waters are surrounded by forested mountains and plenty of swaying palms, with a small village nearby that consists entirely of brightly painted wooden clapboard houses. There's even the perfect Caribbean church on the headland. Best of all, there are not, nor ever will be, any other hotels to share it with. Campbell Gray's Carlisle Bay is the only hotel in this idyllic location and, having negotiated title to the entire beach, he intends to keep it that way.

Even before the two hundred-plus crew started building, the travel world was buzzing with anticipation. Why would such an urban and urbane operator venture to such a remote spot? What could he possibly offer that wasn't already available from the thousands of hotels that already exist in the Caribbean? The answer is a level of luxury and an attention to detail that may be the norm for the world's biggest cities, but is still quite novel in the Caribbean. From

the lights that illuminate the garden at night, to the bleached grey stain of the outdoor timber, to the flowers (orchids, orchids and more orchids), to the custom-made furniture and interiors designed by London-based Mary Fox Linton – no detail large or small has escaped Gordon's magnificent obsession. The swimming pool tiles were brought in from Bali, a black-painted orchid pool defines the entrance, and the shop displays Vilebrequin swimwear. With the proprietor's assured taste, Carlisle Bay has been groomed as a Caribbean option for discerning adults.

The all-suites hotel opened in late 2003, and only time will tell if it can live up to all the pre-launch hype. But one thing is for sure: the guest reaps the benefit of Gordon Campbell Gray's almost manic attention to detail. It's a sexy combination: an ensemble of thoroughly tamed, perfectly trained, preternaturally well turned-out details – in a wild, undomesticated and ruggedly natural setting.

---

address Carlisle Bay, Old Road, St Mary's, Antigua, West Indies

t (1) 268 484 0000 **f** (1) 268 484 0001 **e** info@carlisle-bay.com

room rates suites from US $540 (half board)

the landing

Harbour Island is everything the Bahamas should be and mostly aren't. The Caribbean dream is straightforward: hibiscus and palm trees and beautiful timber houses painted in bright gelato colours, with whitewashed picket fences. Plus of course crystal-clear turquoise waters lapping at the edges of exquisitely deserted beaches. The reality, particularly in Nassau, is (mostly) vastly different. There are endless duty-free tourist emporiums, and more than enough cruise ship passengers on day leave to make them viable. Hotels come in three sizes: large, very large, and way too large. The few cute little houses to survive are forlorn and distinctly out of place.

Then there is Harbour Island. Take a plane from Miami to Eleuthera, a taxi to the local wharf and a small speedboat across the bay and you've arrived at the Bahamian version of Capri – minus the crowds. This island is too remote for daytrippers (minimum two hours by fast ferry from Nassau) and the waters are too shallow for cruise ships. And unlike Mustique, another perfect little Caribbean island, Harbour Island is not exclusively given over to vacation homes for the rich and famous. There's a genuine local culture here which brings together expat residents with indigenous Bahamians. The result is something real – not too perfect and not too

rustic. The other beauty of Harbour Island is the scale: small wooden houses, some dating back two centuries; small roads, mostly covered in sand; small buildings – no high-rise hotels, no apartment blocks, no condominiums, nothing in fact above two storeys high. The whole place is just pink-sand beaches and brightly painted clapboard houses.

When the British first arrived here in the 1700s, they quarried the local coral-stone and used it to build stately houses with wooden verandahs. One such property, one of the most important on the island, is now a hotel called the Landing – because it's literally a stone's throw from the dock where the mailboats and water taxis arrive. It's the perfect Caribbean island guesthouse. With a cool interior of chalk-white walls, mahogany-stained wooden floors and immaculate white linen draped on massive four-poster beds and Chippendale chairs, the style is exactly right, a crisp patrician look with a distinctive British colonial signature.

Places like this always have a special story, and the Landing is no exception. It started with a blind date – a blind date that went wrong. Toby Tyler was a bachelor living the good life in Sydney when friends called to invite him to dinner, hoping to matchmake him with their visitor, a model from New York. Not only was it not love at first sight, but

389

Harbour Island is just the way we like to imagine
the Caribbean – colourful, charming
and unspoilt

Quirky, effortless, authentic – there's
no style formula at work here,
just simple good taste

A stone's throw from the main jetty, the hotel
is housed in one of the island's earliest
colonial buildings

The decor of the Landing never feels 'decorated'; it is casually elegant and convincingly timeless

The restaurant is a real drawcard, with its sophisticated wine list and a world-class chef from Sydney

Designers David Flint Wood and India Hicks fused carefree Caribbean culture with British colonial form and formality

they didn't even particularly like each other. But because of mutual friends they kept meeting, and by the time Tracy Barry – originally from the Bahamas, and the daughter of a former Miss Bahamas – was ready to leave, they were making plans to get married and settle in Sydney. But first Tracy had some loose ends to tie up, which included making some decisions about a family property on Harbour Island, a grand old house that had been run as a hotel – not very successfully. They made the decision to sell the place, and Toby accompanied Tracy to help organize things.

What happened next no doubt happens to a lot of people who come to Harbour Island … they couldn't bear to leave. Toby, a veteran of the catering business in Sydney, convinced Tracy to hold the sale until he had had a look at the books. He was convinced the answer lay in opening a top-class restaurant that would lure future guests, but also help tide them over out of season. He managed to convince one of Sydney's top chefs, Ken Gomes, to move to Harbour Island and he and his new wife set about a massive top-to-toe renovation.

Food aside, the Landing's greatest quality is aesthetic integrity. It feels like old money lightened up and toned down by its laid-back location. The look is a result of collaboration with locals David Flint Wood and India Hicks, whose own hilltop home has featured in just about every interiors magazine worldwide. She is the daughter of the late David Hicks and although she made her name modelling, the design gene eventually reasserted itself. Harbour Island being the place it is, it's no surprise they all ended up working together on the Landing. David and India did the design, Toby created the restaurant, and Tracy runs the place. The result is straight out of a Hemingway story, a relaxed, barefoot destination where life revolves around drinks at six and dinner at eight.

---

address The Landing, PO Box 190, Harbour Island, Bahamas

t (1) 242 333 2707 **f** (1) 242 333 2650 **e** info@harbourislandlanding.com

room rates from US $198

korakia

When I first heard about this hotel I was sceptical. It has had great press over the years, but it looks so Moroccan. Why not build in the style of the region? But admittedly I had never been to Palm Springs, so I just didn't get it. Once I did go there, it didn't take long. There's something about Palm Springs that is strongly reminiscent of Morocco. Perhaps it's the heat, or the palm trees, or the desert that glows red at sunrise and sunset; perhaps it's the laid-back rhythm of a lifestyle where people don't really venture out until the heat of the day has abated.

For lovers of Palm Springs mid-century modernity, Korakia is not for you. But if you are seeking a seductive retreat from day to day reality, it's perfect. The keyword is romance. Unlike the slick air-conditioned atmosphere of most American luxury hotels, this is a place of hand-washed linen sheets, canopied four-poster beds, lace, ceiling fans, slate and wooden floors, furniture from Rajasthan, chairs from Mexico, glassware from France, black-and-white photography and lots of old books. Following a spectacular sunrise (pretty much guaranteed in Palm Springs), the day starts with breakfast in the garden. Small, weathered wooden tables are set with blue gingham cloths and in the shade of citrus trees you are served strong coffee, toast,

pastries and home-made blueberry pancakes. Suddenly the Los Angeles of freeways and fast food seems a million miles away. By night, the impression is of being on the set of Bertolucci's *The Sheltering Sky*. Candlelight flickers, the pool glows between palm trees, and the lights from the guestrooms peek out through small, typically Moroccan windows onto a complex of courtyards and outdoor plazas.

It's a romantic place with an equally romantic past. Dar Marroc, as the villa was originally called, was built in 1924 by the Scottish artist Gordon Coutts in memory of his beloved Tangier. This was Palm Springs before it was discovered by the movie crowd. It was still primarily an artists' colony and the domed desert hideaway of Coutts' Moroccan folly, with its whitewashed battlements and huge wooden doors, became its cultural centre. Diverse artists came from all over the world to visit Coutts and his young wife Gertrude. The flamboyant artist, with his flaming red hair, would tell tall tales of his exotic travels against the spectacular setting of the San Jacinto Mountains. His bohemian guests included Rudolph Valentino and Errol Flynn. Even Winston Churchill is rumoured to have painted in the artist's studio that today is one of Korakia's guestrooms.

Palm Springs' little bohemian secret might eventually have been forgotten had it not been bought fifty years later (albeit in a dreadful state) by another international adventurer, Los Angeles native Douglas Smith. Smith had lived a life every bit as cosmopolitan as Coutts, and what's more he even resembles the younger Coutts. Raised in the suburbs of LA, Smith fled to Newport Beach for a life of racing and skippering yachts along the California coast, before moving to Paris – as Coutts had before him – to study art at the Julian Academy. Smith eventually landed up on the Greek island of Spetses, where he opened the Kalla Café, a big favourite with jetsetters like Jackie O., Mick Jagger and Stavros Niarchos. He returned to the States in 1979 to work as an architect and designer. But just as Coutts had pined for Morocco, so Smith longed for the simple beauty and whitewashed architecture of his Mediterranean hideaway. Palm Springs reminded him of Spetses, and he started to look there for a piece of property for his wife and daughter. That he should end up with Coutts' Tangier-inspired folly was the stuff of a Danielle Steel novel. Needless to say, it took a lot of work to restore the original fibre of the villa. But Smith, with his training in design and his worldly experience, was perfectly placed to provide the property with the type of aesthetic that feels as if it's always been this way. The Moroccan architecture is still evident, but to that Smith has added the influence of the American Southwest, of Mexico, and of the whitewashed walls of Greece – a mixed bag, but a successful one because all these influences share a common spirit.

The Korakia style also now extends to the neighbouring property, a 1937 Mediterranean-style villa built for the early screen star J. Carol Naisch. But, style aside, the secret of Korakia's success is the way it evokes the essence of exotic travel and faraway places.

---

address Korakia Pensione, 257 South Patencio Road, Palm Springs, California 92262, USA

t (1) 760 864 6411 **f** (1) 760 864 4147 **e** info@korakia.com

room rates from US $139

dunton hot springs

Not too many people have heard of Dunton. That's because until only four years ago it was a ghost town. A ramshackle collection of rustic log cabins (including a dance hall, chapel and saloon), it is typical of the makeshift mining towns that sprung up in the Rockies during the gold rush of the late 1800s. It might be a one-horse town to our eyes but Dunton presented a welcome bit of civility to the miners camped out for months on end in the mountainous wilderness of the southern San Juan ranges of Colorado's Rockies.

Situated at the not inconsiderable altitude of 8,900 feet, Dunton remained a mining camp until 1944, when the nearby Emma silver mine closed down. Overlooking El Diente Peak and Mount Wilson, it's situated at the other end of the Lizard Head Pass to Telluride, itself once a ghost town but now a thriving upmarket ski resort favoured by the Hollywood 'A' list. Nestled amid some of the most spectacular scenery of the southern Rockies, Dunton is unexpectedly pretty for a mining town. And it has a bit of a story to go with the setting. Legend has it that Butch Cassidy and the Sundance Kid holed up here after robbing the bank at Telluride. Butch Cassidy's name is still carved in the saloon bar to prove it.

What Christoph Henkel and Bernt Kuhlmann got when they purchased the site in 1994 was picturesque but hardly glamorous. In fact it was a mess, as can be expected of a place that has been abandoned for the better part of four decades. The buildings were in varying stages of ruin and there was no electricity, no gas, no water, no telephone, no sewerage … nothing but the camp and the hot springs that gave the settlement its name. Bubbling up from the earth's core at around 45° Celsius, the mineral-laden springs were about the only feature of the town still working.

Undaunted, Henkel and Kuhlmann – one a film producer, the other a real estate developer – clung to their vision of what it could be rather than what it was. What they wanted it to be was a piece of the old American West brought back to life – without the hardships. Their dream was to recreate the real drawcard of the gold rushes, the promise of adventure. Accessible only by a dirt road so remote that elk roam casually across it, secure in the knowledge that a grand total of four cars travel past each day, Dunton has all the credentials for a unique adventure experience precisely because it is so isolated and so remote.

Kuhlmann and Henkel went to untold lengths to maintain the illusion that they had done hardly anything at

Dunton Hot Springs, a former mining town,
is a collection of restored log cabins
in Colorado's Rocky Mountains

A ground floor bedroom is defined by its
African *kente* cloth patchwork bedspread

The honeymoon cabin is set
right on the river's edge

Fake wolf fur and a Santa Fe-style
antique dresser against the original
bare logs of the cabin walls

Derelict until just a few years ago,
the log cabins have been restored
to appear unrestored

The interior of one cabin is a
Native American-inspired scheme
complete with a buckskin bedspread

Dunton, at an altitude of 8,900 feet,
is a sure bet for powder snow
in the winter

The smallest cabin combines a Turkish kilim,
African masks and *kuta* mud cloth
with American Southwest antiques

The library cabin contains quite a collection
of books on ghost towns
of the Wild West

An exotic Rajasthani carved wooden bed
is the focal point of Dunton's
honeymoon cabin

A rustic double-height cabin
houses Dunton's naturally heated
swimming pool

The pool is fed by a 45°C spring.
The view is of the highest peak
in the area

Part of Dunton's charm is that some of
the 1860s mining camp remains derelict

One cabin has its own hot spring pool –
a great slate trough that takes no more
than twenty minutes to fill

Butch Cassidy and the Sundance Kid are said to
have hidden out in Dunton's saloon
after robbing the Telluride bank

The interior of the library cabin is a cosy
bear-rug-and-fire kind of place

Bernt Kuhlmann, one of the proprietors of Dunton,
was married in the outdoor chapel built
beside a waterfall

Wagon-wheel chandeliers, a pressed-tin ceiling
and a massive full-size pool table
dominate the old saloon

all. From a distance it certainly doesn't look like anything has been 'tarted up'. The roofs are still covered in rusted plates of corrugated iron, and (with the exception of the dance hall and the saloon) most structures are simple cabins made of split, cracked and heavily weathered logs. It takes more than a passing acquaintance with the place to discern the three million dollars spent on renovating it. But that's the beauty. Humbled by the soaring peaks of the San Juan mountains, it looks, feels and smells like a rugged miner's camp. There's nothing obviously luxurious about it … until you venture indoors. Rustic Santa Fe antiques, African masks, Turkish kilims, Rajasthani beds, Chinese chairs and Moroccan rugs are combined in one cross-cultural bundle to give each cabin a style that perfectly complements the ragtag exteriors of these former miners' huts.

They are stylish, yes, but comfortable too. Natural slate floors are heated from below, the bathrooms feature sumptuous baths and showers, and even the loos are of a standard usually reserved to top city hotels. There is direct international dialling and antique cupboards conceal stereo systems. The saloon has a fully equipped professional kitchen and one of the houses reveals a grand indoor spring complete with cold tub and massage centre. A centrepiece of the restored camp is the yellow teepee, a piece of Native American theatre that shelters one of the many hot springs on the grounds. One cabin, plain as can be from the outside, in fact houses a two-storey library with a roaring fireplace, leather armchairs and a not insubstantial collection of books about the American West.

The camp functions primarily as a corporate and executive retreat. This is the wild Wild West with all luxuries laid on, an atmospheric leap back to the romantic days of the gold rush and bar-room brawls.

---

address Dunton Hot Springs, PO Box 818, 52068 West Fork Road #38, Dolores, Colorado 81323, USA
t (1) 970 882 4800 **f** (1) 970 882 7475 **e** info@duntonhotsprings.com
room rates from US $325

the home ranch

Round Mountain Ranch, Big Creek Ranch, Triple Diamond Ranch, Yampa Valley Ranch – Steamboat Springs is ranch country. These are not just big houses by another name, they are real working ranches. This part of Colorado is Marlboro Country in the snow. Everybody – and I mean everybody – wears cowboy boots, tooled leather belts with big shiny buckles and big hats. And everybody drives a pickup truck.

I grew up skiing on the East Coast, in New England, and I used to dream of going to Steamboat Springs. The horses in the snow, the white-capped red barns and the famous powder snow seemed like the ultimate combination. I couldn't wait to head out west with my skis, a Ford Bronco and a pair of Tony Llama boots. Alas, my parents had other plans and, before I ever had a chance, we moved to Australia. So it was with great anticipation that I drove from Denver to Steamboat last winter.

Steamboat is situated on what they call high prairie, flat land that happens to be at an altitude of almost 9,000 feet (2,750 metres). Nowhere else in the world is there such a vast fertile plateau at such an altitude. The town of Steamboat Springs got its name in the mid-1800s, when trappers trudging up the Yampa River heard a gurgling

sound that they thought was a steamboat, but which turned out to be natural hot springs. Until recently it was a cattle town. Its main street, lined with weathered clapboard houses, is broad enough to allow a herd to be driven through. Today, however, skiing and ski tourism are the chief business, and ski tourism demands facilities that Steamboat provides in a style that's more big city than rodeo. Most of the architecture owes more to Starbucks than the Last Chance Saloon. Brochures still feature cowboys and rustic red barns, but the reality is that the Wild West flavour doesn't extend much beyond the old town and main street.

What a pity! I was really looking forward to the whole cowboy cattle-ranch thing. But once out of Steamboat, on the road to tiny Clark, the fantasy was back on track. At the northern end of the Elk River valley, with Hahn's Peak in the distance, the Home Ranch is a step back in time. There are no condominiums or hotels or even houses in this area, just the odd ranch. Clark is straight out of cowboy folklore. It has a general store, a saloon bar and a sign that says 'Welcome to Clark. Elevation 7,271 feet. Population ?' (It seems they never got around to counting.) The only hangout is the local bar, where the menu is real cowpoke stuff: chicken, fried steak, fried catfish sandwiches, and pork belly chilli.

In summer, you can ride one of the Home Ranch's 140 horses through the surrounding birch forest. In winter the emphasis changes to skiing. For downhill enthusiasts, it's a thirty-minute drive past all the other ranches back to Steamboat. Directly exposed to any weather travelling across America, particularly fronts from the Pacific – the ones that bring snow – Steamboat is the place where they invented the term 'Champagne powder'. The main mountain is smallish by European standards, but the real attraction is the back country – the off-piste terrain in the forest glades. Cross-country skiers need not leave the grounds of the Home Ranch. Summer riding trails are transformed into cross-country trails in the winter.

Most importantly, the Home Ranch is not a hotel that happens to resemble a ranch. It is a ranch and a home that graciously opens its doors to guests. Ken Jones (proprietor and, it is said, a bit of a horse whisperer) explains that the tradition of receiving guests on a ranch goes back to the very earliest settlers, who were always glad of the company and an extra pair of hands. The accommodation includes eight private cabins and six rooms in the main house. Eating here is truly a 'come and get it' cowboy experience. You rise in the morning to a roaring fire in the cosy dining room, and as you settle in to the panoramic view someone emerges from the kitchen and announces that they're making blueberry pancakes and would you like some. It's a 'what's on the griddle today' kind of breakfast. On Mondays the restaurant is often booked out because everyone 'around these parts' knows that Monday night is barbecue night. Ken himself gets behind the biggest barbecue kettle you've ever seen and all the cowboys flock in. How do I know they're cowboys? As they say on the high prairie, 'no matter what you wear, if you wear a cowboy hat on your head you'll be called a cowboy.'

address The Home Ranch, PO Box 822, 54880 RCR 129, Clark, Colorado 80428, USA

t (1) 970 879 1780 **f** (1) 970 879 1795 **e** info@homeranch.com

room rates from US $400

round hill

A former sugar plantation on the outskirts of Montego Bay, Round Hill is where Jacqueline and J.F.K. spent their honeymoon; where Oscar Hammerstein and Richard Rodgers played chess; where Hitchcock got sunburned; where Noel Coward, if egged on enough, would sing for the guests. Bing Crosby, Bob Hope, Errol Flynn, Paul Newman, the Aga Khan, Charlie Chaplin … the list goes on and on and on. In a competition for name-dropping, there are few hotels in the world that could take on Round Hill. Even today the celebrity stakes are high. Stella McCartney, according to staff, practically grew up here, while Beatle dad Paul would play dominoes with the locals, who didn't give a damn if he was a Beatle as long as he could play (dominoes, that is). And whereas Noel Coward was the celebrity most identified with Round Hill in the past, now it's Ralph Lauren and family who have become the new glamour fixture. From November on Lauren is here almost every weekend. With only three hours' flight time, it's quicker to fly from Manhattan to Montego Bay than to drive to the Hamptons. (Though it does help to have your own jet.)

Just what is it about Round Hill that makes it such a magnet, particularly for people utterly spoilt for choice? A significant part of the equation is Jamaica itself. Jamaicans will remind you that they are a nation, not just an island; a nation of three million, with cities and highways and crime and shopping centres and its own very particular culture. Jamaicans are open, friendly, very laid-back, and have a wicked sense of humour. One thing they are not is remotely impressed by fame and celebrity.

But the warmth of the people aside, the success of Round Hill goes back to fifty years ago, when a young Jamaican laid down the blueprint for his development. John Pringle was from one of the island's oldest and most privileged colonial families. He'd been living and working in New York, but for some inexplicable reason he was obsessed with returning to Jamaica to open a hotel. The fact that he had no hotel experience, nor any money to speak of, did not deter him. Through family connections he was made aware of a piece of land about half an hour's drive from the centre of Montego Bay. It was part of a large cattle and farming estate, but this gently sloping rounded plot (hence Round Hill) wasn't exactly stellar in agricultural terms. That of course suited Pringle perfectly because he was mainly interested in the little beach at the end of the site.

His mother paid the deposit, but otherwise Pringle had to resort to imagination to finance his dream. A plan was

hatched with his lawyer: he would parcel off a twenty-five-acre tract to house the hotel and twenty-nine cottages that he could sell off-plan. The revenue generated by the sale of the cottages would pay for the hotel. It was devilishly daring, and it worked – beyond any of Pringle's expectations. His success was boosted immeasurably by the fact that the first sale was to none other than Noel Coward. Although Coward was a friend of his mother, Pringle had never himself met him. But by chance he found himself sitting next to Coward on a flight to New York. Seizing his opportunity, he pulled out drawings and photos of the Round Hill site and spent the flight pitching the scheme. Eventually Coward put his hand on Pringle's knee and said, 'My dear boy, if you will only stop boring me I'll buy one of your blasted cottages.' True to his word, he did.

Having the illustrious Mr Coward as his first client was a huge coup, and it opened the floodgates. So much so that one American magnate agreed to buy a plot on the basis of a photo for a price of £25,000, enough to finance all the real estate in one hit. In fact, by the time the Paleys heard about it, there were really no cottages left. But nobody said no to Bill Paley, the Murdoch of his day, so Pringle blasted a site from an adjacent cliff and built the fantasy of a house that is today owned by Ralph Lauren.

After fifty years Round Hill has a million stories to tell. But the most impressive is how little it has changed. In a world of built-in obsolescence, it's exciting to come across a place that savours its uncomplicated authenticity. There's nothing flash about Round Hill, and there never has been. It still offers the same blend of qualities that has always pulled the famous faces, namely a well-preserved slice of old Jamaica, with sympathetic architecture and a predictably colonial pace of life: lunch at one, tea at four, dinner at eight and lots of swimming, snorkelling and sailing in between.

---

address Round Hill, PO Box 64, Montego Bay, Jamaica, West Indies

t (1) 876 956 7050 **f** (1) 876 956 7505 **e** info@roundhilljamaica.com

room rates from US $260

hotelito desconocido

Only an Italian could create a place like this. Hotelito Desconocido – literally 'Unknown Little Hotel' – is surely the most romantic place in Mexico, if not all of the Americas. The setting couldn't be more seductive. Hotelito's thatched *palafitos* are arranged along a broad lagoon flanked by mountains and palm forests on one side and by a massive virgin beach and the booming surf of the Pacific on the other. The lagoon is home to an extraordinary variety of wildlife, including herons, vultures and pelicans, and each year hundreds of newly hatched *tortugas* (turtles) start their voyage to maturity by making their way across this beach and into the wild surf.

As you pass through the nearby *pueblo* – a place straight out of *El Mariachi* – and descend towards the distant palm trees that tell you the Pacific is not far away, nothing can compete with your first glimpse of this palm-fringed lagoon and its long strip of unending beach. It was this view that prompted Marcello Murzilli to put his life on hold and embark on one of the most ambitious escape destinations I have come across. He first saw the lagoon from the air. He was flying from Careyes just to the south, itself the pioneer of a whole new approach to Pacific development, reintroducing indigenous sensitivity in palm-thatched palapas built without steel, concrete or glass. As he swooped across the 8-mile long lagoon,

the only one along a 49-mile stretch of unbroken sand, Murzilli knew he just had to have a closer look. There were no roads to where he wanted to go, so he hired some *charros* on horseback with machetes, and off they went. When they finally reached the lagoon, like a modern version of Cortes' little band of conquerors, he knew then and there that this was the place where he could realize a dream.

The locals were bemused by this unshaven man with holes in his shirt and a knotted handkerchief on his head, especially when he started making enquiries about buying the land. To people who lived from farming, fishing and ranching, he must have seemed a complete madman. And maybe he was. But he was also creative, persistent, entrepreneurial and, despite appearances, rich. Marcello Murzilli had a jeans company called (ironically enough) Charro, which he sold up after twenty years of hard work, leaving behind a life of helicopters, big business and Formula One sponsorship (yes, really) to restore a wooden yacht and sail around the world for two years. It was during this time that he rethought his life philosophy. 'Once you have every toy and thing you could imagine,' he will tell you, 'the ultimate is to have nothing. To enjoy nature in her pure unspoilt state – to go to bed when it's dark and to wake up when it's light. To enjoy the simple

pleasure of candlelight every day, and to do without computers, cars, newspapers, telephones or television.'

While the village was still scratching its collective head, the Italian with the holes in his shirt had already bought the land and rapidly become the area's biggest employer. Up to two hundred workers toiled for four years. Roads were laid, jungle was cleared, palm trees were planted and lots of buildings went up – none of them like anything else along this coast. Murzilli insisted on building the accommodation in the style and manner of original Mexican dwellings. These palafitos are shacks on stilts made of palm fronds and mud, with roofs of trimmed branches and palm-leaf thatch. Painted bright yellow, they may be authentic but they are anything but plain or basic. They are all different, all wonderfully eccentric, vividly colourful and hopelessly romantic. The interiors ingeniously follow the colours and themes of Mexican bingo. Some are pink, others blue or green or yellow, with impressive four-poster beds swathed in mosquito netting, doors and windows made of woven palm, outdoor showers, bathrooms with colourful tiles, oiled wooden floors, and a riot of naive oil paintings on the walls. And of course, because there is no electricity (just solar power by day), there are lots and lots of candles in all sorts of containers, pots and lamps – more than five hundred, to be exact.

While the palafitos were being built, along with two bars and two restaurants, reception, spa and stables, Marcello Murzilli lived on the beach in a tent. As he talks of those years, you can see from the twinkle in his eye just how special they were. There was much hardship, much expense and many setbacks, but the result speaks for itself.

At night the place is like an adult fairy tale – twinkling and starry and wonderfully flattering (even Northern Europeans look bronzed). By day it's a private paradise, with your own lagoon and an almost endless deserted beach. The only disappointment is having to leave – eventually.

---

address Hotelito Desconocido, Playon de Mismaloya, Jalisco, Mexico
t (52) 322 281 4010 **f** (52) 322 281 4130 **e** hotelito@hotelito.com
room rates from US $290

cotton house

Like most islands in the Caribbean, Mustique in the Grenadines was once a sugar plantation. In the seventeenth and eighteenth centuries sugar was the new commodity and its cultivation could yield vast profits. For the colonial powers, the Caribbean was well suited to growing sugar cane because there was plenty of land and sun, not to mention an indigenous population, the Caribs, whom they could conveniently enslave on the grounds that they were cannibals. When the native population was exhausted, boatloads of slaves were brought from Africa to continue the backbreaking work. But in time, with the shift of large-scale sugar cane cultivation to Asia, the West Indies became less competitive and the plantations, including that of Mustique, were abandoned. Today its restored remains, including the windmill and warehouse, form the core of the Cotton House hotel.

So why, you may ask, is it called the Cotton House? The story behind the name is, in a sense, the story of modern Mustique. This three-square-mile island just south of St Vincent was by the fifties just an abandoned bit of sunburned scrub inhabited by the odd fisherman and his family. And so it might have remained if a young Colin Tennant, a.k.a. Lord Glenconner, had not adopted it.

The scion of a wealthy aristocratic family from Scotland, he had set out for the West Indies to inspect long-forgotten family holdings. While in St Lucia, he heard about an island that was for sale and immediately took the first mail boat out to see it. Despite its craggy, unkempt appearance his imagination was fired and he promptly cabled his father to advise him of his plan to buy. His father replied that he was 'in full accordance providing there is water'. There wasn't, but that didn't stop the young lord from paying £45,000 sterling (a small fortune in 1959) for an island without buildings, services or water.

Fuelled by enthusiasm, Tennant set about making the island habitable. His first grand plan was to convert the ruins of the sugar plantation into a working cotton plantation. Against great odds (and at enormous expense) he managed to bring in a crop, but only one: he was forced to stop when his accountants calculated that every shirt woven from his fine cotton had cost £3,000.

Undaunted, Tennant turned his manic drive and extravagant imagination to a more sybaritic goal – that of turning Mustique into an earthly paradise for family and friends. In those days nobody had heard of Mustique. Awareness of the island was given a boost when Tennant

The Great House, now the living/dining
room and bar, was the old sugar
plantation's warehouse

Shabby chic in the Caribbean:
Indian silk, white cotton slip covers
and dark wood colonial chairs

Guests are accommodated in a collection
of small cottages spread
around the estate

In true colonial fashion, dinner
is served on the veranda
of the Great House

Theatre set designer Oliver Messel was responsible
for the design of the pool house,
known as Messel's Folly

A fondness for French doors with oval
fanlights is a typical design signature
of Messel's work

The Cotton House estate is the prime location
on Mustique, located between L'Ansecoy Bay
and Endeavour Bay

Colonial eclecticism extends to the smallest details,
including this velvet cushion depicting
an exotic scene

The diving school specializes in classes
for absolute beginners

Coutinot House has a wraparound terrace
that overlooks Endeavour Bay

Beyond the mill, on a point overlooking
the rugged Atlantic coast of L'Ansecoy Bay,
is Baliceau Cottage with four suites

Beach baroque – a shell-encrusted cupboard
in the Great House is typical of Messel's
eccentric excess

The Cotton House diving school on
Endeavour Bay is a typical
Caribbean shed on the beach

The Monkey Bar in the Great House has been
Mustique's main place of mischief
for over two decades

From the balcony of Coutinot House,
the view takes in the quiet Caribbean
(as opposed to Atlantic surfing beaches)

The Cotton House is furnished in classic
colonial style with linens, cottons, rattan
furniture and polished wooden floors

The stone windmill, workhorse of the
original sugar plantation, is still a
landmark on the property

Without being too formal, the ambience
of the Great Room has a sense
of elegant heritage

gave Princess Margaret (a distant relative) a parcel of land as a wedding present. There were no roads to speak of at that time, nor even electricity until 1972. Yet the newly formed Mustique Company pressed ahead with creating a hotel to house guests invited to the island to consider buying land.

The imposing storage house with its foot-thick stone walls and typical veranda became the dining room, the ballroom, and the popular Monkey Bar. In true colonial style, the 'rough and ready' was set aside at night, when guests would dress for dinner and be entertained by some sort of show that the irrepressible Tennant had managed to conjure. Attracted by Mustique's promise of privacy, ideal weather and perfect beaches, as well as the advantage of being out of the hurricane zone, many big names signed on the dotted line. Mick Jagger, David Bowie and Tommy Hilfiger are among those who were approved (while the Aga Khan and the Shah of Iran were apparently rejected).

Cotton House is a collection of houses dotted around a lush estate, each with a view, and guests are accommodated in a house of their own. It has the best location on the island, on a promontory that divides windswept L'Ansecoy Bay from the calm green waters the other side.

Despite the stories of wild times and crazy parties, Mustique's present-day appearance – immaculate and unspoilt – is the result of rigorous efforts. No helicopters are allowed on the island and the landing strip accommodates nothing bigger than a six-seater. The airport, like the nearby church, was built in bamboo, and there is no traffic to speak of – everyone gets around on a Mule. This is not quite as rustic as it sounds: Mule is the brand name of Kawasaki's motorized golf carts. These only have two gears (forward and back) but there are still speed bumps all over the island – noise is micro-managed like everything else here. Paradise, it seems, takes relentless planning.

---

address Cotton House, PO Box 349, Mustique, St Vincent, West Indies

t (1) 784 456 4777 **f** (1) 784 456 5887 **e** cottonhouse@caribsurf.com

room rates from US $460 (including breakfast)

the wawbeek

New York high society didn't always escape to the Hamptons. A hundred years ago the majestic Adirondack mountains were the preferred retreat. With their lakes, beaches and cool forests – a welcome respite from New York's heat and humidity in summer – and their pristine ice and snow in winter, the Adirondacks were an established part of the seasonal society escape. But it wasn't just the summer climate or the spectacular beauty that made the Adirondacks so popular; they were given an additional boost by property developer Thomas Durant, who made the mountains accessible to city folk by building the Adirondack railway line, completed in 1871.

Even so, it was a few years before Durant, or rather his son William, caught the attention of New York's millionaires. In 1879, William Durant showed the rich something really fantastical they could do with their money. He commissioned an incredibly elaborate and luxurious compound in this wilderness destination built largely out of unskinned logs. The idea swiftly caught on. It was the first 'great camp', and soon every tycoon just had to have one. These baroque creations in logs were very grand, very eccentric and very expensive. For the first time, American money had found its own equivalent of the Alpine *Schloss*.

Builders of the great camps set out not only to copy but to outdo the aristocratic splendour of a European castle in the snow. They had enormous fireplaces built in riverstone, chandeliers made from antlers, bearskin rugs and countless hunting trophies (shot or bought – it didn't matter, so long as it was impressive.) The grandest of all the great camps was, appropriately enough, built by the richest man in America, William Avery Rockefeller. Logs were used to construct everything from a private service station and a boathouse for an entire fleet of boats to a formal dining room with a thirty-foot ceiling and a monumental riverstone fireplace at either end.

Today, Rockefeller's camp on Lake Saranac thrives as an exclusive hotel called the Point. It's a sensational place with equally sensational levels of luxury and, of course, a price tag to match. As a hotel experience, it is largely limited to mini-Rockefellers. On the very same lake, however, in an equally idyllic location, is another great camp that offers the same enchanting log cabin experience at far more affordable rates. The Wawbeek, on Upper Saranac Lake, is the real thing – a turn-of-the-century forty-acre property that features both individual log cabins and spacious rooms in a larger Lake House. Its interiors have abundant fireplaces, endless cosy nooks for reading, and plenty of antler lamps and hunting trophies. In addition to the two living rooms packed with card tables, games, books, and cushion-filled corners (but no TVs – anywhere), most of the rooms in the Lake House have their own fireside sitting areas. The views across lake and mountains are magnificent. It's a homely aesthetic designed to allow the stressed-out New Yorker to regain some balance of life.

Even so, the best place to be is outdoors. As the locals say, 'here in the north country, all seasons are intense.' Walk, hike, swim, bike, and sail in the summer (all gear is included in the price, by the way) and cross-country ski, skate, snow-shoe and fish in the winter. There's even downhill skiing not far away. The nearest mountain is Big Tupper, only eight miles from the Wawbeek, and thirty miles away is Lake Placid, the venue for not one but two Winter Olympics. For some just the air and the unspoiled natural beauty of the place is stimulus enough.

Active or not, all guests have the food to look forward to in the evening. The Wawbeek restaurant, located in the camp's original dining cabin on a rocky promontory overlooking the lake, has a considerable culinary reputation. Chef Richard Brosseau is a local boy who cooked the length and breadth of the United States before coming back home to the Adirondacks, and anyone who has eaten at the Wawbeek will be grateful that he did. Whatever the season, the menu is always entirely in step with the outdoor life, offering hearty, meaty dishes like pheasant, rabbit, venison and aged steak, accompanied by North Country vegetables, fruits and local cheeses.

A 'great camp' is undoubtedly a great experience. Of all the travel fantasies that exist, retreating like Hemingway to a log cabin on a wooded lake nestled into surrounding mountains must be high on the list.

---

address The Wawbeek, 553 Hawk Ridge, Upper Saranac Lake, Tupper Lake, New York 12986, USA

t (1) 518 359 2656 (1 800 953 2656) **f** (1) 518 359 2475 **e** info@wawbeek.com

room rates from US $140 (including breakfast and use of boats)

hix island house

It all started with Hurricane Hugo. After years of vacationing on the quiet Puerto Rican island of Vieques, Toronto-based architect John Hix had finally purchased his dream piece of land – thirteen hilltop acres of Vieques's tropical jungle with panoramic views of the Caribbean. As Hugo hit the headlines, the builders were ready, but Hix had not submitted working plans. According to meteorologists, the hurricane would miss Vieques … but it didn't. Hix stayed up all night glued to the TV following its progress. It was a wake-up call. He literally went back to the drawing board to design a house that could withstand a hurricane.

The triangle, as Hix will tell you, is the strongest shape in nature, and so a triangular house it was – in reinforced concrete with enormous cutouts to maximize the view, and strategically placed metal roll-down shutters in case another tropical tempest should come along. Hix also decided to leave the outside raw and unpainted. What he created was both practically and aesthetically a tropical bunker – a poignant design direction in light of the island's recent history. Vieques, a twenty-minute flight from Puerto Rico's capital San Juan, didn't used to be much of a tourist destination. That's because most of the island served as a base for the United States navy, who used it for combat exercise and shooting practice. Even the beaches were codenamed for war-games, hence Red Beach, Blue Beach, Purple Beach, etc. It was paradise wasted. The locals certainly thought so: the navy's presence was highly unpopular, and whenever they could, the citizens of Vieques would venture out in little boats and enter restricted zones just to make their message felt. Even the island's mayor did a stretch in the brig. In the end it was a tragic accident that triggered the US forces to pull up stakes. A navy employee was killed when he left his bunker for a smoke during bombing exercises. When the navy departed, it handed over to the American fish and wildlife authority, who turned the entire area of the base into the largest wildlife reserve in the Caribbean. Which is great news for travellers, because it means none of the island's unspoilt beaches are available for development – not a house, not a hotel, not even a snack shack. The beaches are as they should be: totally empty.

As so often with highly individual places, Hix Island House was never planned as a hotel. It evolved into one because John Hix figured it was high time some of his friends started to pay. So he built more villas, each in his signature bunker style. At first glance, the suites of Hix Island House have more in common with a big city loft than a Caribbean

Owner-architect John Hix has designed sophisticated spaces perfectly suited to a tropical environment

Towering blade-like walls that alternately hide and reveal tropical vistas are one of many modernist tricks used at the house

Design details at Hix Island House are pervasively linear, like this floating day bed suspended by stainless-steel cables

Intersecting planes highlighted by dramatic shadow – the visual intricacy is a treat for photographers

The massive concrete walls and panoramic cutouts of the loft-like spaces combine enclosure and exposure

DIY Rietveldt. A design classic made from marine ply – simple and affordable, just as modern design was meant to be

The luxury of the interior is in the space, the location and the view rather than the raw materials

All of the loft-like studios are in raw concrete, except for this single room rendered in adobe-coloured wash

Bathrooms are stylishly composed of thick slabs of polished concrete – powerful geometry in the tropics

Without the surrounding dense greenery, the expanses of bare concrete could have been depressing

There's nothing conventionally Caribbean about these Philippe Starck armchairs and angle-poise tripod lamps

The monochromatic calm of concrete floors, walls and ceilings is interrupted only by vivid Marimekko bedspreads

The first of John Hix's hurricane-proof buildings was based on the triangle, the strongest geometrical shape

The cleverly conceived studios feel as if they are open to the elements, yet during a storm the bed will remain dry

A studio entrance ascends through a two-storey void. This is an architecture of ritual and drama

Like a true bunker, Hix Island House is almost entirely hidden by the surrounding jungle

Massive architectural cutouts bring tropical breezes and views of the jungle into the pared-down interiors

Formerly the site of a huge US naval base, Vieques is home to the biggest wildlife reserve in the Caribbean

island hideaway. Yet these open-plan shapes, with polished concrete floors and huge unglazed cutouts framing postcard views, are perfect for the tropics. The building's design allows the reliable trade winds to circulate, eliminating the need for air-conditioning. Which is typical of the ecologically sensitive spirit of Hix Island House. Electricity is generated by solar panels, the water from the showers irrigates the lush tropical fruit garden, and the handsomely designed swimming pool uses a low-chemical cleaning system.

The impression created by these Caribbean lofts is that of being on a boat, and at night it's like sleeping on deck. The architecture blurs the distinction between outside and inside. One end of your loft is exposed to the elements, yet your bed is far enough inside never to get wet. You can experience a tropical downpour without closing a single window – there are none. Hix Island House is the tropics amplified by modern architecture and design. It's not just

that each loft is around four times the size of a typical hotel room, but the sense of space is boosted by the openness to the elements. It's all about visual sensation – a far more sophisticated tool than merely fluffy towels or Frette linens (though you do get these too).

A certain sort of rugged simplicity asserts itself with the fact that the hotel has no room service, no restaurant, no café and no bar. The message is clear. We give you a great space to stay, you entertain and feed yourself. Each suite has a fully equipped kitchen and a well-stocked fridge, and the bread delivered to your room each morning is baked fresh on the premises. The hotel is run by a couple who have both done their fair share of globetrotting. They will give you directions to the island's most remote beaches at the drop of a hat, but they are not likely to send into town for your favourite painkiller or designer vodka. This, after all, is no place for princesses.

---

address Hix Island House, HC-02 Box 14902, Vieques, Puerto Rico 00765

t (1) 787 741 2302   **f** (1) 787 741 2797   **e** info@hixislandhouse.com

room rates from US $190

cibolo creek ranch

Big hats, big boots, big stakes, big egos, big ranches, big money – the vast state of Texas conjures some vivid images. Even before *Dallas* brought the Southfork brand of Texas lifestyle into hundreds of millions of homes around the globe, we had exotic expectations of this one-time Mexican territory. Think of Texas and we think of its distinctive longhorn cattle, of ranches the size of small countries, of roping, riding, rodeo-loving cowboys, of dust storms, oil derricks, and self-made millionaires chewing tobacco and riding their horses to the doors of their private planes.

In reality, Texas is much more like the world we inhabit, full of shopping malls, freeways and suburban sprawl. Even outside the continually expanding urban areas, Texas these days is more a state of "ranchettes" than ranches. These are not the dusty, never-ending spreads featured in the movie *Giant* – more like big suburban houses that happen to have huge yards and miles of neat white fencing.

There really aren't too many big ranches left in Texas. So it's lucky that one of the most authentic and impressive takes paying guests. Cibolo Creek is 30,000 acres of perfection, a three-dimensional expression of all our most romantic Texas fantasies. Its authenticity is only accentuated by the time it takes to get there. A twelve-hour drive from Houston or four hours from the nearest commercial airport at El Paso, El Cibolo is situated in El Despoblado (literally, the uninhabited), an enormous, virtually empty tract of land in Texas's Big Bend. This is and always was the perfect place to be a cattle baron.

Almost two hundred years ago Milton Faver, or Don Melitón as he came to be known, arrived at the border town of Presidio del Norte, apparently on the run after killing a man in a duel. He married a Mexican woman from an influential family and made some money trading Mexican goods with newly arrived settlers. When the United States army built Fort Davis in Big Bend, it was clear they would need beef and other provisions, and Don Melitón saw his opportunity to launch a cattle ranching venture. The terrain he selected was half-way between the fort and the Mexican border in a mountainous region that benefitted not just from a cooler climate but also from a creek that continued to flow even in the most arid weather. Don Melitón approached the development of his 30,000 acres with more care and forethought than one might expect in the Wild West. First and foremost, to protect against marauding bands of Apache and the even more ruthless Comanche, he built a rectangular adobe fort with walls over three feet thick.

This structure was large enough to house his family and shelter his horses and livestock in the event of a raid. As his operation grew Faver built two more forts (La Cienega and La Morita) and diversified into goats and sheep as well as the famous longhorn. By his death, Don Melitón had indeed become a proper cattle baron.

When Houstonian John Poindexter came across El Cibolo in 1990, it was a pale shadow of its former self. But the creek still flowed, and it was this constant supply of clear fresh water that clinched his decision to pick up where Faver had left off. What was left of the old main fort had been whitewashed, and Poindexter found it surrounded by rusting junk, its fences long since fallen down and its roads barely passable. But Poindexter had made his fortune picking up down-and-out companies and turning them around, so he was not fazed by the scale of his task. He brought in an army of workers from Mexico to painstakingly reconstruct the three forts using hand-made sunbaked adobe bricks. He invested in irrigation, built extensive stretches of dry wall, and reintroduced the longhorn herd.

But Poindexter was interested in recreating the lifestyle as well as the look. So at night all of El Cibolo's guests eat together at one enormous table. Instead of television and telephones (guestrooms have neither) there's coffee around an outdoor open fire after dinner. Rooms have adobe fireplaces and big old frontier beds, verandas are adorned with saddles and colourful horse blankets and the floors are laid with traditional baked tiles.

El Cibolo has the vast untouched landscape, the endless sky, the crystal-clear air, and the deafening silence we all crave. This is a ranch where you can rope a calf, climb a canyon, or raft down the nearby Rio Grande. Or you can do nothing at all. Either way, you won't ever get closer than this to your own private Ponderosa.

address Cibolo Creek Ranch, PO Box 44, Marfa, Texas 79843, USA

t (1) 432 229 3737 **f** (1) 432 229 3653 **e** reservations@cibolocreekranch.com

room rates from US $400 (including meals)

sundance

The sign on Interstate 15 to Salt Lake City pointed to Sundance. I took the turn-off and immediately started to worry. If Sundance was signposted so prominently perhaps it wasn't the perfectly preserved little mountain hideaway I had hoped for. Less than forty minutes later, my fears were put to rest. My rentacar was slipping backwards down a narrow mountain pass at an alarming rate, and another car coming down had just slid into the canyon's creek. Even big rugged four-wheel drives were coming down the twisting mountain road like toboggans. Believe it or not, this mayhem was a welcome sign. Here was a mountain road that looked like a mountain road, unlike the six-lane freeways to resorts like Vail, Colorado. If the road isn't compromised, I thought, then the place itself probably isn't either.

I was right. Located on the slopes of the breathtaking 12,000-foot (3,600-metre) Mount Timpanogos, Sundance is as authentic as the treacherous road that leads there. Robert Redford's commitment to the environment and his sensitivity to the creative process – to design, architecture and landscaping – make it unique in the American West. It all started over thirty years ago, when Redford was looking for a place to live and raise his children. It was known as Timphaven then, a small ski resort tucked away in the folds of Utah's spectacular Wasatch mountains. Redford knew the terrain and he decided to purchase a parcel of land to build a house for his wife and family. But the close proximity to Salt Lake City worried him. He feared it was only a matter of time before property developers stepped in and ruined the place. So he made a trip to New York and managed to secure enough investors to buy the entire valley. That way he could ensure that Sundance, as he renamed it, would stay just as it was.

The name refers to a ritual of the local Ute Indians – but obviously also pays tribute to one of Redford's most memorable roles in *Butch Cassidy and the Sundance Kid*. Appropriately enough, Sundance is a place that was created with a film director's eye. Wherever you look, from the strategically placed Native American art and Wild West craft, to the rustic barn-like architecture, the carefully landscaped paths that connect cabins and restaurants, even the graphics on the staff t-shirts, it's clear that compromise is not a word Redford chooses to be familiar with. The Owl Bar, for instance, is the original 1890s rosewood bar rescued from Thermopolis, an old Wyoming town once frequented by Butch Cassidy's Hole in the Wall gang. There are also two restaurants, the Tree Room and the Foundry Grill, as

THE OWL BAR

Sundance, Utah

OPENING TIMES

MONDAY - FRIDAY 4:00 PM ~ 12:00 AM

well as the General Store, the mountaintop 'snack shack' Bear Claw's Cabin and the equipment rental shop. Sundance has been an evolving project since 1969. The first job was to get rid of the remnants of Timphaven, which included a 1960s burger joint named Ki-Te-Kai, Samoan for 'come and get it'. The only thing that has survived from old Timphaven is Ray's Lift, which is still called Ray's Lift.

As far as the skiing goes, I was without expectations. But it snowed all night and the potential for fresh tracks was motivation to set the alarm early. Much as many locals will not thank me for exposing their secret – Sundance is simply a great place for experiencing Utah's legendary powder. It's true there are only three lifts, but they go for miles and ultimately take you to a mountain that's surprisingly steep and with surprisingly long runs. My absolute favourite is Bishop's Bowl, which ends in a long half-pipe-like gully. In larger resorts such a beautiful open bowl would be

'skied out' in minutes. At Sundance they limit the number of people on the mountain.

The plan from the beginning was to make Sundance both a recreational and an arts community. It was not all, as one might assume, smooth sailing. In Redford's own words: 'The first year I couldn't get a loan from the bank. The waiters didn't show up…. Vehicles stalled, sewers backed up, we were robbed, and the tree in the Tree Room died.' Despite all, Redford has managed not only to maintain the beauty of the place but to preserve the character of a small local village. A guy I met in the Owl Bar had been skiing here since before it was Sundance and more than thirty years later it's still his favourite mountain. 'You should see it on a Sunday,' he said with a grin, 'it's the best place to ski in the entire Rockies.' Why Sunday? Because Provo, the nearest town, ten minutes down the road, is ninety per cent Mormon – and Mormons do not ski on Sundays.

---

address Sundance, RR3, A-1 Sundance, Utah 84604, USA

t (1) 801 225 4100 **f** (1) 801 226 1937 **e** Reservations@Sundance-Utah.com

room rates from US $215

canoe bay

Wisconsin? Why go to Wisconsin?

One very good reason is that Frank Lloyd Wright designed no fewer than two hundred houses here. This was also where he built Taliesin, the groundbreaking compound he used as retreat, design laboratory, showcase, intellectual hub and the counterpart to his winter compound in Arizona, Taliesin West. Wisconsin was the creative breeding ground for Wright's innovative Prairie Style, and yet sadly today the state is better known for its cheese and its football team, the Green Bay Packers. Fortunately, there are enthusiasts keeping the legacy of this great American architect alive. Dan Dobrowolski, proprietor of Canoe Bay, is a self-confessed Frank Lloyd Wright fanatic, and should you have any time to spare after you leave his compound he can provide you with a detailed tour itinerary of all the most important Wright buildings that can still be visited in the state.

Situated in the northwest corner of Wisconsin, a six-hour drive north of Chicago and not too far from Lake Superior, Canoe Bay is located on three private lakes in a setting that is eerily reminiscent of *On Golden Pond*. It's an idyllic situation of virgin forests and pure waters. In fact the privacy and beauty are such that really any old shack would do here. But not for Dan Dobrowolski and his wife Lisa. His laid-back, easy-going style belies a total commitment to aesthetic standards and a mentality more like that of an artist than a hotelier. It was quite a gutsy move, for instance, to design a hotel in which none of the rooms has a telephone, especially given that each guest cabin is quite remote from the next (not to mention the reception house). But Dobrowolski wants his guests to leave behind their city lifestyles. So if you want something from reception, you have to walk there.

The real testament to Dobrowolski's remarkable sensibility is the architecture. One of the most beautiful of Canoe Bay's cabins looks convincingly like a Frank Lloyd Wright design in miniature, and not by coincidence. It was designed by John Rattenbury, one of Wright's best and most trusted students, who still lives at Taliesin West in Arizona. Apart from his own work as an architect, Rattenbury is a senior fellow of the Frank Lloyd Wright School of Architecture. This cabin is essentially a studio in layout, and the design is thoroughly bewitching in its use of materials and intersecting planes and angles. Indeed, architecturally speaking, it is to a shack what Fabergé is to an egg.

You certainly don't have to be an architecture junkie to appreciate Canoe Bay. Nature is the premier drawing card here. There are kayaks and rowboats in which to explore Lake Wahdoon, and in winter you can ice-skate or go cross-country skiing. The restaurant is almost as spectacular as the scenery, built and furnished in a style that again borrows from Wright (although not in this case designed by Rattenbury). It specializes in stylized versions of local produce: dishes such as shiitake and cremini mushroom soup, locally caught rainbow trout in cranberry butter, and rack of lamb with hazelnut crust.

So just how did Rusk County, Wisconsin, end up with the only Relais & Châteaux property in the American Midwest? Canoe Bay's estate, comprising 280 acres of lush forest and three private lakes, originally belonged to Ezra Cornell, who donated it in 1874 to Cornell University in New York. Proceeds from the sale of the land and its timber provided funds to construct the university's first buildings. In the 1960s the property was developed as a retreat, but it had fallen into disuse by the late 1980s. Dobrowolski had explored these forests and fished on Lake Wahdoon in his childhood. In 1992 he bought the entire property and left behind his career as an Emmy-award winning meteorologist with ABC and Fox to concentrate on building his vision of a wilderness retreat for grown-ups.

The couples-only policy makes this one of the United States' most romantic retreats. Just how good is Canoe Bay? Well, *Condé Nast Traveler* voted it one of the best three lakeshore hotels in North America, *Travel & Leisure* named it Inn of the Month, and *Bon Appétit* praised its extraordinary comfort and cuisine. But ask Dan Dobrowolski about his creation and he'll give you a cheeky smile. 'What do I know?' he'll reply. 'I'm just a guy who lives in the woods.'

address Canoe Bay, PO Box 28, Chetek, Wisconsin 54728, USA
t (1) 715 924 4594   **f** (1) 715 924 2078   **e** mail@canoebay.com
room rates from US $325

Frédéric Legrip del.   Schroeder Sculp.

SOUTH AMERICA

When, during the first half of the twentieth century, the world turned itself upside down with a world war, a financial depression and then another world war, people turned to South America as a place to start again. Brazil, Uruguay, Argentina, Chile and Peru attracted millions of displaced Europeans, exhausted by bitter battles and desperate to start over in a land not yet jaded by cynicism.

Unlike the Orient, South America never really captured popular imagination because of its exoticism (with the exception, of course, of Rio and Carnival), but there's a seductive optimism to the place that's reflected in the architecture and design, as well as the lifestyle. When we think of South America, from the sleepy beach-shack aesthetic of Brazil's Bahia, to the vast *estancia* country of the Argentinian gaucho, to the wild virgin frontier of Patagonia, we think of a culture inextricably linked to a way of life.

Mention Brazil and the mind conjures up beach life and the captivating refrains of the samba, or the beach-born lambada. Mention Argentina and it's the tango – a lilting, mesmerising combination of Italian showmanship and Spanish heat. We associate North America with physical manifestations, such as the skyscrapers of New York City or the mountains and canyons of America's West … but South America is the only continent defined as much by music and dance as by its natural beauty. It's a simple but significant difference. South America is a destination for doing, as much as merely watching.

Sure, you can go just to see the famous Iguazú Falls, or the magnificent ruins of Machu Picchu, but if you only go for the sights you will have missed the most appealing aspect of South America – its people. Only in this continent have the world's populations been truly mixed.

We now know that the people of pre-Columbian South America, the Incas of the mighty Andes, for instance, descended from nomadic tribes that made their way over from China via the Bering Sea. Then came the bearded white conquerors from Europe, as well as the slave labour brought over from Africa to work the plantations and mines established by the imperial Spanish. Add to this the significant number of Japanese who came to work in the burgeoning paper industry of the 1900s and you have a complete global melting pot of race, colour and culture. Perhaps it's this lack of hereditary homogeneity that has set the place free – a population where variety is not a reason for suspicion, but a source of celebration.

yacutinga lodge

A Jesuit priest tied to an enormous wooden cross, floating down the Iguazú River, heading towards a cacophony of roaring water, and then tumbling spectacularly, for an eternity, down the awe-inspiring Iguazú Falls.... This for me is the most memorable and enduring image from *The Mission*.

The story depicted in the film, or at least much of it, is true. Jesuits came to this part of South America, built missions and worked with the Guaraní Indians, but the order was ultimately persecuted and expelled. Despite the eventual destruction of the missions, the area to this day retains the name Misiones, and Iguazú in Misiones has become one of the most popular destinations in South America.

Who would not want to visit a place as phenomenal as this? Together with North America's Niagara and Africa's Victoria, the Falls of Iguazú are the most famous in the world. As a spectacle they can't be equalled, nor can they be separated from their exotic geography. They are located in a splendid subtropical rainforest. Yet Iguazú tourism seems to take little notice of this jungle setting. The town has a shiny new airport, hotels are big concrete boxes with lots of glass and the odd casino, and the Falls, sadly, are treated like a Las Vegas show – a vehicle to get people to come and gamble and spend money; something to do in between poker, dinner and drinks. No one saw the rainforest as a unique experience in its own right ... until the arrival, in 1998, of an adventure tour operator from Patagonia.

Carlos 'Charlie' Sandoval started out as a ski instructor in Bariloche and eventually built a company that specialized in taking people into the wilds of Patagonia to ski, kayak, climb and hike; to interact with the area's natural beauty, not just admire it. Then he moved to Paraguay and started another travel operation that specialized in logistics for scientific expeditions. Ultimately his experience with adventure and science was combined in what today is Yacutinga Lodge – a private slice of intriguing and inspiring rainforest on the banks of the Iguazú River.

Convinced that the extraordinary fauna and flora concealed beneath the jungle's vivid green canopy would be an exciting alternative to air-conditioned 'couch-potato' tourism, Charlie began to plan the creation of his jungle lodge. Architecturally it had to fit in with the organic chaos of the jungle, and symbolically it had to be ready for the year of the millennium. Both goals were achieved – a remarkable feat considering the difficulties involved in working in an area that is virtually inaccessible.

Soaring height, beautiful light, earthy colours....
The organic style is inspired by, and a direct result of,
the surrounding rainforest

Situated alongside the Iguazú River,
the lodge is about forty miles upstream
from the famous Falls

Discarded glass is used to create unique
decorative walls of colour, shape and light –
an inspired example of recycling

The vibrant reds, oranges and yellows of heliconia
are all the more extravagant amongst Yacutinga's
dense jungle green

The long, rectangular, organic-tribal guestrooms
feature an open-plan bathroom
and a private veranda

Almost completely hidden by the jungle,
cleverly camouflaged pavilions emerge only
upon closer inspection

Natural, rugged, and with not a straight line in sight,
the construction is a perfect mirror of the
surrounding subtropical jungle

To get to Yacutinga, a hot, eerily quiet hour
is spent gliding on a narrow river boat down
to the lodge's private dock

In the upstairs dining room, which has a view
onto the living area below, exotic Brazilian timbers
create a warm ambience

The big, brawny Mercedes truck used as
hotel transport is driven by Antonio,
an Argentine version of Crocodile Dundee

Tree trunks, branches and twigs – atmospheric jungle
debris – have played their part in the unusual
construction of the lodge

The road into the jungle is a ribbon of dark red earth,
weaving its way through a semi-tunnel
of leafy green foliage

Trees are used to support the structure and
walls are plastered in a natural ochre.
Lamps, pots and urns are made locally

Even the swimming pool, perfectly camouflaged
by exotic trees, is more of a swimming hole
from *The Jungle Book*

The interior of the main lodge is a surprisingly
spacious and airy affair, considering it is situated
in the deep, dark depths of the jungle

ght green, dark green, emerald green … all green.
The experience of Yacutinga is a uniquely
monochromatic one

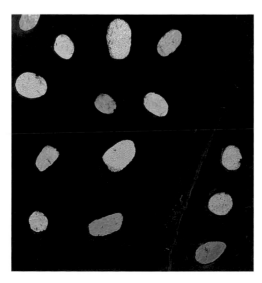

Yacutinga's highly original decoration:
as if Gaudí had turned up to create his
version of Art Nouveau in the jungle

A long plate of glass and a staircase cut from
cleared logs are the only hints that a
sizeable building is hiding here

All the guest bungalows and the main lodge are disguised by the creeping green of jungle climbers, and utilizing found timber and building in local materials such as mud brick and corrugated sheet iron, a style evolved that could be called 'camouflage organic'. Gaudí in the jungle.

But Yacutinga, as Charlie is quick to point out, is not about the style of the lodge. It's about the rainforest. All over the world rainforests are a threatened phenomenon and yet, with their incredible diversity of plants and animals, they may hold the key to important discoveries, such as new pharmaceuticals. The master plan behind Yacutinga is to raise awareness of the importance of rainforests by turning them into a travel experience; a travel experience that does not harm the fragile eco-balance of the jungle but at the same time does not hold back either.

One look at Yacutinga's idea of hotel transport – a big old Mercedes truck with a camouflage paint job and rows of schoolbenches bolted to its flat-plate (looking like a prop from an Indiana Jones film) – tells you this is no ordinary hotel experience.

Whilst in residence, guests are taken on rafting trips down forgotten tributaries of the Iguazú and on hikes along carefully monitored jungle paths which are likely to reveal monkeys, parrots and other neighbours. Even in the camp itself, I almost tripped several times over a bunch of iguanas the size of poodles, baking in the humid heat.

My award for Most Original Jungle Experience, however, has to go to the after-dinner lecture by the resident scientist from Yacutinga's own *estación biológica*. The theme was what to do if you encounter a big snake, and the stars were a collection of extraordinarily impressive reptiles, making their début in the bar to help illustrate basic do's and don'ts. Snake lover or no, you could not fail to be impressed by this reptilian version of Siegfried and Roy.

---

address Yacutinga Lodge, Lote 7 A, Colonia Andresito, 3371 Almirante Brown, Misiones, Argentina

e yacutinga@yacutinga.net

room rates from US $385 (2 nights, all-inclusive)

los notros

'Everything here breathes the solitary air of the end of the world. Everything here has the aroma of the first day of the planet.' The elegant words of Sylvia Iparraguirre sum up Patagonia as best as mere words can. So many writers, including Paul Theroux and the late Bruce Chatwin, have devoted lengthy tomes to this wild, empty, captivating terrain in the southern extreme of South America. And still it continues to elude capture (in the literary sense).

Patagonia is like nowhere else. By virtue of its individuality and odd beauty, it defies description as well as comparison with any other destination on the planet. You can't say, it reminds me of Switzerland or New Zealand or Scotland or wherever, because it doesn't. Nor is there one single outstanding element to its uniqueness. It is a sum of its peculiarly diverse parts: of its barren, unending steppes (named after the Russian steppes), its snow-capped mountains and massive blue ice glaciers, its beaches that extend thousands of feet at low tide, its salmon-filled rivers in strange luminescent greens, its dense verdant forests that adorn granite-capped peaks with trees of unusual shapes and unpronounceable names. It's a world unto itself … and it's a world you're not obliged to share with very many others.

Despite being twice as large as California in terms of land mass, Patagonia has one of the lowest population densities on earth. The state of Santa Cruz, for instance, is the same size as all of Great Britain, and yet only 160,000 people live here. This great emptiness only amplifies the majesty of the place. It's not a region that lends itself to human proportion, and perhaps therein lies its mesmerising power. Like the cathedrals of the Middle Ages, this vast wilderness inspires awe – even in people who've had their fair share of adventure and travel.

But where to start? You could spend a couple of years in a car, drive more than 9,000 miles along routes 40 or 3, and you still would not have seen all of the Provincia de Santa Cruz. And this is the beauty of Los Notros. As the only hotel in the Parque Nacional Los Glaciares, situated bang opposite one of Patagonia's most impressive glaciers, it provides a powerful intro. From every room, every window, any table, chair or couch, even from the bathtub, you are bewitched by a sea of glowing blue ice that is slowly creeping towards you. Because of its size and the dazzling way it reflects light, you can't stop looking at it.

And yet the view from Los Notros, spellbinding as it may be, is nothing compared to getting up close. Just in

Warm, rustic, cocoon-like, the guestrooms
are a welcome contrast to the imposing
brutality of the surrounding nature

From the front terrace, the immense expanse of
Perito Moreno's blue ice comes straight at you –
if only at a speed of a few centimetres a day

The interior's rich reds and bright greens are inspired
by Patagonia's original hand-built timber shacks,
usually painted with leftover boat paint

Unlike the rest of the province of Santa Cruz, which is extremely arid, the area near the mountains is extremely wet – hence all the ice

As the only hotel inside the Parque Nacional Los Glaciares, Los Notros showcases the extraordinary natural beauty of this southern tip of Argentina

Over three miles long, and rising seventy metres above the milky water of Lago Argentino, the Perito Moreno glacier is as large as the city of Buenos Aires

front of the hotel, you can embark on a boat that takes you to within spitting distance of the seventy-metre-high wall of ice that extends for a length of three miles and occupies roughly the same area in square miles as the entire city of Buenos Aires (which is saying something, because the city of over ten million is *vast*). Occasionally the silence is broken by a thunderous clap as a few thousand tons of ice tumble into the milky glacial water of Lago Argentino, the third largest lake in South America. If you're feeling more adventurous, you can disembark at the southern end of the glacier, strap on crampons and hike along the crevasses and shiny, diamond-like faces of the Perito Moreno glacier.

The purpose of Los Notros is to provide adventure, and the hotel's extraordinary location is a great start. In fact, from the moment you arrive, the emphasis is on how best to tailor your discovery expeditions. Checking in is more about establishing activity priorities than filling in a guest register.

The message is clear: you, as visitor, are privileged to lodge in such incredible surroundings and you should definitely make the best of it. And visitors do. During the day the hotel is virtually deserted: guests are off on glacier trips, climbing expeditions, boat excursions to remote ranches and so on. The diverse experiences on offer are as exciting and as dangerous as you want them to be.

At the end of the day Los Notros is a brilliant hotel to come home to. In contrast to Patagonia's severe beauty, it is cosy and on a distinctly human scale. The kitchen is excellent, but not too exotic (there's lots of lamb: the area is famous for it). The bedrooms are warm and cocoon-like, with a touch of that Alpine *Gemütlichkeit*.

Perhaps most importantly Los Notros is a sterling example that tourism doesn't have to spoil a place. Michel Biquard's lodge doesn't intrude into this divine wilderness, it merely makes it more accessible … and more enjoyable.

---

address Los Notros, Perito Moreno Glacier, Patagonia, Argentina
t (54) 11 4814 3934 **f** (54) 11 4815 7645 **e** info@losnotros.com
room rates from US $885 (2 nights, all-inclusive)

pousada picinguaba

Mention Picinguaba to most Brazilians and the likely response will be, Picin where? Fishermen and the odd foreigner in search of the unspoiled, pure beauty of Brazil's Atlantic coast know about it; nobody else does. Located exactly halfway between São Paulo and Rio de Janeiro, just north of the Tropic of Capricorn, Picinguaba is the best-kept secret in Brazil.

To call this area breathtakingly beautiful does not do it justice. Big mountains, clad in the vivid glistening emerald green of primal (as in, never having been forested) tropical rainforest, tumble down into the swimming-pool blue of the Atlantic, forming a continuous series of bends and curves, defining one hidden gem of a beach after another. It's the kind of setting that would be perfect for a film about the first European explorers, because there are no people, no houses, no buildings, no telegraph poles, no sign in fact of this century: just nature in its most extravagant livery.

But if you look very carefully, tucked into one little corner of this virgin coastline is the tiny fishing village of Picinguaba: ten houses, two churches, a couple of bars and a *padaria* (bakery) just about sum the whole place up.

In the morning the men push their traditional hollowed log canoes into the water, paddle to their colourful wooden fishing boats, and do what their fathers and their fathers' fathers did before them – catch squid, grouper and other local fish, and then wait for the merchants to arrive in their trucks to sell the catch (the locals have no cars and so are dependent on the wholesalers from the city).

It's hard to believe, when you're here, that the giant metropolis of São Paulo (twenty million-plus inhabitants) is only a three-and-a-half-hour drive away.... That's exactly what expat Frenchman Emmanuel Rengade thought when he first stumbled across Picinguaba, by accident, on one last trip along the Brazilian coast before heading off to London to take on a new corporate assignment. An enthusiastic fan of South America, Rengade had worked for a year in Bolivia, followed by four years in São Paulo. Careerwise he was making his way up the ladder of a large multinational corporation, but his heart wasn't in it. Secretly he longed for something more adventurous, a life out of the box ... which he found in the form of a colonial mansion hidden away amongst the jungle foliage of the forgotten town of Picinguaba.

Immediately Rengade knew exactly what to do with the property: make it an escape destination for people with a taste for adventure. With its whitewashed walls and

traditional facade, the result is a romantic reminder of Brazil's colonial Portuguese past.

Considering its idyllic location, perched high on a hill with sweeping views of an immense stretch of beach in the distance, it would be tempting to stay within the compound, lounge by the pool and enjoy the fantastic food, which consists largely of the catch of the day. But not if Emmanuel can help it. He wants guests to experience the truly unique attributes of the surroundings. That's why the hotel has its own forty-foot schooner anchored directly below. Guests can take the boat to picnic on an empty beach, or to watch schools of porpoises at play.

The hotel also organizes mini-expeditions into the rainforest to find waterfalls, as well as sea-kayaking trips to explore uncharted beaches. The difference at Picinguaba is that when they say these attractions are next door, it's not a euphemism for a forty-five-minute drive.

One morning, for example, Emmanuel and I checked out the local surf beach, five minutes by car from the hotel, and then disappeared into the jungle to climb a moss-covered pile of gigantic boulders to get to a spectacular waterfall, complete with its own swimming hole. After sliding on our *derrières* back down the slippery stone path of another waterfall, we made our way out of the jungle towards a headland where a local river empties into the Atlantic. By swimming across the headland, we managed to arrive back at the beach directly underneath the hotel. Total time taken by these mini-adventures: two hours. Length of time they will remain a fond memory: forever.

And therein lies the real appeal of Picinguaba. For those travellers who want to escape to a destination where nature is uncultivated, untamed and in large part unexplored, and which doesn't take half a work-week to get to, Picinguaba is hard, if not impossible, to beat.

---

address Pousada Picinguaba, Rua G, 130, Vila Picinguaba, 11680-000 Ubatuba-SP, Brazil
t & f (55) 12 3836 9105 **e** info@picinguaba.com
room rates from BRL 540

vila naiá

If Charles and Ray Eames had decided to drop out and live in a shack on the beach in Brazil, this is what their place might have looked like. In fact Vila Naiá would appeal to most designers and architects because it has real architectural and aesthetic integrity, i.e. it's very well designed. With lots of timber, lots of space and plenty of privacy, it's intelligently laid out and follows architect Glen Murcutt's famous dictum of 'touching the earth lightly'.

The hotel is bang on the beach but thankfully, for once, the preservation of beach ecology was a primary consideration – to the degree that this 42-hectare compound is classified by the government as an ecological wildlife sanctuary.

All over the world, time and time again, property developers make the same mistake. They fail to take into account that a beach is a constantly changing environment; that sand moves in two directions – up into the dunes and back down towards the water. When a great big block of concrete goes up, the sand can't shift as it's supposed to and the beach eventually disappears. At Vila Naiá they have understood this very well, and that is why the entire complex has been built on wooden stilts – even the walkways between various buildings, with trees growing through their elevated timber slats, to ensure that people don't disturb the natural state of the environment. It sounds strict but in reality guests aren't dragooned into the environmental aspect; they probably just think it's a good way to stop dragging sand into their room.

The interiors of Vila Naiá are equally exceptional – a curious but clever mix of Eames pieces and other design classics, such as oval Saarinen tables, with rugged timber walls, and wooden floors, and concrete (polished and plain), and the odd fifties lamp or vase or glass object. Innovative, unusual, superbly comfortable but appropriately simple, Vila Naiá is how a beach shack should be … and Ponta do Corumbau on Bahia's southern coast is *where* that beach shack should be.

Corumbau is a small fishing town, and nothing more. It's not the next Punta, or South America's answer to St-Tropez. It's a fishing village … people fish … that's it. There are no roads, no hippies, and when you fly over you wouldn't notice it if it weren't for its crescent-shaped sand-bank protruding half a mile into the light blue Atlantic.

This is predominantly ranch country and from the air all you see are mahogany-coloured rivers, sizeable clearings for cattle and the odd strip of dense, untouched green leading

As far as the eye can see, there is nothing on the beach … just sand, sea and sun

The guest apartment bathrooms blend the submerged mosaic-tiled soaking-tub Japanese aesthetic with the ruggedness of a beach shack

Elevating the bleached wooden pathways on big beams allows the sand to shift as nature intended

Eames classics, modern lamps and walls of local timber left dark and untreated: the prevailing design signature of Vila Naiá

This part of Bahia's coast is still so pristine and undeveloped that the only footprints in the sand are likely to be yours

Exceptional visual detail: a splash of colour distinguishes each guestroom

Running alongside the beach is the area's only road, a palm-tree-lined, red-dirt track that, seemingly, leads to infinity

A small living room divides each of the four guest apartments: a cool but cosy place to 'kick back' after a day on the beach

Timber decking, thatched roofs, terracotta tiles, white sand and plenty of palm trees define Vila Naiá's outdoor aesthetic

The dining pavilion is a funky combination of Brazilian beach cabaña and classic international modernism – definitely for beach bums with refined taste

The only hint in the surroundings that Vila Naiá exists is its discreet organic timber fence

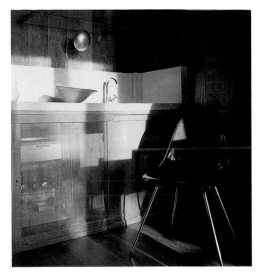

Even the kitchens in the three guest bungalows reflect the signature interior treatment of roughly textured timber, modern lighting and design classics

An elevated timber-planked pathway leads straight to the beach: easy on the eye, easy on the environment and easy on your feet

Adjacent to the swimming pool, there's a pavilion partially paved in white marble, which at night becomes the après-dinner reading room

In constructing Vila Naiá, not a single tree was touched. The jetty-like pathways that connect the pavilions circumvent existing trees

The guest apartments are arranged parallel to the beach to allow ocean breezes to waft straight through

The small hut is the spa, where you can have a massage facing out to sea (the basket on the roof houses wild peacocks)

The four apartments have been allotted the same space and architecture, but the decor is unique to each room

to the sea. The beaches go on for miles and miles, with not a person or building to be seen. People who want a lively town to go with their fabulous beach escape should not come here. If, however, you want to be in a place where the only footprints in the sand are yours, then you should – but don't forget to bring a good book. Vila Naiá is definitely for people who know how to entertain themselves and who understand the value of a place that you don't have to share with busloads of others.

There are two ways to get to Naiá – by private plane or by private boat. Both will leave you with plenty of dinner-party material. The boat picked me up – as in, I waded to it with my camera bag on my shoulder – from the beach at Trancoso. The crew spoke no English. But it's not that complicated. You sit on deck (in the shade) and watch endless beaches go by. Every hour on the hour the engine breaks down, but the crew don't seem too worried by it.

Relax, they say, this is Bahia! Eventually, just past the sand-banks of Corumbau, you wade back in.

Flying back to Porto Seguro is more of an adventure. First you climb into a car that has seen better days, then you hurtle down a dusty red path that is not so much a road as a treeless ribbon of earth. The car bounces along until you come to a hut, a fence and a cow. Open the fence, drive through the middle of a paddock, purposefully scaring the goats and sheep witless, and, hey presto, you're on the local airstrip – a rough little stretch of red dirt with palm trees either side and the azure Atlantic at one end.

What's impressive about the plane journey is the view of never-ending crescents of sand with no one on them. There's probably a ratio of one person per every 20 miles of beach. For the truly adventurous, you could get a horse in Trancoso and gallop along the shore for two days while your bags come by boat. Try doing that in the south of France....

---

address Vila Naiá, Corumbau, Bahia, Brazil

t (55) 73 573 1006 **f** (55) 11 3088 4252 **e** info@vilanaia.com.br

room rates from BRL 680 (including meals)

pousada etnia

Hippy chic, with a samba rhythm, in Brazilian crayon colours. That's the appeal of Trancoso. Thirty years ago you'd be forgiven for never having heard of the place. It was a simple fishing village on the endlessly picturesque (i.e. blessed with long, long beaches) coast of Bahia. There were no roads to it – at least, not paved ones – and that suited the alternative community just fine. Getting away from Brazil's conservative military regime was part of their plan, and it worked, because, as Brazilians will tell you, they were not in Brazil; they were in Bahia. A real hippy culture flourished, with little sophistication and no mod cons: a case of, 'I have a chicken. You have some marijuana. Let's trade.'

It may not have been sophisticated but there was a reason why the hippies chose Trancoso. It was, and still is – thanks to a UNESCO Heritage listing – very beautiful. The tiny town consists of nothing more than wooden fishermen's shacks, painted impossibly bright colours, and a whitewashed church, but it has the distinction that all of its buildings are arranged along a *quadrado* – a barefoot interpretation of a village square. Except that this square is really a rather long rectangle with grass in the middle (where the donkeys and horses graze), sand on the edges and exotic trees, like frangipani, providing shade for the paintbox

fishermen's cottages on either side. At the far end of the quadrado stands the church, and both it and the cemetery next to it – perhaps predictably – have the best view of the beaches below.

With such charm and ethnic beauty, simple though it may be, word was bound to get out, and sure enough in the eighties a different kind of individual started coming here to escape: one with money, and a day job, and the desire to drop out – but only for a while, or as long as their boss would let them. In the same way that artists are often the catalyst for the subsequent gentrification of city areas that were once considered dangerous or undesirable, so the hippies initiated Trancoso's transformation. Afterwards the rich, the chic, the VIPs all started to arrive, and in such a steady stream that airlines began to fly directly to nearby Porto Seguro, and three years ago they paved the road. That, sceptics might say, was the beginning of the end. But this is not so. Because, along with the chic, the town has retained its hippy credentials. For once, billionaires, movie stars (can't tell you which ones), models and backpackers are together and the same, i.e. shirtless and shoeless. And everyone who comes to Trancoso strives for one thing – simplicity. Nobody gets dressed up, nobody

drives their car (unless it's a beach buggy to get to the sea), and everybody hangs out on the quadrado at night.

That said, simple does not have to mean basic. Everything, including the garden, the pool and the spa, adheres to an Oscar Wilde philosophy of simplicity, i.e. 'I have very simple taste; only the best will do'. At Pousada Etnia your own private bungalow is a minimal haven, decorated with no fuss, just plenty of space; and even breakfast, featuring every cake, crêpe, cookie, biscuit or baguette that has ever been called Brazilian, is beautifully (and simply) presented. Pousada Etnia is clearly for people who prefer their simplicity stylish. And it makes sense that an Italian couple is behind it, considering Italians seem to be almost genetically incapable of mediocrity.

Ironically, Conrado Tini and Brazilian-born André Zanonato moved to Trancoso because they'd had enough of the worlds of design and fashion (Conrado had worked for Jean-Paul Gaultier; André had worked in ceramics). They craved sun and tranquillity, bought a piece of land, and spent two years creating a series of bungalows set in a tropical garden where once there was only jungle. The beach is a ten- to fifteen-minute walk from the property, but more importantly Trancoso's quadrado is virtually next door.

It's a great combination – peace, serenity and seclusion when you want it; barefoot outdoor dining, in any number of casual beach shacks, when you don't. Evenings on the quadrado are a special experience, and it's for this reason that Pousada Etnia doesn't serve dinner. They want guests to experience after-dark Trancoso, quadrado-style.

Trancoso may not yet be as famous as Punta, but in South America it's the place everyone wants to go. These days, for instance, the big prize in an Argentinian game-show might be … a week in Trancoso. Hippy chic Brazilian-style, it seems, is catching on.

---

address Pousada Etnia, CX.P. 142, Trancoso, BA 45818-000, Brazil
t (55) 73 668 1137 **f** (55) 73 668 1549 **e** etniabrasil@etniabrasil.com.br
room rates from BRL 350 (including breakfast)

explora atacama

The Atacama is the driest desert on earth. Situated at 2,500 to 3,000 metres altitude, it's in the northeast corner of Chile, 25 miles from the border of Bolivia and 95 miles from Argentina. The Spanish conquistadores, spurred on by tales of silver and gold, tried three times to get to this inhospitable part of South America. The first two times they all died.

Remote, wild, inaccessible, intimidating, Atacama is, in a word, perfect for Explora. As far as Señor Pedro Ibáñez is concerned, the more remote the better. A businessman, entrepreneur, industrialist and scion of a successful Chilean family, he invented a new way to travel when he founded Explora in 1994. He and friends – photographers, artists, musicians, creative types – had all been lamenting the dire direction travel and tourism seemed to have taken. They hated the queues, the overcrowding, the ranks of tour buses. Baking by the pool or vegetating on a beach was not their idea of travelling. Thus, Explora was created as a counter-cultural alternative – to rediscover, as per the company slogan, 'the art of travel'.

Words, of course, are easy but Pedro Ibáñez also put his money behind his imagination. It's not often you find someone who is fearless and who also has deep pockets.

But that's exactly what Explora Atacama benefits from. That, and some amazing locations.

It's true that it takes some commitment to get to San Pedro de Atacama, but it's worth it as few places on this planet are. Atacama may be a high desert but it's certainly not barren, in the sense of devoid of beauty. San Pedro, in fact, is an oasis – a splash of unexpected green amidst a wondrous landscape of sand dunes, gorges, canyons, rock formations, dry salt beds, geysers, flamingo marshes and hot springs … all of it framed by a monumental row of snow-capped, 6,000-metre-high volcanoes. If you're thinking that it sounds like a setting for the next instalment of *Star Wars*, you're not far off. High on top of the 5,900-metre peak of Licancabur, the nearest volcano to San Pedro de Atacama, NASA maintains a top-secret (well, not that secret, obviously) research station, where they carry out experiments in environments that closely resemble the landscape of Mars.

I admit the place took me completely by surprise – on two levels. First, I had expected a lunar landscape, a great stretch of dry, flat nothingness spreading to infinity. Instead the geography and geology are so breathtaking it took me twice as long as it should have done to get from Calama

airport to San Pedro because I kept stopping to take photographs. Second, I had not expected a hotel of such uncompromising contemporaneity, or on such a scale.

Inspired by the cattle haciendas of Mexico and South America, Explora is a 42-acre complex that combines cutting-edge architecture with traditional *pueblo* colours. Despite the linear geometry of its modernism, the complex is not out of place in San Pedro, partially because its simple wooden and rattan furniture retains an element of ethnic handcraft. Indeed Explora could be a working hacienda – and it is, except that here the work is adventure.

If you're at the hotel at any time other than breakfast, lunch or dinner, something is wrong. The list of places to explore and things to do is so extensive you're unlikely to do everything unless you're staying for a month. You can, for example, take one of Explora's fleet of four-wheel-drives up an old mining road to a hot spring oasis hidden in a narrow stone canyon at an altitude of 3,500 metres; take the horses for a trek through the dunes; head out on mountain bikes to the flamingo reserve; hike to the high Andes border of Bolivia; climb a volcano; walk into the picturesque but authentic centre of San Pedro…. The adventures are limited only by your time and your ability.

For all its outdoor options and bold architecture, this Explora is also an extremely good hotel, in the old-fashioned sense. The food is very fine, the wine list surprisingly sophisticated, the service impeccable. Even the most demanding 'princess' would be hard-pressed to find something to complain about, except perhaps saddle sores.

Inspiring design, extraterrestrial landscapes and compelling adventure, with the odd sprinkle of danger. Explora Atacama is the perfect place if you've ever dreamed of being Obi-Wan Kenobi. In this desert, the force is definitely with you.

---

address Explora Atacama, c/o Américo Vespucio Sur 80, Piso 5, Santiago, Chile

t (56) 2 206 6060 **f** (56) 2 228 4655 **e** reservexplora@explora.com

room rates from US $2,060 (4 nights, including meals, transfers and activities)

hotel monasterio

The Incas thought Cuzco was the centre of the universe. Flying over the Andes from Peru's Pacific coast, it's easy to understand why. Situated at an altitude of 3,400 metres, the valley of Cuzco is a green fertile bowl of terraced farms and forests, guarded in the distance by sentinels of mighty snow-capped peaks. Beyond these mountains (some of the highest in the world) are tropical jungles where the Incas once hunted extravagantly coloured birds and exotic beasts, prized for their feathers and their skins. Everything and anything they could possibly want could be found, or cultivated, in their immediate surroundings. Gold, silver, copper, the world's finest wools of alpaca and vicuña, a mahogany-coloured soil that yielded most crops in abundance, and a climate that provided both sun and rain without extremes: they had it all. How could this not be the centre of the universe? For the Incas it was, until the arrival of the conquistadores turned the dream into a nightmare.

The Spanish had no interest in Inca culture. All they wanted was silver and gold. Their king was fighting a holy war in Europe on many fronts and needed to pay his mercenary soldiers. Since the wars in Europe were in the name of religion, the Spaniards rationalized conquest of the New World with the same imperative. The agenda was straightforward: find the gold and silver, ship it back to Spain and convert the locals to Catholicism, whether they want to or not. The Inca rulers were captured and executed, and their palaces and temples razed, to be replaced by churches and cathedrals.

That's how a monastery ended up with the best location in Cuzco. It was built on the site of the fomer palace of Inca Amaru Qhata by the sixth bishop of Cuzco, Monsignor Antonio de la Raya, as a place to train priests. The most beautiful Inca city was in the process of being converted into one of South America's most beautiful colonial cities.

More than four hundred years later, this is what makes Cuzco so attractive. From its cobblestone streets and its Spanish-style townhouses, complete with wrought-iron trelliswork, to the Plaza de Armas, dominated by two cathedrals resplendent with Andean Baroque gilded and frescoed interiors, Cuzco is a historic city like few others. On the surface it's classic Spanish Renaissance, but underneath bubbles the colour and character of the highland-dwelling Incas. It's a fascinating town with a wealth of handcraft. Perhaps not surprisingly, the very heart of the town – its centre in spirit and geography – is a building owned by the

Catholic Church ... except you no longer need to be a priest to stay here. The Orient-Express Group leases the property from Cuzco's archbishop and operates the historic monastery as a hotel.

From a location point of view you can't do better. Plaza de Armas is around the corner, as are the famous Inca stones of Hatunrumiyoc. One block away, uphill, is the part of town known as San Blas, the arts and crafts district.

But the real star is the monastery itself. Much to the credit of Orient-Express, they have managed to retain the look and the feel of a sober but magnificent Spanish stone monastery. In the morning Gregorian chanting, albeit a recorded version, reverberates along the stone columns and arches that define one of three courtyards, sending a shiver of authenticity down your spine. Yet there's nothing severe or pious about the way guests are treated. All the luxuries are there, they've just been reinvented to suit the site.

Breakfast, for instance, is served in the very same refectory where the seminarians used to break daily bread.

You can opt for monastic silence in the courtyard beneath a three-hundred-year-old cedar, or order a pisco sour in the bar of one of the former cloisters. The magnificently over-the-top Baroque chapel is open for private prayer, and the courtyard restaurant is open for private indulgence. The Monasterio is the kind of place that captures the imagination and transports the guest, by way of its chapel and its collection of paintings, to a time and place normally found in history books and museums.

The only problem you may have is sleeping. At 3,300 metres almost everyone has to adjust to an altitude that has 30% less oxygen than at sea level. The Monasterio has come up with a solution which is even better than praying. It is currently the only hotel in the world that pumps oxygen-enriched air into the guest rooms.

---

address Hotel Monasterio, Calle Palacios 136, Plazoleta Nazarenas, Cuzco, Peru
t (51) 84 24 1777 **f** (51) 84 23 7111 **e** info@peruorientexpress.com.pe
room rates from US $360 (including breakfast)

machu picchu lodge

It doesn't matter how many photographs you've seen, how many books you've read or how many stories you've heard. Nothing can possibly convey what it's like to experience the ruins of Machu Picchu for the first time. Actually, ruins is the wrong word to describe this city, perched on a ridge at 2,400 metres, between the dominating peaks of Machu Picchu and Huayna Picchu, and encircled on three sides by the Urubamba River, particularly considering it's pretty much the only city to have survived intact the devastation the Spaniards usually brought to Inca sites of importance.

Just how this monument to the spectacular beauty of the Peruvian Andes managed to avoid destruction of its temples and looting of its treasures is just one of the mysteries that have made this 'lost city', discovered in 1911 by Yale professor Hiram Bingham, enduringly compelling.

But did Hiram Bingham really 'discover' Machu Picchu? The fact that there were farmers living in cleared portions of the site when he got there would suggest that the city was never really lost. At the same time it might have remained local knowledge forever had Bingham not found himself clambering behind a farmer – perspiring, exhausted and sceptical – up the overgrown stone steps to the majestic city in the clouds that we now know as Machu Picchu.

Even the small areas that were cleared of encroaching jungle had Bingham reaching for superlatives. The stone masonry was of a scale and quality the likes of which he had never seen – thirty-ton blocks of granite stacked in interlocking fashion with such precision that even the thin blade of a knife would not fit in between.

Yet the discovery brought more questions than answers. If this was an important Inca city – which it obviously was, judging by the amount of work that had gone into it and the fact that the population was estimated at between 1,000 and 2,000 – then why didn't the Spanish conquistadores know about it? And if it was built by the Inca king Pachacuti, whose seat of power was Cuzco, why did he choose to build in such a remote location? Then there was the question of what happened to all the gold and silver. Such a seat of nobility and higher learning would certainly have had residents with fine attire, exquisite jewelry and beautiful domestic artifacts, yet none of these was found, with the exception, quite recently, of one gold necklace.

Almost a century after Bingham's discovery, a lot more research and study has provided some plausible explanations. The most popular belief today is that, in an effort to spare Machu Picchu, the most spiritual of all sites,

513

Much has been written about Machu Picchu's stonemasonry, yet the large, intricately interlocking blocks were used only for temples and palaces

In the hotel's light and airy private dining room, the stone floors mimic the stonework of the national monument that is, literally, next door

An isolated watch-keeper's hut is a vivid example of what Machu Picchu's houses would have looked like at the time that the city was still inhabited

Guest bedrooms are appropriately simple and contemporary. Any attempt to compete with the charismatic beauty of Machu Picchu would be a folly

Much of this Inca city in the sky is as it was five centuries ago: in most cases the only things missing are the thatched roofs and the interior plasterwork

The single most striking detail of Machu Picchu Lodge is its location. You live with the same view and surroundings as the Incas did

the Inca ordered the city to be evacuated. This would explain the lack of valuables found and the fact that today 80% of Machu Picchu is just as it was at the time, minus the thatched roofs and polished plastered walls.

The stories, the mysteries, the legends, the heart-stopping beauty of the surrounding nature.... Machu Picchu is extraordinarily beguiling, but, like all things that are exquisite, it is not without its price. The price Machu Picchu asks is time, money and patience.

For those without the will or the time to hike the Inca Trail, there is only one way to get to Aguas Calientes, the local town in the valley of Machu Picchu, and that is by special train from Cuzco. The journey takes four hours, through increasingly spectacular scenery, following the raging rapids of the Urubamba River all the way. Upon arrival you are required to buy a ticket for the half-hour bus journey up the Hiram Bingham Highway (despite its name, a rather discreet

dirt road). Then you have to wait in line to buy your entrance ticket. All in all it would have to be the most exhilarating and exhausting day trip imaginable. If you leave your hotel in Cuzco at 5.30am you can expect to be back at 8pm.

And here's where the pure magic of the Lodge lies. Instead of making the long journey home, you get to stay. Located right next to the lost city, the Lodge is Machu Picchu's only hotel, and it will remain so because National Heritage has no intention of allowing any more here. The Lodge isn't grand or extravagant, and neither should it be; any attempt to compete with Machu Picchu's charisma would be terribly inappropriate. But it is cosy, contemporary and comfortable, and there is no hotel on earth situated in a more privileged location. Before 10am and after 4pm you have Machu Picchu all to yourself. You can wander round the temples, houses and palaces, alone with their many mysteries. Even the mighty Inca Pachacuti couldn't do that.

---

address Machu Picchu Sanctuary Lodge, Monumento Arqueológico de Machu Picchu, Machu Picchu, Cuzco, Peru

t (51) 84 21 1039/38 **f** (51) 84 21 1053 **e** info@peruorientexpress.com.pe

room rates from US $474 (including meals)

la posada del faro

Ten years ago the idea of Punta del Este being anything other than a beach destination for Argentinians, weekend commuters from Montevideo and the odd jetset Brazilian was so unlikely as to be absurd…. OK, perhaps the occasional Spaniard with family in South America, but that was about the extent of the presence of 'Los Continentales'. Now Punta is on the tip of everyone's tongue. Americans, Germans, Dutch, British, Italians, Canadians, Japanese … even the French, not renowned for their willingness to leave their *pays*, are heading to Uruguay's beautiful beaches.

To announce with some nonchalance that you're off to 'Punta' is all of a sudden very chic. The perfect reply would be, 'Really? Which punta?', because Punta del Este is a cumulative term; like 'the Hamptons'. It includes Punta Ballena, La Barra, the town of Punta, and José Ignacio.

Punta Ballena is famous for the odd whale and the very odd Casapueblo – a Gaudíesque piece of organic sculpture perched on a cliff, which started as a house for the artist who built it, by hand, and ended up as a hotel.

The town of Punta, a few miles up the road from Ballena, is for those who like their sand with concrete; lots of concrete. What was once a tiny fishing village is now a mini-Miami, dominated by a skyline of high-rise apartment buildings and big casino hotels. Brazilians love it because it's flash: not everybody else does.

Further northeast, across a bridge with two humps (no joke) is La Barra, a low-rise village with plenty of boutiques, sushi bars and fashion models. It's a lot like East Hampton but more multicultural and exotic, i.e. the bikinis are smaller.

Furthest away, on the road to Gazon, all by itself, is José Ignacio, a funny name for a town but the perfect spot if you like your beaches wild, unspoiled and … beautiful. José Ignacio, and more specifically La Posada del Faro, is the place you'd rather not tell your friends about. Let them stay in La Barra instead.

Simply put, José Ignacio is nothing more than a small clump of houses on a point dividing two splendid crescent-shaped beaches. The point is defined by a *faro*, or lighthouse, and from a distance the houses of the town disappear behind the dunes. The prevailing ambience here is pure beach. There's a *mercado* in a red wooden shack; a boutique in a white wooden shack; a beach club on wooden stilts with a spectacular vista of the surfing beach; and for the grown-ups there's a handful of laid-back restaurants in vividly coloured wooden shacks that just happen to feature some of the famous chefs of South America.

Is this paradise? It is if you aspire to be a beach bum with *bon goût* – to never wear shoes (even at night), to wander around in your boardies, catch a few waves, take the kids for a swim, and eat lots of fish that's been caught by the guy who has his boat at the far end of the beach. It's a lifestyle that appeals as much to the locals as to the visitors. And that, no doubt, is the secret of La Posada del Faro's charm. The proprietors José and Carla García Arocena are locals. As a child, José spent all his summers on Punta and one of his best friends, son of the artist Carlos Páez Vilaró, lived in Casapueblo. These days the Arocenas live in José Ignacio all year round, their children grew up here and, despite the fact that they've travelled quite a lot, they wouldn't live anywhere else. The posada, which they opened in 1991, is for all intents and purposes their beach house. In fact they live next door, but the hotel is very much an extension of their love for the area.

Apart from being, architecturally speaking, the most attractive house in José Ignacio (inside and out), it's completely in tune with the beach-shack freedom that makes this place so compellingly appealing. White linen sofas, rugged floorboards, whitewashed walls, bamboo sun shelters: nothing is too sophisticated and yet there is enough comfort and luxury to spoil you in a way that staying with friends never can.

José Ignacio's posada is a magic place – the kind you don't want to leave – and I'm not the only writer to think so. A few doors down is the house of British author Martin Amis. I was surprised to discover he lives in Ignacio all year round too. Well, perhaps more envious than surprised.

Even in the winter, when the weather is colder and the Argentinians stay in Argentina, José Ignacio still has its dunes and its ocean, and people meet by a fireplace instead of on a beach. Sounds like the perfect place for a writer….

---

address La Posada del Faro, Calle de la Bahía esq. Timonel, José Ignacio, Uruguay
t (598) 486 2110 **f** (598) 486 2111 **e** info@posadadelfaro.com
room rates from US $120 (including breakfast)

INDEX

HIP™
HOTELS

All Rights Reserved. No part of this publication may be reproduced or transmitted in any form or by any means, electronic or mechanical, including photocopy, recording or any other information storage and retrieval system, without prior permission in writing from the publisher.

© 2005 Herbert Ypma

First published in 2005 in hardcover in the United States of America by Thames & Hudson Inc., 500 Fifth Avenue, New York, New York 10110

thamesandhudsonusa.com

Library of Congress Catalog Card Number
2005900863
ISBN-13: 978-0-500-51248-7
ISBN-10: 0-500-51248-5

Printed and bound in Singapore by CS Graphics

Designed by Maggi Smith